e-Merchant

Addison-Wesley Information Technology Series
Capers Jones and David S. Linthicum, Consulting Editors

The information technology (IT) industry is in the public eye now more than ever before because of a number of major issues in which software technology and national policies are closely related. As the use of software expands, there is a continuing need for business and software professionals to stay current with the state of the art in software methodologies and technologies. The goal of the Addison-Wesley Information Technology Series is to cover any and all topics that affect the IT community: These books illustrate and explore how information technology can be aligned with business practices to achieve business goals and support business imperatives. Addison-Wesley has created this innovative series to empower you with the benefits of the industry experts' experience.

For more information point your browser to http://www.awl.com/cseng/series/it/

Sid Adelman, Larissa Terpeluk Moss, *Data Warehouse Project Management.* ISBN: 0-201-61635-1

Wayne Applehans, Alden Globe, and Greg Laugero, *Managing Knowledge: A Practical Web-Based Approach.* ISBN: 0-201-43315-X

Michael H. Brackett, *Data Resource Quality: Turning Bad Habits into Good Practices.* ISBN: 0-201-71306-3

Frank Coyle, *Wireless Web: A Manager's Guide.* ISBN: 0-201-72217-8

James Craig and Dawn Jutla, *e-Business Readiness: A Customer-Focused Framework.* ISBN: 0-201-71006-4

Gregory C. Dennis and James R. Rubin, *Mission-Critical Java™ Project Management: Business Strategies, Applications, and Development.* ISBN: 0-201-32573-X

Kevin Dick, *XML: A Manager's Guide.* ISBN: 0-201-43335-4

Jill Dyché, *e-Data: Turning Data into Information with Data Warehousing.* ISBN: 0-201-65780-5

Dr. Nick V. Flor, *Web Business Engineering: Using Offline Activites to Drive Internet Strategies.* ISBN: 0-201-60468-X

David Garmus and David Herron, *Function Point Analysis: Measurement Practices for Successful Software Projects.* ISBN: 0-201-69944-3

Capers Jones, *Software Assessments, Benchmarks, and Best Practices.* ISBN: 0-201-48542-7

Capers Jones, *The Year 2000 Software Problem: Quantifying the Costs and Assessing the Consequences.* ISBN: 0-201-30964-5

Ravi Kalakota and Marcia Robinson, *e-Business 2.0: Roadmap for Success.* ISBN: 0-201-72165-1

David S. Linthicum, *B2B Application Integration: e-Business-Enable Your Enterprise.* ISBN: 0-201-70936-8

Sergio Lozinsky, *Enterprise-Wide Software Solutions: Integration Strategies and Practices.* ISBN: 0-201-30971-8

Joanne Neidorf and Robin Neidorf, *e-Merchant: Retail Strategies for e-Commerce.* ISBN: 0-201-72169-4

Patrick O'Beirne, *Managing the Euro in Information Systems: Strategies for Successful Changeover.* ISBN: 0-201-60482-5

Mai-lan Tomsen, *Killer Content: Strategies for Web Content and E-Commerce.* ISBN: 0-201-65786-4

Bill Wiley, *Essential System Requirements: A Practical Guide to Event-Driven Methods.* ISBN: 0-201-61606-8

Ralph R. Young, *Effective Requirements Practices.* ISBN: 0-201-70912-0

Bill Zoellick, *Web Engagement: Connecting to Customers in e-Business.* ISBN: 0-201-65766-X

e-Merchant

Retail Strategies
for e-Commerce

Joanne Neidorf

Robin Neidorf

Addison-Wesley

Boston • San Francisco • New York • Toronto • Montreal
London • Munich • Paris • Madrid
Capetown • Sydney • Tokyo • Singapore • Mexico City

The publisher offers discounts on this book when ordered in quantity for special sales. For more information, please contact:

Pearson Education Corporate Sales Division
One Lake Street
Upper Saddle River, NJ 07458
(800) 382-3419
corpsales@pearsontechgroup.com

Visit AW on the Web: www.awl.com/cseng/

Library of Congress Cataloging-in-Publication Data

Neidorf, Joanne.
    E-merchant : retail strategies for e-commerce/Joanne Neidorf,
Robin Neidorf.
        p.   cm.—(Addison-Wesley information technology series)
    Includes index.
    ISBN 0-201-72169-4
        1. Electronic commerce.   2. Retail trade—Computer network
resources.   I. Neidorf, Robin.   II. Title.   III. Series.

HF5548.32.N44 2001
658.8'4—dc21   00–054837

ISBN 0-201-72169-4
Text printed on recycled paper
1 2 3 4 5 6 7 8 9 10—CRS—0504030201
First printing, April 2001

*To our colleagues and mentors who guide and support our decisions
and who celebrate our successes.*

Contents

CHAPTER FIVE   **INVENTORY   107**

CHAPTER SIX PRICING AND PROMOTIONAL STRATEGY   127

CHAPTER SEVEN PROFITABILITY   145

CHAPTER EIGHT VENDOR RELATIONS 171

CHAPTER NINE   RUNNING A RETAIL ORGANIZATION   195

CHAPTER TEN   THE VIRTUAL REAL WORLD: e-RETAIL CASE STUDIES   209

Preface

What This Book Is

The Web is an interactive, collaborative environment. Fittingly, this book is both interactive and collaborative as well. We two authors entered our partnership, each with our specialties and insights, and together have created something neither of us could have described when we started.

As collaborations go, ours faced some unique challenges. We are sisters—a factor that could simplify and/or complicate our work together. Throughout the research and writing process, Joanne lived in Sweden while Robin lived in Minneapolis. We communicated, trading outlines, chapters, notes, ideas, and more, primarily via e-mail.

From the perspective of the culmination of the project, we find that our work on this book has been a fairly precise microcosm of how electronic communication, trust, and focus can enable effective collaborations. The promise of the Internet age can be fulfilled, as long as we are willing and able to adapt our methods, not only for working and research but also for shopping.

What This Book *Isn't*

With so many e-related books available, it seems important to add a few words about where this book fits into the landscape of resources: This is not "the only book you will need" to plan and run an e-retail site. Our focus is strictly on merchant functions and merchandising, touching on topics like business plans, site design, customer service, and order fulfillment only as they intersect with the merchant's responsibilities.

Why this restriction? In our review of the existing resources, we found that the merchant element of e-retail has been given scant (if any) attention. Joanne's hands-on experience as a buyer made the work of the merchant familiar territory, even in an unfamiliar medium. At the same time, Robin's work as a Web researcher and content analyst and writer gave her insight into the way people effectively use the online environment to advance their business goals.

To cover other subjects ranging from general business planning, marketing and promotion, to warehouse management would have taxed our partnership. More to the point, we saw no reason to reinvent the Web, so to speak. Others have covered and will cover those topics better than we ever could.

Who Should Read This Book

Anyone who works in any capacity with an e-retail site but does not understand the fundamentals of retail will benefit from this book. Entrepreneurs, business owners seeking to diversify their online revenue streams, consultants, and Web designers and programmers will also find an easy-to-understand introduction to the principals of retail.

In researching this book, particularly the case studies in Chapter 10, we heard the frequent lament that e-retail organizations must overcome a gaping cultural disconnect before they can be effective. Merchants must understand the strategy, construction, and maintenance of a Web store, just as they understand brick-and-mortar stores. Programmers and designers must understand the goals of the Web merchant to create and implement sites that further those goals. Our intent is that *e-Merchant: Retail Strategies for e-Commerce* helps organizations of all sizes and types overcome the language barriers that have tripped them in the past.

Acknowledgments

Many people influenced the creation of this book and supported our efforts along the way. Those who generously offered their time, expertise, and insights include Josh Litwin; Anne-Marie Otey of FashionDish.com; Philip Clark of

SmartCard; Michael Schmier of BabyCenter; Katherine Lee of WeddingChannel; Brad Roberts; Soon-Chart Yu of Gazoontite; Bill Pond and Meg Hays of Garden.com; Martin McClanan and Amy Burke-Bessette of RedEnvelope; Rachel Elson of Tradeweave; P. Kelly Mooney, Ed Johns, and Keriake Lucas of Resource Marketing; and Jane Smith of LiSimba Consulting.

Nearly a dozen technical reviewers took time from their busy schedules to give us frank and helpful advice on a draft of the manuscript. Randi Lachter provided early research assistance, and Meredith Hinke provided an invaluable "lay" reading of the manuscript.

Mary O'Brien, Mariann Kourafas, and Mamata Reddy at Addison-Wesley helped us express and communicate our ideas clearly. Our agent, Dianne Littwin, immediately saw the promise of our proposal and worked like lightning to find a home for our book.

In Robin's household, Andrew patiently supported yet another major project, playing for hours with Talia while Robin worked in the next room. In Joanne's household, Peter tolerated international phone calls and willingly read the growing pile of papers on an industry he had never had much interest in before.

To all, our gratitude.

Joanne Neidorf
Robin Neidorf

About the Authors

Joanne Neidorf holds an MBA from Stanford University Graduate School of Business and has worked with internationally known retailers such as Macy's (where she was responsible for more than $30 million in annual sales), Gymboree, and The Walt Disney Company. After working as a buyer/category manager for a retail start-up in Sweden, she has returned to the United States and joined the merchandising department at DFS Galleria, a global retailer specializing in merchandising to the traveling public. Her buying expertise, coupled with her business analysis background, has also made her an in-demand consultant for Internet start-ups.

Robin Neidorf provides Web-based intelligence to small and mid-sized organizations through her company, Electric Muse. Additionally, she provides content analysis, strategic planning, and copywriting services for the Web and for print media. As a business journalist for nearly ten years, she has specialized in rendering complex ideas clearly for a wide variety of audiences. Robin holds an MFA in creative nonfiction from the Bennington Writing Seminars and has taught research and writing (creative and technical) at the University of Minnesota, Hennepin Technical College, and the Bennington Alumni Retreat.

CHAPTER ONE

Introduction

You are an e-retailer . . .

You have to do everything required to run an e-commerce operation *and* simultaneously integrate sound retail concepts.

You have to compete in a quicksilver Internet environment in a quicksilver retail industry.

You are up against some of the strongest established brand names in commercial history—Sears, J.C. Penney, and Wal-Mart. These are traditional retailers that know their markets and have the funds to hire the people who can introduce them to the secrets of e-commerce.

You are also up against some energetic adolescent companies that are on their way to becoming household names, such as Amazon.com, eBay, and Fogdog Sports.

Oh, yeah . . . one more thing—the angels who threw obscene amounts of capital at e-retailers throughout the late 1990s have decided to sit on their hands for awhile and see if anyone can actually make money selling consumer goods over the Internet.

In a sense, you are in a position much like that of Ginger Rogers, doing a difficult dance backward and in high heels!

Other books and resources can guide you through the fireswamp of setting up an effective e-commerce operation. Clearly, the choices you make and the infrastructure you devise will be critical—from the software you choose to the customer service policies you elect to the fulfillment logistics you employ. You can follow every piece of advice you get through those resources, but will they make you a better *retailer*?

The concept of retail is based on a four-pronged mission: The *right product* in the *right place* at the *right price* at the *right time*.

With this essential mission in place, issues like customer service, technology, and fulfillment are tangential. True, they are absolutely vital to successful business operations, but at the same time, they are not, in the tired language of our day, your *core business*. They are not the essence of what it means to conduct retail operations successfully, online or off.

Thus, the focus of this book is on basic, sound retail principles, as they can be adapted to the peculiar medium we know as the World Wide Web. Issues like customer service, fulfillment, and technology are considered only as they directly relate to retail principles; the Appendix at the end of the book provides more information on these topics and can guide you to further resources.

What has not been covered in other resources is your core business, retail, or more specifically, *e*-retail. Don't let the "e" distract you. The key to success and profitability lies in the understanding and application of the elements of *retail*: strategy, assortment planning, merchandising, inventory management, vendor negotiations, and so on.

So what about the "e"? There is no doubt that the Web has changed the landscape of the retail industry. The Web is what Harvard Business School professors Christopher M. Christensen and Richard S. Tedlow call a "disruptive innovation."[1] As such, we must pay special attention to the way retail concepts apply to the medium. The retail industry has adapted to disruptive innovations before. The upscale department store, the mail-order catalog, and the discount department store were earlier disruptive innovations that forced retailers to rethink how they did business and for whom. The full impact the Web will have on retail will not be completely clear for several hyped-up holiday shopping seasons—in other words, for several years. However, even at this stage, we can begin to think of the Web like the telephone, a tool that soon no business can afford to be without, that makes every step of business more efficient, and which enhances rather than replaces existing retail prospects.

How all this will unfold is far from clear. New technologies enabling better online customer experiences appear regularly, and just as regularly, they disappear. Connectivity itself is changing, with high-speed access and broadband capabilities becoming more common. Interactive television, which today is still something of a novelty, may become as commonplace as the remote control.

Meanwhile, the online consumer population changes rapidly. Every Web demographic report shows more women, more young and older people, and more mass-market users accessing the Web to accomplish more tasks; that means more communication, more research, and of course, more shopping.

As consumers, we are still getting used to the Web, in much the same way consumers had to learn to shop from a catalog or understand the nature of a discount department store. These earlier disruptive innovations are now so much a part of our shopping experience that we hardly notice how we are selecting a particular sales channel over another, making those choices based on convenience and value. Web-based shopping is moving in the same direction. The real challenge facing the online retail industry today is not the development and deployment of technology to make e-retail possible. It is to change consumer behavior, to get consumers to consider Web stores equally with their other options.

Next to all this uncertainty, one thing is very clear: there are distinct competitive advantages to launching a Web-based retail operation. This book will help you discover and maximize them, while minimizing the inherent disadvantages of the medium.

No Internet-focused book can get beyond its first few pages without launching into a breathless citation of statistics on the quadrillions of dollars soon to be spent online, the hordes of middle-class families making their first tentative online purchases, the dramatic rise of online spending and retail-focused Web sites, and so on. Odds are, you already know the news, or you wouldn't be reading this book.

Instead of the laundry list, we have decided to focus on one industry forecast that is simple and relatively conservative: By 2010, close to 20 percent of retail spending in the United States may be conducted via the Internet.[2] That is an estimated $660 billion chunk of an overall $3.3 trillion retail marketplace. The United States is expected to continue to dominate Web-based retailing throughout the first decade of the twenty-first century, but growing international markets also exist in Germany, Japan, Scandinavia, France, Great Britain, and South Korea.[3]

Who's in the Game?

Anyone with a modem can set up shop in Cyberspace, but as the shakeouts of early 2000 made plain, the gold rush is slowing down. Clearly, there is more to e-retail than coining a catchy dot-com name and creating some sassy, ironic advertising. Web-based retail may have altered the superficial appearance of the industry and may have broadened the options for the way shoppers and retailers can interact, but the underlying structure of successful retail has not shifted one iota. A careful mix of know-how in technology, marketing, consumer behavior, merchandising, and logistics will support a successful e-retail organization

So what has changed? There is no doubt that shopping online is a different psychological experience than shopping at a mall, in a Main Street shop, or from a catalog. e-Retail creates hybrid forms of the consumer/merchant relationship, forms that offer different kinds of sales opportunities than existing media offer. Table 1.1 compares the three most common retail sales channels—brick-and-mortar, catalog, and the Web—across the elements that characterize the shopping and business ownership experience.

e-Retail + Traditional Retail Operations ("Clicks-and-Mortar")

Sites like macys.com and gap.com, as well as relative latecomers walmart.com and jcpenney.com, are evolving into online branches of brick-and-mortar operations. This kind of site is not limited to the rich, famous, and nationally well-branded. Many smaller stores have used the Web to broaden their market by opening online branches, which make available to Web shoppers goods that were once only accessible to people near the store.

The inverse image of this model is also evident: businesses that started out as Web e-retailers but have since added brick-and-mortar operations to their sales channels. Gazoontite launched its Web site selling hypoallergenic products before opening its flagship store in San Francisco. Additional stores have opened on both coasts and in the Chicago area. Originally intended to reinforce the site's branding and credibility, the brick-and-mortar operations have proven to be a huge success, even as the e-retail site has stopped selling. (For more on Gazoontite, see Chapter 10.)

The concepts outlined in this book apply to traditional retail stores and e-retail sites. If your site would benefit from a storefront, the same skills and metrics should guide your decisions. For the purposes of this book, however, we focus on the e-retail component of the business.

e-Retail + Catalog Operations

In this category are well-known catalog merchants like Lands' End, which has expanded its popular direct merchant business through landsend.com. For catalog retailers, expansion to the Web is a relatively easy development. They already conduct most of their sales through remote media and are already equipped to handle customer service and order fulfillment.

Table 1-1   Channel Comparison

	Bricks-and-mortar-retail	Catalog retail	e-Retail
Location and presence	Physical buildings branded and easily identified and found Most traditional and oldest location for retail Commands attention in the retail landscape	Print materials "Portable store" Sent to targeted mailing lists	Location is the Web address, available globally through any Internet connection Can establish a presence through partnerships and cross-promotions (links between sites)
How merchandising is accomplished	Use of store space and "fixturing" Signage and other product information tools	Page layouts Organization of catalog Relationship between product and text	Web page layout Relationship between product and text Signage and other product information tools Category, search, and sorting mechanisms Interactive product locators
Options for promotional activity	Pricing strategies and campaigns can be implemented on a daily basis	Pricing strategies and campaigns can only be implemented as frequently as new catalogs are distributed	Pricing strategies and campaigns can be implemented "instantaneously," depending on internal organizational
Options for inventory	Product must be available at multiple store locations to maximize purchasing opportunities (with the exception of products intended for special order)	Product is held at warehouse until ordered and shipped to customer	Multiple inventory ownership options, with most prominent being traditional, "just-in-time," and a hybrid of the two

This model also has an inverse, in the form of dot coms that have added print catalogs or other print sales tools to their online site offerings. Print sales tools can serve as a tangible reiteration of an e-retail brand and its product offerings. Garden.com, for example, added a print catalog to the many merchandising techniques the company used to drive sales at its Web site before ceasing operations. (For more on garden.com, see Chapter 10.)

The consistent, physical reminder of your name and brand can be an important aspect of your marketing, regardless of whether you intend to achieve sales through both a print catalog and your retail site.

e-Retail + Web Site Content

Selling goods is a complementary component of business for these sites, which may rely on other sources of revenue for some portion of their business. Other components may include community building, editorial and informational content, product reviews, and recommendations or other features to draw users to the site.

The combination of targeted information and retail is a powerful one that cannot be easily replicated offline. To be sure, many traditional retailers of all kinds offer their customers print newsletters, loyalty programs, educational opportunities, and more. However, the Web uniquely enables customization of that content, allowing customers to pull from the site exactly the content they want and need, when they want it, and many times, in the form they want it. From the e-retailer's perspective, this customization is automated; the company need not employ envelope stuffers to select and mail the appropriate materials to a customer on a regular basis. From the customer's perspective, this feature creates the experience of becoming a "market of one," with a direct relationship to the retailer.

Content and e-retail sites may mix their revenue streams in a variety of ways with any number of tools such as membership programs, advertising, sponsorships, retail, subscriptions, and syndication of content. Affiliate programs, which credit a referring Web site for sales made through the site, can make almost any site a *de facto* e-commerce site. For the purposes of this book, we considered sites that rely on product sales of 50 percent or more of their revenues.

FashionDish.com and BabyCenter.com are both content-driven e-retail sites. Both sites rely on targeted content (e.g., celebrity gossip, parenting information) to bring customers to the site and keep them coming back. (For more on FashionDish and BabyCenter, see Chapter 10.)

What format best suits your business? What sales channels will prove successful for you? The balance between Web sites, brick-and-mortar stores, and catalogs depends on your retail strategy, goals, and budget. Although our focus throughout the book will be on the Web-based retail operation, take some time to consider whether additional sales channels make sense for your product, market, and unique selling proposition (especially in our exploration of retail strategy in Chapter 2).

From Consumer to e-Retailer

We have all been on the customer side of the customer-retailer relationship, so we all know something about how that relationship unfolds, successfully or unsuccessfully. However, the actual metrics of running a retail operation profitably are not revealed through that relationship; they exist only behind the scenes, in the planning and execution, of managing the holiday hype and the summer doldrums. The secrets of retail are not arcane. In fact, they are not even secrets. Yet like any apprenticed profession, retail management can best be learned by heart through practice. This book will start your practice by showing you exactly which muscles you need to find and flex.

The heat of the early days of e-retail is cooling down, and the first of the madness seems to have passed. Let's all take a deep breath of fresh reality!

Reality comes with a few lessons. The most important one is this: you cannot conduct retail, online or off, without a foundation in retail principles. That is, maybe you can; just not for very long. As too many e-retailers have learned, all you get to show from the shoot-from-the-hip approach is a bloody ledger of red ink. Not a pleasant holiday bonus! And your investors will *not* thank you.

We start at the beginning with retail strategy. Define your business. Differentiate it from your competitors. Fill a niche. Then we build your e-retail operations logically based on this strategy: assortment planning (which items, how many, and what will they cost you); merchandising (presenting goods for sale); inventory management (controlling the investment your goods represent); pricing and promotions (what to charge and what message it sends); profitability (analyzing operations to realize a profit); vendor relations (working with your suppliers); and organizational structure (the employees and how they need to communicate).

In addition to this step-by-step escorted tour through the world of retail management, we have created two hypothetical e-retailers: ShoeWeb and WebKidCare.

Each chapter applies the practical knowledge of the chapter to these two hypothetical e-retailers, demonstrating the decision-making processes the management teams would employ to make solid business decisions. You can also read the stories of the hypothetical e-retailers beginning to end by opening the ShoeWeb or WebKidCare files on the accompanying CD-ROM.

Keep in mind that the hypothetical e-retailers were created solely for the purpose of illustrating retail principles in a controlled environment. Please do not create a retail plan based on either of these hypothetical sites. Any resemblance to existing or planned companies is purely coincidental. (Honestly, we just made them up!) However, the purpose of them is to walk you through examples of how these principles might be applied in the process of setting up an e-retail organization.

The case studies in Chapter 10, however, are all based on research and interviews with the leaders of e-retail organizations, all but two of which are still in business as of the publication of this book. While the hypothetical sites lay out decisions in a theoretical world, the case studies show how e-retailers have modified, adapted, and applied retail knowledge to the Web environment.

Clearly, there are many paths to success in e-retail, but the shortest and most profitable paths have a common foundation. They put the *retail* in e-retail.

Endnotes

1. "Patterns of Disruption in Retailing," *Harvard Business Review,* Jan/Feb 2000.
2. "Survey: E-Commerce: We're Off to the Online Mall," *The Economist,* February 26, 2000.
3. "Survey: E-Commerce: First America, Then the World," *The Economist,* February 26, 2000.

CHAPTER TWO

Retail Strategy

Chapter Preview

Defining and drafting a detailed retail strategy is based on simple questions but makes a world of difference in creating your e-retail site. Once the strategy is in place, the more tactical and practical assortment, resource, and financial planning can begin. Our hypothetical e-retailers work out the elements of their strategies.

Defining Your Retail Strategy

Retail strategy can be summed up in three critical questions:

- WHAT are you going to sell?
- WHO are you going to sell to?
- WHY will a customer buy from you?

Retail strategy is a vital component of business planning. Like many struggling businesses that neglect to record and follow their business plans, amateur e-retailers may not bother to hammer out a logical retail strategy either. As simple as these questions sound (What? Who? Why?) the effort you put into coming up with answers will make a significant difference in the rest of your planning and implementation process.

WHAT Are You Going to Sell?

Your first response to this question may be very broad or specific, depending on the genesis of your e-retail concept. Table 2.1 presents examples of potential e-retail concepts that are broad and specific.

Table 2-1   Potential e-Retail Concepts

Broad	Specific
Books	Fiction and nonfiction by contemporary women authors
Cooking supplies	Hard-to-find spices from around the world
All things Asian	Imported Asian handcrafts and home décor

Many e-retailers begin planning with the "what." *Hey, wouldn't it be neat to sell glow-in-the-dark dog biscuits over the Internet?!* Where you begin is not as important as the process you use to flesh out the idea, getting past the "wouldn't it be neat . . ." stage and into a strategy that can be profitably implemented.

What are you going to sell? Answer this question from the most general to the most detailed level. Try to sum up your product line in a few words. See how your strategy suggests an identity, logic, and focus for your e-retail establishment.

Many e-retailers will find success in identifying a niche they can passionately serve. Marketing your e-retail site to a virtual community of folks worldwide who all share the same interests is a natural way to take advantage of the "everywhere and nowhere" quality of the Internet. If you have spent much time on the Web, you have probably run across this kind of site: fridgedoor.com (sells only refrigerator door magnets), mustardstore.com (sells hundreds of varieties of mustard) and justballs.com (sells only sports balls), to name but a few. The economics of setting up a traditional retail storefront dedicated to such a narrow niche is not encouraging. Tackle the niche on the Web, however, where physical geography does not limit your potential customer base, and you have a business plan.

Let us examine a few well-known retailers, online and off, to see how their "what" is realized. Table 2.2 lays out the "what," both general and specific, for a variety of organizations.

It is important to establish your identity and parameters; just do not become a slave to your initial concept. The ability to adapt your strategy without losing focus is the hallmark of a well-run retail organization, online and off. Compare, for example, the many incarnations of The Gap with the adolescent growing pains of Amazon.com. Since its inception as a shop for Levi Strauss jeans in 1969, The Gap has evolved into a brick-and-mortar and dot com international fashion presence. Amazon.com began life as the world's largest bookstore. It added music and video, followed by the auction block. Home improvement was added later.

Table 2.2   What Do They Sell?

Retailer	General	Specific (more specific)
The Gap and gap.com	Fashion	Apparel (clothing and accessories) Personal care (fragrances, skin care, and so on)
Ikea	Home furnishings	Furniture Tabletop accessories Linens Decorating supplies Housewares
Toys-R-Us	Children's retail	Toys Clothing Books Videos Infant care items
Fogdog (www.fogdog.com)	Sporting goods	Clothing Equipment Accessories Sports nutrition
BabyCenter.com	Baby and toddler paraphernalia	Maternity and breastfeeding aids Travel gear Health care Clothing Nursery furnishings Toys, books, and so on
WeddingChannel.com	Wedding paraphernalia	Bridal accessories Gear for groom Guests' interests

STARTING WITH RIVETS:
A BRIEF HISTORY OF THE GAP

In 1969, The Gap started as a shop for Levi Strauss, Inc. It was simple to describe the organization to shoppers: "This is the place to buy your cool jeans." Product categories were limited to the different styles they carried. Assortment simply meant sizes.

In the mid-1970s, The Gap began shifting its product mix to feature jeans manufactured under its private label. Soon, casual tops were added to the mix. Who was going to wear these cool jeans without something equally cool and comfortable on top? Their "what" then changed from "jeans" to "casual fashion apparel." Categories now included men's and women's fashions, including pants, tops, and limited accessories.

Visit a Gap store today, and you will immediately see the effect the workplace revolution has had on the organization from the mid-1980s to the present. In addition to jeans and casual tops, there are various product categories that have little to do with the original concept of The Gap from 1969, such as dressier selections, khakis, cotton pants and skirts, shoes, hats, underwear, scarves, and hosiery. However, if you examine the selection, The Gap's strong sense of identity is evident. With the increase in product categories that can be qualified as "fashion apparel," The Gap has not lost its logic, focus on its customer, or identity.

The most recent evolution at The Gap has been the introduction of fragrances, soaps, and other personal care products. From apparel, the organization has broadened the definition of "fashion" to encompass personal care products as well, creating a whole line that could be described as "branded lifestyle." Meanwhile, GapKids and babyGap catch the youngest consumers before they have even identified a personal style.

In 1997 The Gap has operated e-retail stores, starting with www.gap.com, followed by www.gapkids.com and www.babygap.com in 1998. The Gap's other brands, Old Navy and Banana Republic, also operate online. Banana Republic's Web site is an extension of the brand's catalog operations; the Old Navy site, originally used primarily for brand promotion, is now a fully functional e-retail store as well.

> "The online . . . business is offered as an extension of our store experiences and is intended to strengthen our relationship with our customers," notes the company's 1999 10K, filed with the Securities and Exchange Commission in April 2000. The lesson? Even well-established brands do not launch into e-retail simply for the sake of e-retail, any more than they would create a catalog simply for the sake of having a catalog. There is a focused business purpose to the endeavor: to make the Web one more medium for customer connection.

With each addition to the assortment, it has become more difficult to define Amazon.com. The most recent industry analyses of the organization reflect the growing confusion about just what *is* Amazon.com.

Yet, you must start somewhere. As you define what you are going to sell, you can begin either from the top (your *theme* or one-word description that encompasses all categories) or bottom (a specific product or group of products that you believe will sell well and around which you want to build a concept). Whether your e-retail operation is currently live or not, evaluate your product assortment as it exists right now. Is it logical? Can shoppers understand what you are all about?

Use Worksheet 2.1, Product Assortment Worksheet, to begin analyzing your product assortment. Copy the worksheet in the book or use the one provided on the accompanying CD. Follow the pattern shown in Tables 2.3 and 2.4, which are sample worksheets based on existing retailers.

Worksheet 2.1 Product Assortment Worksheet

What are you going to sell?
(One- or two-word description of product offerings or theme)

Product categories	Subcategories	Logic

Table 2.3   Sample Product Assortment Worksheet

BabyCenter.com

Infant/Toddler World		
Product categories	Subcategories	Logic
For Mother	Pregnancy aids Breastfeeding equipment Maternity apparel Skin care and health and beauty items	Mothers are most likely doing the shopping; items are placed conveniently and specifically to her needs.
Nursery	Bedding Furniture Home décor	Little ones need a well-equipped place to sleep and play.
Gear	Car seats Strollers Carriers Activity centers Safety	On the go and playing at home, infants and toddlers require an amazing amount of equipment. Safety is of the utmost importance!
Clothing	All items for targeted ages	This offers the convenience of purchasing known brands at the same time as purchasing other children's goods.
Health care	Feeding supplies Diapering supplies Over-the-counter pharmaceuticals	The basic necessities can be difficult to shop for; this offers the convenience of shopping at one's leisure for necessary items.
Entertainment	Toys Books Music Videos	Full range and selection of entertainment for infants and toddlers is available.

Table 2.4   Sample Product Assortment Worksheet

Garden.com

Gardening supplies		
Product categories	Subcategories	Logic
Plants	Annuals Perennials Trees and shrubs	The heart and soul of the garden
New growth	Bulbs Seeds	For those willing to wait longer for results
Tools and essentials	Hand tools Power tools Fertilizer and mulch Plant stakes and labels Gardening clothes	One-stop shopping for all garden needs
Garden décor	Fountains Metal ornaments Stone ornaments	Not just for plants, the garden is an "outdoor room"
Floral gifts	Wreaths Blooming plants	Those who love gardening also love to give garden-related gifts
Fresh stem	Bouquets and cut flowers	An appropriate gift for gardeners and those who love gardeners

Practice using this organizational tool by reviewing the offerings of retailers, e-retailers, and catalog merchants. Once you are comfortable with defining product categories, fill out the worksheet with your proposed retail store product categories. Once you have defined what you are going to sell, you can move on to the next question: WHO you are going to sell to.

WHO Are You Going to Sell To?

Who are the potential purchasers of your products? Are you targeting a broad spectrum of the population, or do you have a niche market to address? What will most of your customers have in common? Do your customers already know they need your product, or do you need to educate them about its value or existence? Are they repeat buyers, or is your product a once-in-a-lifetime purchase?

You need to know and learn everything you can about your potential customers. This is one of the places where your business plan dovetails with your retail plan. Before you open your e-retail site, obtain a realistic understanding, based on research, of the size of your potential market, the buying patterns of your ideal customers, and the factors that motivate their purchases.

If you were operating a shop on Main Street, a defining parameter of your research would be the geography of your location. Obviously, geography is not a primary consideration for your e-retail store, but the following are other categories to be considered and are not traditional components of research with a traditional store:

- Is your target audience already online or likely to go online soon? What would compel them to go online if they are not there already?
- Does your target market have and use credit cards for purchases? Are they credit-worthy?
- Do members of your target audience already make purchases online? What is their level of readiness to do so?
- What kinds of sites, e-retail and other types as well, do members of your target audience visit on a regular basis? On an occasional basis?

It helps to be able to slice and dice your overall potential market (in this case, all once and future Web users) into broad types that you can then study further. A useful breakdown of Web users reveals[1]:

Simplifiers visit only a select few sites and have no tolerance for any extra effort. They spend an average of seven hours per month online. Simplifiers will identify the e-retail sites they like and bookmark them, and they will rarely seek out a new source or shopping experience. They demand end-to-end convenience and dislike features (e.g., chat rooms or pop-up advertisements) that may distract them from their primary purpose.

Surfers spend a great deal of time and money on the Web. Constituting only 8 percent of the active users, they account for 32 percent of total online time. Surfers are constantly seeking new experiences, new information, and whatever is HOT, HOT, HOT!

Connectors are still experimenting with the Web and learning what it can do for them. They comprise approximately 36 percent of active online users. Only 42 percent of them have already made online purchases. Connectors tend to seek out established brands they know and trust when they are ready to make online purchases.

Bargainers use the Web primarily to seek bargains and secondarily for the thrill of the hunt. To appeal to bargainers, a site must respond to their need to shop for the deal, get a great price, and "hobnob" with like-minded bargainers. Small wonder this group makes up more than 50 percent of all users of eBay, the greatest flea market in the universe!

Routiners and **sportsters** are both types who use the Web primarily for information, unique content, and up-to-date knowledge they cannot find elsewhere. Routiners hang out at news and financial sites, while sportsters exhibit the same behavior at sports-oriented sites. These users are the least likely to have made online purchases and the least likely to do so soon.

This list is only one potential breakdown of Web users, and there are others. Compare a few, until you find one that resonates for you.

Locating this kind of information can be challenging but fun. This research is nothing like the dutiful term papers you may have been forced to do in high school. Retail is about having a relationship with customers, one customer at a time. By researching your customer, you are beginning that relationship.

But I'm a Department Store . . . Do I Really Need to Do All This Work?

You may be reading through this material, thinking, "I don't need to go through this. I'm a department store, so I carry everything. I can skip to assortment planning." Think again. Unless you have vast resources behind you (and in your bank account) be very wary of the "all-things-to-all-people" strategy.

Since the Web is global and reaches consumers across virtually all demographics, it is tempting to try to make the most of the marketplace by offering a little of everything. Hence, at the point of creating retail strategy, it may seem like an easy way to avoid slogging through the work of market definition and research. Later in the process, however, you will not find this to your advantage at all.

How do you market an e-retail site that is all things to all people? It is possible but will require a lot of cash. You have to be present wherever "all people" are present, that is, *everywhere*. How do you keep track of inventory across different departments? How do you organize a purchasing system so that your efforts are coordinated? How do you communicate with vendors who you are and assure them that you will get consumers to your site to buy the products?

Keep in mind the lessons offered by example of The Gap and Amazon.com. Both companies started their retail life as something specific (selling Levi's jeans and selling books) and have since expanded their offerings, customer bases, and revenues. Yet they began with a tight focus. Each expanded to new product lines and departments with the right combination of market factors, sales history, and consumer trends.

You can always expand. It is pretty difficult to contract successfully. In the real world (as real as the Web gets, anyway), the winners of the first round have *not* been the e-retailers that began with a generalist approach. Now-defunct operations like ValueAmerica, a company that tried to transfer the discount department store concept directly to the Web, failed in part because they were not specific enough to differentiate themselves in the minds of consumers. While building an online brand, identity, and presence, the word of the day every day is FOCUS.

Resources for Research

Government Publications

Some of the resources you can use to begin researching your market include government publications such as the *Statistical Abstract of the United States,* the *United States Industrial Outlook,* and the *Marketing Information Guide.*

These can all be found in the business section of your public library. The reference librarians in the business section are your greatest allies in conducting such research.

For other types of government statistics, such as census information, industry data, the *Federal Reserve Bulletin,* and others, visit www.fedstats.gov. Fedstats is an easy-to-use one-stop Web site providing free access to government data. You can search Fedstats by keyword or agency, or browse an alphabetical list of all the reports available on the site.

Other Publications

Other publications available to the public for conducting research include the following:

Standard & Poor's Industry Surveys

Moody's Manuals

Encyclopedia of Associations

Journal of Marketing

Journal of Marketing Research

Journal of Consumer Research

ERetail.net

emarket.com

Journal of eCommerce

Other helpful tools include trade or special-interest magazines that address your field or are of interest to your audience.

This list is only a bare-bones place to start. Many publications are now available online, as well as in the library. Online research offers the capability to search a document or publication by keywords, saving you the time of scanning the entire text.

Online Resources

The online resources for research are almost mind-boggling. The following are a few suggestions that help subdivide the ocean of information.

THE INTERNET PUBLIC LIBRARY (www.ipl.org)

A project of the School of Information at the University of Michigan, the Internet Public Library provides a reliable launch pad for Web research. In addition to the basic reference collection, the librarians have organized information available on the Web by categories, and the "catalog" is updated regularly.

LIBRARIANS' INDEX TO THE INTERNET (www.lii.org)

Can you trust the information you find on the Web? If you found it through the Librarians' Index to the Internet, you have confirmation of the accuracy of the information. The Index is just that—a subject index of information, vetted by librarians, guiding you to reliable Web resources. The Librarian's Index to the Internet is supported by the U.S. Institute of Museum and Library Services and maintained through the Berkeley Digital Library SunSITE, a divison of the Library of California.

NORTHERN LIGHT RESEARCH (www.nlresearch.com)

Northern Light allows you to search freely available Web pages and "special collection" documents, which you do have to pay to view, on what seems to be a limitless universe of subjects. The searching capabilities of this site allow you to enter queries in plain language ("How many people had face lifts last year?") or through keywords ("cosmetic surgery AND men") and thoughtfully organizes your results into topical folders, making it easier to find the kind of information for which you are searching.

INTERNET STATISTICS AND RESEARCH SITES

A number of these sites are out there, and you can find a few to start with at Northern Light or any other search engine. Two useful ones include www. intercongroup.com and www.internetstats.com, both of which provide data, news, and reports on worldwide usage of the Internet, as well as e-commerce, e-business, and various user trends. Some of the information available is free; other information is contained in reports that must be purchased. You should not have to pay for basic statistical information. In fact, comparing statistical information from two or three different free sources is wise. If you are seeking more detailed information or more complete reporting on consumer behavior and trends, however, expect to pay for that kind of industry intelligence. It is true that there is a lot of free information floating around Cyberspace, but unless you know and trust the source, using free advice means risky business.

HOOVER'S ONLINE (www.hoovers.com)

Hoover's provides company information on public and privately held companies—a great way to check out the competition! Hoover's also provides direct links to Securities and Exchange Commission files at www.sec.gov, where you can look up SEC filings for publicly traded companies. The most comprehensive filing a company provides is the 10K, an annual report on the industry, business, finances, and forecasts for the coming year. If you can identify a publicly traded company in your industry or a related industry, 10Ks are a great way to get summary information on the state of the industry and the market. Look especially for the sections entitled "Industry Background" or "Industry Outlook."

LISTSERVS, USENETS, WEB SITES, AND SPECIAL INTEREST CHAT GROUPS RELATED TO YOUR BUSINESS

The global popularity of the Internet is in large part due to its unique ability to connect individuals with common interests. Listservs and Usenets are both international topical communications systems whereby registered users can read and respond to the comments and questions of other users. Trade association sites or private special-interest Web sites are another variation on the theme. Most Internet service providers (e.g., America Online or Compuserve) offer their users "chat rooms," where like-minded users can connect with each other and discuss everything from current events to model rockets. You can find affinity groups by checking out the major Internet service providers, typing keywords into search engines, or exploring directories of Listservs and Usenets. Try the directories at CataList (www.lsoft.com/lists/listref.html) and RemarQ (www.remarq.com) for starters.

You can find groups as specific as the needle or as general as the haystack. If your e-retail site is selling handmade dog sweaters, you could look for affinity sites devoted to pet talk in general, dogs in general, or specific breeds. If you are selling a new type of women's running shorts, you might find groups discussing health and fitness, women's groups discussing exercise, or groups of female runners.

The users of these features and services are your potential customers, but remember that your purpose at this stage is not to sell anything to them but to engage in their community. Learn their vocabulary. Understand their issues. Find out the latest hot topic, and learn which recently released products your market loves and hates. *Do NOT use these sites to post advertising or marketing messages to draw users to your e-retail site.* This is considered a *very* serious breach of "Netiquette," and you may well be thrown off the site if you do so. In fact, it is not a bad idea to review a Netiquette resource to learn more about the rules of engagement for these virtual communities before you participate. Visit any site on the Netiquette Webring (a collection of sites all devoted to explicating Netiquette: www.netiquette.freeservers.com) to learn proper behavior.

Other Resources

SHOP THE COMPETITION, ONLINE AND OFF

No matter what you are planning to sell, *someone* out there is selling it too, or selling something like it. Find out who and where and to whom. Visit competitors' sites and learn as much as you can about their *modus operandi*. Go to brick-and-mortar establishments that your customers are used to visiting. Make note of where and how your competitors are marketing their stores. What messages are they using to attract customers? Are you aiming for the same customer, or do you plan to julienne the market differently?

Look for complementary businesses too. Stores that cater to your customer but fill different needs may be able to help you. For example, if you are selling custom-designed golf shoes and you find a store selling custom-selected golf clubs, the possibilities for fruitful partnerships are immediately apparent.

HELPFUL TIPS FOR ONLINE RESEARCH

The Internet has proven to be a researcher's nirvana. Much of the information that was once only available through tedious hours at the library can now be pulled up right on a personal desktop. The federal data alone, collected at Fedstats (www.fedstats.gov), is worth its memory capacity in gold to a market researcher. Add in all the trade organizations, special interest Web pages, service provider content channels, and search engines (both specialized and general), and you have some very powerful, comprehensive research tools literally at your fingertips.

This bonanza comes with a caveat, however. Because of the ease of point-and-click research to follow link after link after link, it is easy to get sucked into the sheer volume of information available. It is important to know when to step back from the computer, take the dog for a walk, think about what you have learned, and begin putting the information into some kind of useful order.

Set aside a specific amount of time for your research sessions. Put a kitchen timer next to the desk if you need it to stay on task. Write down the specific question you want to answer during this session. It is best to have only one question before you at a time, and try to narrow your question's focus enough so that it is possible to make some headway. Instead of "What criteria do parents use to select children's equipment?", try "What criteria do parents use to select strollers?"

Log on, take a deep breath, and take charge! Depending on the targeted question during a given research session, you may start from a search engine (again, it is best to be as specific as possible, unless you feel like wading through 300,000 hits), a trade site, a competitor site, or a service provider's content channel, to name a few. When you find a particularly helpful site, bookmark it. You can also save pages to an external disk or to your hard drive with the "save" feature of your browser. Saving material this way allows you to review it at leisure when you are offline. Saving will also help you create a research archive that you can use as a starting point in a future research session.

Document all salient information as you find it. To print or not to print is a matter of personal preference. Despite the promise of the paperless office, printed documents still allow us to take notes, highlight points, file by subject, and read on the bus or at the doctor's office. If you are printing, be sure that your browser's print options allow you to print the site address and the date of printing for each document you keep. There is nothing worse than having a piece of information on your desk and not knowing where it came from or how to back it up.

Follow links that seem helpful, but if the first few pages do not live up to your expectations, backtrack to your last helpful site and try again. This will help you avoid chasing too many rabbits down holes and will keep you working with material you find helpful.

Remember that the Internet is an entertainment medium *and* an advertising medium. Any commercial site you visit (including most search engines) is designed with eye-catching advertising and games designed to keep you on the site or get you to visit the site's sponsors. Do your best to stay on task and ignore these appeals to come outside and play.

When your time is up, immediately log off and write down your initial thoughts on what you learned in this session. This debriefing makes it much easier to go back through your saved and printed materials and remember what you were thinking at the time.

Research can be time-consuming, but it is also a wonderful process of discovery; just remember to drop the breadcrumbs on the path so you can find your way back.

The resources for research are vast. You will find the more you learn in general, the more you learn about new sources. At the same time, be creative in your approach to research. Talk about your project with friends and colleagues. You will be amazed at how often you may hear, "You know, I just read something about that the other day . . ."

By gathering this information from all available sources, you are planning from a position of knowledge rather than from guesswork. If you are attempting to get financing for your e-retail start-up operation, you will need to show the bank your market research and demonstrate that it supports your business plan. Even if you are not seeking financing, getting as much information as you can find about your customers can only help you. How old are they? Where do they live? Where do they shop? What motivates them to purchase goods and services?

You are not simply gathering data indiscriminately, however. Once you have the data, you must also identify which demographics and "psychographics" *matter* to your customer in their relationship with you, the e-retailer. Some products and categories are bought on the basis of gender, ages, or interests of the consumers. Other product purchases are defined by price sensitivities, brands, or consumption habits. Table 2.5 illustrates the different motivators behind a few different kinds of product purchases.

Many retail and e-retail operations cater to several markets, although one is generally defined as the primary market. For each distinct market, you will want to be able to lay out demographics and "psychographics" in a way that helps you communicate with your customer. To do this, you need to rely on your research, experience, and brainstorming. Remember to repeat this process for each market segment to which your e-retail site will cater. Copy Worksheet 2.2, Customer Demographics and "Psychographics," from the book or the CD-ROM to brainstorm about your own primary and secondary markets. When you are done, you will be able to create a visual reference that suggests what the common denominators are between your markets so that you can craft your assortment and marketing to maximize sales accordingly. The sample in Table 2.6 characterizes the primary market for a well-known retailer.

Once you have outlined what you are going to sell and to whom, you can turn to the third question: WHY will customers purchase from your e-retail site?

Table 2.5   Product Purchase Motivation

Product	Primary purchase motivator	Secondary purchase motivator
Towels	Color	Price
Lingerie	Gender	Age
Motorcycles	Interest	Brand
Greeting cards	Brand	Season, occasion

Worksheet 2.2 Customer Demographics and "Psychographics"

[Name of Business]

_____ *Market*	
Age	
Gender	
Primary function of product	
Secondary functions of product	
Features sought in product	
Where they currently purchase	
Price-sensitive?	
Brand-conscious?	
Fashion-conscious?	
Frequent or casual user?	
Web behavior category	
Other:	

Table 2.6 Sample Customer Demographics and "Psychographics" Worksheet

The Gap and gap.com

Primary Market	
Age	20 to 30
Gender	Female
Primary function of product	Fashion
Secondary functions of product	Apparel
Features sought in product	Comfort, casual but elegant styling
Where they currently purchase	Gap and competitors
Price-sensitive?	Medium
Brand-conscious?	Very
Fashion-conscious?	Medium to Very
Frequent or casual user?	Medium
Web behavior category	Connector

Why Will a Customer Buy From You?

You should be able to answer this question in three or four clear sentences. This is the part where your retail strategy comes together. *What* and to *whom* establish the essence of your e-retail site. *Why* speaks to the relationship you have with your customers. Being able to answer this question demonstrates a clear understanding of your customer's purchase patterns, needs, and how you will meet those needs. The *why* establishes why consumers shop for items at different places. It is the reason Neiman Marcus and Sam's Wholesale Club are both big businesses. You can buy a dress at either store. Obviously, effective retail is not just about customers needing dresses. It is also about different customers looking for different things in their shopping experience, merchandise selection, and budget.

Determining why a customer will shop at your e-retail site rather than use any alternative method to acquire the kind of merchandise you are carrying establishes your competitive advantage. It is imperative that you do not proceed with assortment planning until you have a thorough understanding of your competitive advantage.

LOCATION, LOCATION, LOCATION

Considered the three most important elements in traditional brick-and-mortar retail, location-location-location is, surprisingly, just as important for Web-based retail. Despite the ease with which users can clickety-click from New York to Milan to Johannesburg in seconds, the location you choose will affect how easily they find and get to *your* site.

At this initial strategic stage, you want to give some thought to location. Perhaps you are considering tenancy in an online mall. Perhaps you have yet to name your enterprise. Even if your business is already live and selling, you may be considering different hosting/server options that may affect the availability and functionality of your site.

The Power of Naming

In the discourse of philosophy, the naming of a thing grounds it in reality. Nowhere is this more apparent than in e-culture, where your name is literally your *address*. Consider carefully, then, the impact your name has on the user. It should be descriptive, strongly branded, and *easy to type*. Your name is your real estate. Choose wisely.

e-Commerce consultant David Strom notes that when Barnes & Noble launched barnesandnoble.com in 1997, the company had moniker troubles. "You'd think that a brand like Barnes & Noble is worth lots in Cyberspace," Strom wrote in *Web Informant,* his online newsletter, while summing up a scathing review of the site's gala launch in New York. "Unfortunately, it is a pain in the carpal tunnel to type in as a URL: www.barnesandnoble.com. It looks funny on the page. No, I am not being small-minded here. Maybe lazy. But I made lots of mistakes trying to type in their name in my browser, and I am a pretty accurate typist. It just doesn't work. Indeed, the whole 'and' thing in a domain name really doesn't flow for me. As Emperor Josef says in Amadeus, there are just too many notes."[2]

It is worth noting that since Strom wrote that piece, barnesandnoble.com has changed its name to the snappier bn.com (AOL keyword *bn* for short). The trade-off, of course, is existing brand-equity for ease of use.

Getting "Malled"?

It was probably inevitable that Cyberdevelopers would take the successful mall concept and apply it to e-retail. The problem is, the model does not work as effectively on the Web as it does in suburbia. The mall concept originated as a way to put a wide variety of stores in a single easy-access location, making shopping an easier experience for consumers. People can go to the mall, even if they are not quite sure what they are looking for, and find a plethora of reasons to part with their money all under one roof.

On the Web, however, customers do not need a Cybermall to explore a wide range of choices. In fact, most Cybermalls are cumbersome to navigate and, for the most part, do not provide the cohesion, logic, and compelling shopping experience of their real-world counterparts.

The upside is that renting space in a Cybermall may give you access to store-building tools and some marketing support. If you need this sort of structure to test an idea or launch a small-scale version before setting out on your own, this option is worth exploring. Be sure to read the lease's fine print carefully. As a Cybermall tenant, you should expect and receive the same kind of service as a

(continued)

Location, Location, Location (*continued*)

tenant in a brick-and-mortar mall. Verify traffic counts, talk to other tenants about their experiences with the landlord, visit the site to see if it is a place you can imagine your customers visiting, and take all the legal precautions with the lease as with any other rental arrangement.

Service, Please

Remember that there is still a physical presence to e-everything. Somewhere, circuits and wires and communications equipment are humming with your transactions. Some companies will opt for keeping the messy physicality in-house. They will need to hire the gurus who can choose the equipment, program it, and keep it running.

Outsourcing your server and hosting functions is another option. Countless companies are ready, willing, and able to provide these services for you. All are not created equal. Make sure that your technical host can provide the kind of home you seek for your systems over the long haul, because moving, even virtually, is expensive and problematic. The Appendix provides more information and a guide to resources, but we raise the issue here as part of your grand vision and front-end planning.

Here are examples of retail differentiation that may apply to your concept:

- Low/best price
- Broad selection (wide range of categories, features, price points, and so on)
- Deep selection (lots of colors and sizes of each item)
- Special/niche selection (e.g., special sizes, special-interest items)
- Delivery speed
- Customer service and support
- Product information/guarantees
- Rare or unique items
- Leverage from partners
- Brand recognition and loyalty
- Convenience/easy-to-find location
- Value of site content to users
- Loyalty programs

The competitive advantage is a key feature, or combination of key features, that your customers want or need in their shopping. Each feature correlates to specific benefits to the customer. The features are your competitive advantage; the benefits create the relationship with your customer. Use the same format to brainstorm your e-retail site's competitive advantages on Worksheet 2.3, Competitive Advantage Analysis.

Table 2.7 lays out the different competitive advantages of two retailers: Sam's Wholesale Club and Neiman Marcus, whereas Table 2.8 applies the same concepts to e-retailers Amazon.com and FashionDish.

Worksheet 2.3   Competitive Advantage Analysis

[Name]

Feature	Benefit

Table 2.7   Competitive Advantage Analysis

Sam's Wholesale Club

Feature	Benefit
Bulk Items	Useful to both business and private customers
Self-serve	Lowers prices by reducing sales staff overhead
One-stop shopping	Broad range of product categories under one roof
Membership shopping	Targeted marketing
Low prices	Saves money, increases buying power

Neiman Marcus

Feature	Benefit
Haute couture, designer and unique items	Customers can get the latest fashions and wear unique, well-made clothing to express their individuality
Well-trained sales staff	Assistance selecting between many expensive items; customers feel well-cared-for in the store
Many departments with complementary products	Ability to coordinate décor, outfits, gifts, and so on
Personal shopping services	Busy customers can save time by having a trained shopper make selections
Corporate credit program	Makes it easy to purchase items and pay costs over time, if desired

Table 2.8   Competitive Advantage Analysis

Amazon.com

Feature	Benefit
Almost unlimited selection	Meets the practical needs of a wide range of customers; customers can shop at the same site for many kinds of items
Product reviews by actual customers as well as staff	Customer can get a preview of the product's features and usability, helping to make an informed buying decision
Quick delivery	Customer gets product soon after order
Targeted product recommendations	Assistance with selecting additional items, finding related items
Low prices	Saves money, increases buying power
Easy to find	Easy-to-remember name and lots of partner placement mean that the customer does not have to hunt around the Web to find the e-retail site

FashionDish.com

Feature	Benefit
Fashion/gossip content	Unique and sassy editorial aimed to interest, advise, and entertain target market
Personal shopping service	Personalized follow-up on customers' questions and specific requests
New/fashion items	Customers have access to fashionable products
Limited assortment	Creates focused identity and reduces time needed to find fashion items
Site discounts on hot accessories	Stretches customer's spending power for unique, targeted items
Celebrity-identified products	Customers can identify with their favorite celebrities and put themselves on the cutting edge of fashion

How Do You Sell?

There are many ways to sell a product, through different media and with different tools. Our primary concern throughout this book is on Web-based retail sales of consumer products, but you should not limit yourself to this singular focus. As noted in Chapter 1, successful retailers big and small have integrated their sales channels to maximize customers' opportunities to buy. A Web site may send a print catalog or have a brick-and-mortar store grounding its brand. Catalogs may expand to the Web or establish real-world shopping opportunities such as a simple outlet store.

How you sell depends on your customers, products, budget, and a host of other variables. The appeal of Web-based retail is that it seems to have fewer inherent barriers to entry than other sales channels (lower start-up costs, wider distribution capabilities). However, Web-based retail demands minute attention to customer service and the changing technologies that support the medium.

Choose sales channels based on where your customers are, how they are accustomed to shopping, and what works for your product assortment. Keep in mind that Web shoppers may research a product online, then choose to buy it in a traditional store, or vice versa. A consumer contemplating the purchase of a complex tool may want to play with one at a store, but he or she may ultimately purchase it through the Web. Another consumer may use the Web to compare features of different manufacturers' appliances, then hit the local brick-and-mortar establishment to make the purchase.

Your challenge is to become the consumer's retailer of choice for each and every touch point in the purchase process. If your retail strategy includes such elements as a loyalty program, you want that program to be integrated across your various sales channels. Most importantly, customers should recognize you in any medium because your message, your logic, and the experience of shopping with you are consistent across all media.

Looking Ahead to Profitability

Each decision you make while defining your retail strategy will of course have a practical and financial impact on the way you eventually run your operation. Consider the impact each of these variables, which are critical to the development of your retail strategy, may have on your overall business operations. Table 2.9 demonstrates the profit considerations inherent in several strategic positions.

Table 2.9   Strategic Components/Profit Considerations

Strategic component	Practical profit considerations
Wide selection	Requires merchants with expertise in many areas or more merchants
	Increases warehouse space demands
	Increases inventory stock of slower-moving sizes and styles, thereby slowing down your inventory turn
Fast delivery	Requires own warehouse and sometimes multiple warehouses
Fashion-conscious products or customers; highly seasonal stock	Increases chance that particular items will be slow or nonsellers
	Requires continual updating of merchandise and inventory
	Clearing old stock will involve increased markdowns and sales
Complex products	Extensive pre- or post-sale customer support required
Valuable site content	Adds an important editorial arm to your operations and requires policies regarding editorial content

These factors do raise costs, but that does not mean you should avoid them. In fact, these may form the core of your competitive edge. If developed and sustained, these elements can set you apart from your rivals. However, you must be aware of the increase in cost that accompanies them so that you can price your goods accordingly to remain profitable.

Achieving Harmony between Your Retail Strategy Elements

You may have already noticed, in going through these exercises and worksheets, that the elements of retail strategy (the *what, who, why,* and even *how*) develop in tandem. Each element interacts with and affects the others. As you fine-tune your retail strategy, continue to refer to your worksheets and modify each one as you go. Each change must confirm and complement your overall strategy.

While you work through your retail strategy, get into brainstorming mode. Do not self-censor your ideas until they have had time to blossom. Then you can work backward from your dream to figure out what resources you will need in order to make it come true.

Remember that every decision you make with regard to your e-retail business may impact other aspects of the strategy. Building and sustaining a profitable retail operation involves constant change and adaptation, but the decisions and changes you make must always refer back to a logical, coherent strategy, or the entire enterprise can collapse. It is an incredibly dynamic and fast-moving industry, which is both the thrill and the challenge of making all the pieces work together.

Table 2.10   Product Assortment Worksheet

ShoeWeb

Shoes for men and women		
Product categories	Subcategories	Logic
Men's shoes	Dress Casual Athletic Seasonal	Shoes for all aspects of life; one-stop shopping
Women's shoes	Dress Casual Athletic Seasonal	Shoes for all aspects of life; one-stop shopping
Shoe care	Leather care products Polishes Laces Shoe trees	Expert assistance in caring for and maintaining good looking shoes
Accessories	Coordinating handbags and belts	Appropriate items to finish an outfit

Hypothetical Cases

Retail Strategy for ShoeWeb

ShoeWeb plans to begin e-retail operations with a full line of men's and women's shoes. The store will feature a wide variety of styles and sizes of shoes suitable for all occasions (Table 2.10).

Although the owners of ShoeWeb intend to sell to all adults, they want to segment their market to improve their financial planning and marketing efforts. Some market research reveals that their primary market will be comprised of women. Additional details of the primary market are defined in Table 2.11.

Table 2.11   Customer Demographics and "Psychographics"
ShoeWeb

Primary Market	
Age	25 to 45
Gender	Women
Primary function of product	Fashion
Secondary functions of product	Comfortable footwear
Features sought in product	New, attractive, and comfortable.
Where they currently purchase	Shoe stores, department stores
Price-sensitive?	Medium: Expect well-made shoe to cost between $75 and $200
Brand-conscious?	Yes
Fashion-conscious?	Extremely
Frequent or casual user?	Medium; on average, purchases eight pairs of shoes each year
Web behavior category and details	Simplifier: Is familiar with Internet usage, mostly through work; spends on average 3 hours per week online outside of work; does product research, but rarely makes purchases on the Web; those at the younger end of the target market do the most web shopping

The owners of ShoeWeb know the kind of organization they are trying to build; they want to have a reputation for great service, unlimited selection, and close customer relationships. They brainstorm on the features of their business, coming up with the customer benefits that will translate into sales.

By laying out the retail strategy on these worksheets, our shoe e-retailers quickly find conflicting elements in their dreams for ShoeWeb:

- Quick delivery means owning a lot of stock in warehouse.
- A wide range of styles in so many sizes also means taking on a lot of inventory.
- Highly fashion-conscious product lines involve risky inventory.

Together, these three elements contradict the "lowest prices" feature. ShoeWeb has a couple of options here. If they still feel that "lowest price" is the key factor to their success, they must retool the other elements of the strategy to

Table 2.12   Competitive Advantage Analysis
ShoeWeb

Primary Market	
Feature	Benefit
Wide, fashionable selection	Best availability of the latest styles and colors
Guaranteed sizes	Hard-to-fit customers know their sizes are always in stock (from size 4 to 11, in widths A to DDDD)
Fast, reliable delivery "in time for the weekend" for orders placed by Wednesday night	Although Web shopping is less immediate than bringing a purchase home from the mall, ShoeWeb gives customers the speediest possible delivery of merchandise
Generous return policy	Since it can be seen as risky to buy shoes without trying them on, customers have options regarding their purchases
Lowest prices	Increases customer spending power

reduce some of the costs related to stocking inventory. This might mean more limited selections in styles and/or colors or a longer delivery time.

Another alternative is to revisit their customer definition. Since their primary market is only "moderately" price sensitive, perhaps it is appropriate to eliminate the "lowest prices" feature of the competitive strategy.

How ShoeWeb will sell products is a particularly important question for this particular e-retail strategy. Since customers assume they will want to try on shoes before buying, ShoeWeb has a challenge on its hands to make sense of itself in the online environment. The management team briefly considers adding a print catalog to its sales channels, since customers are at least familiar with the concept of ordering shoes from a catalog, but ultimately decides to focus all its efforts on the Web site. Clearly, effective education on the benefits of Web shopping for shoes should be a major component of marketing.

When the owners of ShoeWeb negotiate with vendors in Chapter 8, they can explore other ways to reduce their inventory costs. For instance, many footwear manufacturers want early tests on their products to determine the correct quantities for second-wave production. ShoeWeb might propose providing this valuable market-testing opportunity in exchange for sharing the inventory risk.

The bottom line is that there is no "right" answer, but ShoeWeb will live or die by a logical retail strategy.

Retail Strategy for WebKidCare

WebKidCare is a content-based site providing information on child care and development. Its revenue model relies on an extensive e-retail operation selling toys, books, and equipment. Caregivers visit the site to get information on caring for their young charges and to acquire the many supplies and amusements required at the early stages of child-rearing (up to age 6). Table 2.13 outlines the product assortment for the e-retail component of the business.

The owners of WebKidCare have already laid out their retail strategy. To differentiate themselves in a crowded and fragmented marketplace, WebKidCare focuses on the needs of professional and semiprofessional caregivers. These caregivers are looking for a streamlined method to review and order equipment. They are busy people who want to ensure they are making sound purchases for work. WebKidCare offers a full line of equipment, along with expert and user reviews of products sold on the site.

Home-based day care, organizational day care, small businesses, and franchises are among the markets targeted. Within these markets, various individuals

Table 2.13   Product Assortment Worksheet

WebKidCare

Child care equipment		
Product categories	Subcategories	Logic
Infant	Gross motor skills Fine motor skills Language Music Reasoning Health and Safety	Appropriate accessories and equipment for creating a stimulating, professional caregiving environment
Toddler	Gross motor skills Fine motor skills Language Music Reasoning Health and safety	Appropriate accessories and equipment for creating a stimulating, professional caregiving environment
Preschool	Gross motor skills Fine motor skills Language Music Reasoning Health and safety	Appropriate accessories and equipment for creating a stimulating, professional caregiving environment

may be making the purchases for a child-care facility. Table 2.14 focuses on one primary market: directors and/or lead teachers at small child-care centers (up to 24 children of varying ages).

In its competitive advantage analysis, WebKidCare identified a number of effective features and benefits, as outlined in Table 2.15.

The *how* is less important for WebKidCare than it is for ShoeWeb, but the WebKidCare management team will look into the possibility of adding a print component to its sales channels. Eventually, a brick-and-mortar showroom may add another "real-world" dimension to WebKidCare's efforts.

Table 2.14   Customer Demographics and "Psychographics"

WebKidCare

Primary Market	
Age	35 to 45
Gender	Female
Primary function of product	Safe entertainment for multiple children
Secondary functions of product	Kid-friendly facility décor
Features sought in product	Long-lasting, easy-to-clean/care for, safe, fun
Where they currently purchase	Catalog suppliers and showrooms
Price-sensitive?	Very to moderate
Brand-conscious?	No
Fashion conscious?	No
Frequent or casual user?	Frequent by seasons
Web behavior category and details	Simplifier: Generally juggling many distinct tasks over the course of a busy week; has little time for in-depth shopping and yet wants to make informed decisions. Seeks sites that enable more effective child care environments; not interested in "fluff" or flash.

Table 2.15   Competitive Advantage Analysis

WebKidCare

Feature	Benefit
Classroom-grade equipment	Withstands repeated use by groups
Specialty items for use with multiple children	Customers can directly access products pertaining to group child care
Corporate accounts	Customer saves time by entering order and delivery information once; corporate credit to worthy customers means that customers can plan cash flow better
Guaranteed low price	No need to shop the competition, which saves the customer time
Informative, targeted content providing information on the business of child care, tips, and advice	Unique and useful resource for professional and semiprofessional caregivers
Wide range of quality equipment and supplies all in one place	Saves time for busy professionals
Product review board	Customers know they are purchasing equipment that has already been reviewed by objective experts for safety and effectiveness

RETAIL STRATEGY CHECKLIST

❑ Retail strategy is about *what, who,* and *why*: *What* are you going to sell? *Who* are you going to sell to? *Why* should a customer buy from you?
❑ Define the *what*:
   ❑ Complete Worksheet 2.1, Product Assortment Worksheet
   ❑ List broad categories and more specific subcategories
   ❑ Aim for a logical assortment that tells potential customers what you are all about.
❑ Define the *why*:
   ❑ Begin researching your target market through publications, online resources, and other sources
   ❑ Shop the competition
   ❑ Complete Worksheet 2.2, Customer Demographics and "Psychographics," for each market you are targeting
❑ Define the *why*:
   ❑ Review potential competitive advantages that you can offer your customers through unique features.
   ❑ Translate your features into customer benefits.
   ❑ Complete Worksheet 2.3, Competitive Advantage Analysis.
❑ Consider *how* you sell: Which channels and which ownership models apply to your business?
❑ Review your strategy work to date: Are there inconsistencies between your strategic components? Is a logic gelling for your e-retail site?

Endnotes

1. "All Visitors Are Not Created Equal," a proprietary study by *McKinsey Research and Media Metrix,* April 2000. The research surveyed 50,000 U.S. active users of the Web.
2. "The Makings of a Mediocre Web Site," *Web Informant* 68:13, May 1997. (www.strom.com)

CHAPTER THREE

Assortment Planning

Chapter Preview

With the strategy in place, the more tactical and practical assortment and financial planning can begin. Our hypothetical e-retailers strive to create product assortments that reflect and enhance their strategies.

So, What *Are* You Selling?

Once you have played with, researched, and established your retail strategy, you can plan the assortment of products you want to carry in your e-retail store. You are now moving from the strategic plan into the tactical plan. If you are selling books by contemporary women authors, it is time to decide *which* authors and *which* books. If you are selling cooking supplies, it is time to decide *which* supplies and *which* manufacturers. Once your strategy is in place, you can start to select products, set prices, and create preliminary financial plans to make your operation profitable.

Assortment planning is comprised of two steps: (1) defining the products and (2) developing the financial plans to support your product choices.

It is important to stress that assortment planning is NOT optional. Regardless of whether you plan on owning your inventory, assortment planning fills in a central piece of your plan: *what* you are actually selling, that is, brands, styles, colors, and so on. Most e-retailers own some or all of their assortments, which is why the assortment planning process is tied so closely to the financial-planning process. You must remember, though, that even if you do not own a buck's worth of stock, your product sources will require sales forecasts in order to plan supplies. The forecasting component of the financial plans, then, remains an important tool, regardless of the business and inventory model you select.

GOING HYBRID: ASSORTMENT PLANNING WITHOUT OWNING ASSORTMENT

If you plan to offer items that you do not own as inventory, assortment planning and sales forecasting become *more* important in creating a profitable operation. Consider the following:

- **Researching and sourcing product:** Your relationship with your customer (and your bank) demands that you identify and offer products that your customer wants and is willing to pay for. Your relationship with your vendors, however, changes significantly when you ask for unusual shipping and/or ownership arrangements. You are now asking the vendor to share more of the risk associated with products that do not sell, along with the costs of warehousing products. Vendors who agree to these arrangements want to know how much of their products you anticipate selling so that *they* can plan resources and cash flow.
- **Merchandising:** As we explore in Chapter 4, effective merchandising attracts customers to your site, moves them through your site to the items they want (and the ones you want them to want), and encourages them to part with their plastic. The only way to merchandise effectively is if you have a well-defined assortment. The customer selects an item from your fabulously compelling assortment; even though she may not know if the item is in your warehouse, *you* need to know.

Eventually, you will be making decisions about how much of your assortment you will own as inventory and how much you will be able to arrange for "just-in-time" supplies in response to customer orders. That is the great promise of the Web environment—to have the freedom to market and sell items that are not "on the shelf."

Assortment planning lies at the very heart of what a merchant does for a retail organization, and it is a skill learned best by practice over the course of a career. Keep in mind that it is unrealistic to expect to get assortment planning precisely right the first time you try it, any more than you could expect to get calculus equations right the first time you try them.

Defining Products

The retail strategy you have created serves as the framework for your product assortment planning. You have already defined your product categories and subcategories. Use Worksheet 3.1, Assortment Planning Worksheet, to create a separate sheet for each subcategory, and start listing all the products you want or may want to carry. The blank worksheet is provided on the CD-ROM, or you can copy the version in the book. Be as specific as you can. If you know what brands you want, list them. If you know what price ranges you want to offer, list them. Tables 3.1 and 3.2 demonstrate the use of the worksheet for subcategories on two e-retail sites: the WeddingChannel and Fogdog Sports. Complete assortment-planning worksheets for every subcategory in your assortment. You will prioritize the importance of each product later, so use this opportunity to brainstorm as many product offerings as you can.

Worksheet 3.1   Assortment Planning Worksheet for [Name of Business]

Category: [Insert here]

Subcategory: [Insert here]

Product	Price	Notes

Table 3.1   Assortment Planning Worksheet for WeddingChannel.com

Category: For the Ceremony

Subcategory: Ring Pillows

Product	Price	Notes
Tres Beau Ringbearer Pillow	$29	All below are through preferred supplier, Beverly Clark
		White/ivory
Amour Collection Ring-bearer Pillow	$39	White/ivory
Flower Petals Square Pillow	$39	White/ivory
Threads of Gold Square Pillow	$33	White/ivory
Classique Ringbearer Pillow	$33	White with red accent
Organza Bow Collection Ringbearer Pillow	$33	White with gold accent
Nontraditional styles		Different colors (pastels) and fabrics (lace) available
Do-it-yourself kit	Approx. $20	Pillow and booklet with ribbon/decoration suggestions and instructions

You will inevitably have to compromise between your "ideal" assortment and the actual products you are able to source. Generate as many options as possible at the front end, and you will improve your chances of creating a full and well-balanced array of products to offer your future customers.

As you work through this exercise, the importance of skilled buying knowledge for each of these categories immediately becomes apparent. Perhaps you are a microretailer, offering only five categories of items, each with no more than two subcategories. With a minimal selection of three products in each subcategory, you should research and prepare an assortment of at least 30 products in order to take your site live. Of course, that is assuming you can find a source for every one of those products. As a point of comparison, Gazoontite, a multichannel retailer specializing in relief for allergy and asthma sufferers, carries 2,000 to 3,000 products. (For more on Gazoontite, see Chapter 10.)

Table 3.2 Assortment Planning Worksheet for Fogdog.com

Category: Apparel

Subcategory: Performance Bottoms

Product	Price	Notes
Hind Women's Munich Tight	$57.99	*Colors:* Black, charcoal, ink
		Sizes: S to XL
Hind Munich Tight	$57.99	Black, charcoal, ink
		S to L
Nike Track Pant	$51.99	Black, Obsidian
		S to XL
Want comparable styles at a lower price point? Look into lighter colors (blue, green) for summer season.		Try Danskin or Moving Comfort

What Is a SKU?

In retail, a product is called a *SKU* (pronounced "skew"), short for "stock keeping unit." A SKU can be anything you define it to be, and products are labeled with a SKU number to define them in the assortment. For the most part, you will want to assign SKUs to the products in your assortment on a one-to-one basis. However, if you are carrying items that come in different sizes and/or colors, you can use SKUs to define your assortment in a way that makes sense for your business.

For example, a manufacturer may decide that a shoe style is available in three colors: brown, black, and burgundy. From the manufacturer's point of view, this is one product with three colors and in multiple sizes. The retailer, on the other hand, may want to consider each color as a separate SKU (in fact, the retailer may only want to buy the black and the burgundy). Thus, instead of stocking one style, the retailer stocks two SKUs with unique SKU numbers. Another retailer may consider the style as one SKU regardless of color, while a third may want to distinguish further and separate SKUs by color and size. It all depends on what the retailer wants to track.

BASICALLY, IT'S FASHION

In addition to identifying the products that fit into each category and subcategory, there are some additional ways to think about your product offerings.

In the fashion world, it is common to divide your products into "basic" and "fashion." Created by the fashion apparel industry, this breakdown can be applied to other markets as well. You simply need to determine which items in your assortment change often, and which items remain the same, season after season. Booksellers always carry dictionaries (basics), but the hot titles change every season (fashion).

Types of Products	
Basic	Always in stock (i.e., able to reorder)
	Often purchased more than once, or in multiples (e.g., socks, underwear, and so on)
	Remains the same from season to season
Fashion	Styles and/or colors change often
	Usually available for one season only

In your assortment, you should mix both basic and fashion items. The basics are the anchor products that your customers *know* they can purchase from you at any time. Thus, when they need it, they will visit your site. The fashion items encourage return visits whenever your customers want to check out "what's new."

The best basic and fashion mix depends on a number of factors, including the following:

- **Speed of your market:** If your market is one in which new styles are introduced rapidly, and the customer is often seeking the latest style, you need to devote more of your assortment to fashion items.
- **Customer profile:** Is your customer more interested in replacing an existing item, or trying something new? Are your shoppers simplifiers, who want

---

easy access to basic products, or are they surfers, constantly seeking new experiences?

- **Your strategy:** Your strategy may dictate an emphasis on one area or another.
- **Profitability requirements:** Basic items are usually less risky to purchase, and are therefore more profitable for you to sell.

Assortment planning is an ongoing process, of course. Once you are open for business, you should keep up with the products available in your field and make appropriate choices for each season's offerings. Fashion items require more creativity and risk taking in your ongoing assortment planning, but even if your assortment is primarily basics, you need to stay on top of things. After all, designers and manufacturers change styles regularly even for such basics as socks and underwear.

Prioritizing Assortment Needs

Once you have listed as many product options as you can, you need to prioritize the importance of each within your assortment. Return to your retail strategy and compare it with your preliminary assortment list. Lay out your growing assortment options visually (e.g., on note cards, with one product per note card) and "read" the assortment for logic, clarity, and alignment with your strategy. Are there redundancies or major gaps? Do you need more breadth or more depth in any given category or across the board? Tweak and tune the assortment, creating as many logical options as possible. Which of your potential products will attract your customers and drive your business? What do you anticipate your bestsellers to be? What one or two products do you want your customers to equate with your name? Answers to these questions help you determine where to put the majority of your effort in sourcing items in the marketplace.

Assortment planning is the practical embodiment of your retail strategy: the *who, what,* and *why* detailed in Chapter 2. As you make preliminary decisions about the specifics of your assortment, keep a list of your who, what, and why handy. Tack it up on your bulletin board. Tattoo it to your eyelids. It is the key to creating an assortment your customers will find compelling.

Sourcing Products

Once you have laid out your product assortment and prioritized your assortment, you can begin to source your products in the market. Time for research again—this time to learn who makes the products you want and who sells them. There are a number of ways to find products and potential vendors. These include:

- Studying competitor assortments
- Participating in online marketplaces (see "The Web of Sources")
- Reviewing trade journals
- Attending trade shows featuring the types of products you want to carry

As you request information from potential sources you are likely to receive catalogs (or *line-lists*), which will vary in their level of detail and information. Mark the items that interest you, and make notes on the additional questions you may have regarding product specifications and pricing. If an item is unfamiliar to you, feel free to request samples and/or product demonstrations.

A Web of Sources

You have probably had some exposure to the way the Web has altered selling relationships between businesses, as well as those between businesses and consumers. The easy connectivity of the Web allows vendors and retailers (e- and otherwise) to forge closer relationships with real-time exchange of information on needs, supplies, production issues, and market intelligence.

Not surprisingly, this environment has fostered the growth of several retail networks that exist to connect retailers and suppliers with each other. As an e-retailer, you can connect with these networks and not only benefit from the retail- and industry-specific content the networks offer but also their access to suppliers of products of all kinds.

These Web-based networks can be a good starting point in finding vendors for the products you want to supply. Try Tradeweave (www.tradeweave.com) or Market Max (www.market4retail.com).

Remember to ask your suppliers for advice as well. They know their products intimately and may have some helpful information to share with regard to their customer segments and competitive advantages. Ask for their product recommendations, given your retail strategy.

In the previous assortment planning worksheet examples (Tables 3.1 and 3.2), the buyers had many specific ideas of products and brands they wanted for their assortments, but also some more general ideas. The WeddingChannel buyer is interested in finding more options for ring pillows—perhaps something in a nontraditional color or fabric. The Fogdog Sports buyer seeks a performance bottom at a lower price than the ones she has already identified. As these buyers identify potential products through research, they can update their assortment planning worksheets appropriately and re-prioritize the assortment.

If you already know what brands you want, you can begin by contacting their sales departments. Keep in mind that many of the largest brands have licensed their names to various manufacturers, so if you want to purchase a single brand's shoes and ties, you will probably deal with two different license holders. For instance, Ralph Lauren licenses the manufacturing of sweaters to one company, underwear and socks to another, and jackets to a third. If you want to carry the whole Lauren line, you will deal with all these manufacturers to obtain the products you need. The best strategy in this case would be to start with the brand owner, and request the appropriate contact information for each product in which you are interested.

In Chapter 8, the topic of contacting and negotiating with vendors is explored in detail. For now, keep in mind the following constraints and delays you may experience in creating an assortment for your store launch:

- **Vendors may not be willing to use your e-retail site as a distribution channel.** The Internet is still a young medium, and vendors may be wary. Vendors may also be concerned about channel conflict; perhaps they are trying to use the Internet to achieve direct-to-customer sales, or perhaps they have established relationships with other retailers and e-retailers whom they do not want to offend by creating a relationship with a newcomer.
- **Larger vendors may be unwilling to work with a small merchant.** Some vendors may feel that small orders are not worthwhile.
- **Vendors may need an extended lead time to fill your orders.** Depending on the point of manufacture, labor conditions, raw material pricing, and a myriad of other factors, vendors may not have complete control over how quickly they can get products to your warehouse.
- **Products you need may be unavailable or delayed in production.** Life happens, for any of the above reasons and more. This is a fact of retail life.

In fact, all of the above can happen. Hence, it is important to generate as many product ideas as possible in the beginning. Inevitably, you will only be able to secure a portion of these items initially, and you do not want to launch your store with a piecemeal or bare-bones assortment.

Traditional retailers and catalog retailers face limitations in assortment planning that do not apply to e-retail sites. For most brick-and-mortar establishments, what you see is what you can get. In other words, the available assortment is on display. Customers can always request special orders, but, for the most part, they are limited to items in stock. As to catalogs, they are expensive to print and mail, and pages cannot be crowded with images and words if they are to sell effectively.

This limitation has a huge impact on the way buyers plan the assortment. Traditional stores and catalogs must stock and merchandise items they think will sell (no kidding) to a range of customers. Any item that is going to take up valuable space had better earn its keep.

e-Retailers, however, have a great deal more freedom in creating and selling a broad and deep assortment, even if every item on the site is not waiting in the warehouse for shipping. This freedom comes at a price, however; it makes assortment planning a bit trickier. In addition to all the other tracking you must do, you will need to be tracking product availability. Use Worksheet 3.2, Hybrid Assortment Planning Worksheet, on the CD-ROM or copy it from the book. Table 3.4 shows the worksheet filled in with sample information. As you move forward, you will need to keep tabs on how much of your assortment is immediately available,

Worksheet 3.2   Hybrid Assortment Planning Worksheet for [Name of Business]

Category: _____

Subcategory: _____

Product	Price	Availability	Notes

Table 3.4   Assortment Planning Worksheet for Widgets-R-Us

Category: Jumbo Widgets

Subcategory: Designer Models

Product	Price	Availability	Notes
Acme XL3	$2.00	Warehouse	
Acme VL3	$2.25	Warehouse	
Vision W2	$4.00	Vendor Stock: 2 weeks	
Vision W3	$4.20	Vendor Stock: 2 weeks	
Titanium 423	$5.00	Special Order: 4 weeks	
Titanium 234	$6.00	Special Order: 4 weeks	
Titanium 1a	$3.00	Warehouse	Vendor arrangement for this season

how much is available within a relatively short period (e.g., two weeks), and how much must be special ordered. The product's availability also becomes part of its selling features, which is discussed in more detail in Chapter 4.

e-Retailers who plan to own and warehouse their own inventory can conduct assortment planning like a traditional retailer. e-Retailers who plan to have some portion of their product assortment available on an as-ordered basis must create tracking mechanisms that alert them to the availability of a product, the length of time before the product can be delivered, and the reliability of the source.

Tracking Assortment

In Chapter 5, we examine different ways of managing your inventory. For now, it is sufficient to learn how to track your assortment as you fill in your plan. When acquiring products for sale, you should keep a list of what you have purchased to check against your list of what you still need. Table 3.5 demonstrates how to track assortment as you source products. Worksheet 3.3, Assortment Tracking, on the CD-ROM provides all the formulas you need to make this document work for you.

Table 3.5 Assortment Tracking

Category	Subcategory	Brand	Distributor	Description	Preliminary order quantity	Cost	Retail	Mark-up percentage
Kids	Bottoms	Sandpiper	KS Fashion	Jeans 2 to 8 yrs	540	7.5	14.99	50.0
Kids	Bottoms	Busiga Barn	Busiga Barn	Sweatpants 2 to 8 yrs	120	9	14.99	40.0
Kids	Bottoms	Osh Kosh	Osh Kosh	Dress 2 to 7 yrs	60	15.5	26.99	42.6
Kids	Bottoms	Osh Kosh	Osh Kosh	Baby overalls 6 mo to 2 yrs	200	18.8	29.99	37.3
Kids	Bottoms	Osh Kosh	Osh Kosh	Jeans 6 to 12 yrs	90	18.4	32.99	44.2
Kids	Bottoms	Osh Kosh	Osh Kosh	Overalls 2 to 12 yrs	148	21.3	34.99	39.1

NOTE: Information sorted by retail price point

Keeping this list updated can help you focus on finding the right products to fill out your assortment offerings. It is also a valuable tool as you create your financial plans.

Assortment Financial Planning

You have identified a product and found a source; you are ready to purchase stock . . . but how much do you want and need? How much can you afford to invest in a particular item? To answer that question, you need to create a financial plan that reflects your sales expectations and turnover requirements.

To create the financial plan, you should look at your assortment plans using both a bottom-up and a top-down approach. First, forecast a plan based on how much you believe you can sell; then, forecast a plan based on how much you need to sell to stay profitable. Finally, work on the two plans until they come together.

Remember that even if you are not planning to own your inventory because of arrangements with vendors who can supply products as ordered, you need to be able to forecast your sales, product demands, revenues, and expenses directly associated with selling product. You *cannot* skip this part! The exact same process quantifies your sales forecasts.

How do you forecast sales? Obviously, if you have historical data with which to work, forecasting is an easier task than starting from zero. Once you have been selling for a few seasons, you can review your sales to determine where your business is growing, stabilizing, or shrinking.

Without historical data from which to work, however, you need to rely on your market research at first. You should have an idea of how large your target market is and which competitors are vying for a share of that market. Your target market may be quite large, since you do not have the location restraints of traditional retailers, but your potential share of that market is probably small, given the wealth of other shopping options available to your customers.

The next estimate you need to make is the number of visits your e-retail site will receive in an average month or in your first season. This estimate will emerge through examining your marketing plans, industry averages, and your overall goals. Finally, think about how many of those visitors will actually purchase something, given the characteristics of your site, market, and assortment.

Now you have a series of estimates with which to work:

- Market size
- Market share size

- Monthly visits (or visits in some other period)
- Visitors who actually make a purchase

You do not need to pinpoint each of these numbers exactly, but try to create a realistic range, best-case scenario to worst-case scenario. If your wildest dreams anticipate 1,000 visitors in the first month, 2 percent of whom will immediately make a purchase, then your best-case projections of even your bestsellers need to be capped at 2 percent of 1,000, or 20 units for the month.

Now consider the specific items in your assortment. Do you have an item that you feel will be your bestseller? What percentage of all visitors do you think can be converted to purchasers for this item? Is there another item that will have a limited appeal but is critical to a small portion of your target market? What percentage of the target market needs this item?

Obviously, you cannot know the answers to these questions, but you can create educated forecasts on which to build your purchasing plans. Build your forecasts by the month (estimating visits and purchases for each month) until the season is filled in, or build your forecasts by the season (estimating visits and purchases for an entire season) and then break sales and units down by months in the season.

Now take the assortment planning spreadsheet you have already developed for tracking your desired assortment and add two more columns: expected sales units and expected sales dollars. Table 3.6 shows a sample; the formulas you need to create this for yourself are on the CD-ROM in Worksheet 3.4, Assortment Financial Planning.

You are unlikely to sell every single item you stock. As you gain experience with your assortment, you will have a better idea of your "sell-through rates," or the percentage of your stock you can expect to get into customer hands one way or another. To start with, find out from others in your industry if there are sell-through standards you can use in your initial planning.

Decide the period for your initial planning. Three months or, at most, six months is a good starting point. If your seasonal business is busiest in April and May, January to June should be your forecasting period, as this period requires you to plan for both slower and busier times. Forecast your sales units for this period, breaking them down by week or month. If you use the formulas provided, the sales dollars calculate automatically, based on the retail data you provide. You can also sum the total dollar sales you project for each category and subcategory.

This financial-planning process gives you a chance to lay out which items you believe will be your bestsellers, as well as the volume you anticipate moving over

Table 3.6   Assortment Financial Planning

Category	Subcategory	Brand	Distributor	Description	Preliminary order quantity	Cost	Retail	Markup percent-age	Expected sales units	Expected sales (in thousands)
Kids	Bottoms	Sandpiper	KS Fashion	Jeans 2 to 8 yrs	540	7.5	14.99	50.0	350	5,247
Kids	Bottoms	Osh Kosh	Osh Kosh	Baby overalls 6 mo to 2 yrs	200	18.8	29.99	37.3	150	4,499
Kids	Bottoms	Osh Kosh	Osh Kosh	Overalls 2 to 12 yrs	148	21.3	34.99	39.1	105	3,674
Kids	Bottoms	Osh Kosh	Osh Kosh	Jeans 6 to 12 yrs	90	18.4	32.99	44.2	65	2,144
Kids	Bottoms	Osh Kosh	Osh Kosh	Dress 2 to 7 yrs	60	15.5	26.99	42.6	50	1,350
Kids	Bottoms	Busiga Barn	Busiga Barn	Sweatpants 2 to 8 yrs	120	9	14.99	40.0	85	1,274

NOTE: Sorted by expected sales $

57

the defined period. It also provides a vital guide for when your e-retail site becomes operational. If you sell seven widgets one month, do you need to reorder? The only way you will know is by revisiting your assortment financial plan. If you planned to sell eight widgets that month, you are pretty close to plan. If you planned to sell twenty-five, you have a challenge on your hands, not to mention a lot of extra widgets. If you planned to sell three, order more, and figure out what market and customer factors contributed to the amazing run on widgets.

Constructing a Buy Plan

Now you can construct "buy plans" to support your sales projections. To create a buy plan, reevaluate the total seasonal sales you are projecting for each item in your assortment. Then break these sales down by month, taking into account seasonal fluctuations, the market, and your promotional plans.

These buy plans can be done at the level of category, subcategory, or any other level you find helpful. For example, if your assortment is coming from eight different vendors, you can create buy plans by vendor rather than by category. The key is to determine which organization makes the most sense for your business.

Table 3.7 is a sample buy plan for a category of goods over a six-month period. Worksheet 3.5, Buy Plan, on the CD-ROM provides all the formulas you need to construct this buy plan for yourself.

The following section outlines the elements that your buy plan should include.

Beginning of Month (or Season) in Stock

Beginning of month or season (BOM or BOS) in stock is the value of goods, expressed in their retail dollar value, which you own at the beginning of each month. In all our financial plans, we will be using retail dollar values to assess everything from purchasing budgets to profitability. The retail dollar value is calculated as the retail price of the item, multiplied by the number of units called for in the plan.

Sales

This is your sales estimate (again in retail dollars) for each month. Keep in mind that with 12 months and 52 weeks in a year, some months have four weeks and some months have five. In the standard retail calendar, the months with five weeks are March, June, September, and December. Therefore, you should plan

Table 3.7 Sample Buy Plan

	Month 1	Month 2	Month 3	Month 4	Month 5	Month 6	
BOM stock	50	65	70	77	77	80	69.9	Average stock
Sales (in thousands)	5	5	10	15	15	20	1.00	Turn
Markdowns	0	0	0	2	2	5	70	Total sales
Receipts	20	10	17	17	20	15	9	Total markdowns
EOM stock	65	70	77	77	80	70	12.9%	Markdown percentage
							99	Total receipts

BOM, beginning of month; *EOM*, end of month.

more sales into these months than in the four-week months. Obviously, you should keep checking back against your spreadsheet to ensure you are on track with the sales you believe your assortment will generate.

You should also factor in holidays or other seasonal events (e.g., back-to-school specials) that might affect your business, and plan your monthly sales accordingly. As a general rule, the retail industry slows down considerably in the summer months. For that matter, so does Internet usage.

Markdowns

You are calculating your sales and stock numbers in retail dollars. However, you will probably not sell all of your inventory at full retail. You may plan for promotional sales periods, membership discounts, or permanent price reductions to help move your stock. Markdowns are where you keep track of and quantify the impact of these activities. If an item normally sells for $100 but you sell it for $90 during a promotion, the $10 difference belongs in the Markdowns row.

Promotional and clearance activity is examined in more detail in Chapters 6 and 7 when we talk about pricing, promotion, and profitability. With that additional knowledge, you may want to return to your first-draft buy plan and make adjustments. Don't worry too much at this point about having every number exact and final. It won't be. Your ability to fit together all the pieces of this kinetic puzzle will improve quickly.

Receipts

This is the value of the fresh stock you plan to purchase each month, again calculated in retail dollars. Generally, with basic products, each month you should purchase the following month's sales and markdowns. In this way, you are continually supplying the product necessary to support your sales and promotional plans.

End of Month (or Season) Stock

The end of month or season (EOM or EOS) stock is calculated as follows:

BOM − SALES − MARKDOWNS + RECEIPTS = EOM

(**Note:** Each month's EOM is carried over to be the following month's BOM.)

At the end of the season, the EOS is the next season's BOS, so you must be careful you are not over- or understocked as you head into the next season. This is particularly critical if your products are highly seasonal. You must plan ahead to minimize the amount of seasonal stock you have on hand at the beginning of the next season.

Turnover (Turn)

Turnover is calculated on this spreadsheet and is defined as *sales/average stock*. Turn tells you how quickly your stock is moving out the virtual door in relation to how quickly you are acquiring fresh stock.

We work more closely with turn in Chapter 7, as we work on managing profitability. At that point, you should return to these spreadsheets and play with the numbers some more, since you will have a better idea of the turn you are targeting. In the meantime, practice using this spreadsheet to plan receipts.

Go back to your assortment planning worksheets and create a list of the items and quantities you plan to have in stock at the beginning of the season. Based on your preliminary quantities and the retail value of the items, calculate the overall retail value of your stock for the beginning of the season. Enter this number as the BOM value for Month 1. Estimate your sales and markdown activity for each month of the season. If you use the spreadsheets provided on the CD-ROM, your EOMs and BOMs will automatically fill in based on the other numbers you enter. You will also be able to see the effect your estimates are having on your overall sales and turn.

Now start playing with the numbers in the receipts row. A good place to begin is with the rule described above: your receipts each month total the projected sales and markdowns of the NEXT month. What does this assumption do to your turn goals, your sales, and your markdown activity?

A turn goal of 1.0 may or may not be appropriate for your business. The same process works no matter what your turn goal turns out to be. For example, Table 3.8 shows a sample buy plan that results in a 1.2 turn.

In this example, the higher turn was achieved by lowering the BOS stock and reducing receipts by $9,000.

If you are relying on just-in-time inventory for some portion of your sales, you will enter your receipts, sales, and markdowns for those items in the months they move through your operation. For example, if the e-retailer using the buy plan in Table 3.7 does twice as much business, and each month and half of its sales rely on just-in-time inventory, the overall plan would look like Table 3.9.

Table 3.8   Sample Buy Plan: 1.2 Turn

	Month 1	Month 2	Month 3	Month 4	Month 5	Month 6		
BOM stock	45	55	60	65	63	66	58.6	Average stock
Sales (in thousands)	5	5	10	15	15	20	1.20	Turn
Markdowns	0	0	0	2	2	5	70	Total sales
Receipts	15	10	15	15	20	15	9	Total markdowns
EOM stock	55	60	65	63	66	56	12.9%	Markdown percentage
							90	Total receipts

Table 3.9 Sample Buy Plan: Combination Traditional Stock and Just-In-Time Inventory

	Month 1	Month 2	Month 3	Month 4	Month 5	Month 6		
BOM stock	50	80	90	104	104	110	89.7	Average stock
Sales	10	10	20	30	30	40	1.56	Turn
Markdowns	0	0	0	4	4	10	140	Total sales
Receipts	40	20	34	34	40	30	18	Total markdowns
EOM stock	80	90	104	104	110	90	12.9%	Markdown percentage
							198	Total receipts

The impact this hybrid model has on turn is discussed further in Chapter 7, with a closer look at profitability.

The important thing is to understand your receipt options, then choose a plan which best supports your sales and markdown expectations, your turn goals, and the nuances of your business and suppliers.

A Quick Note about Turn

You may be tempted to go for speed-of-lightning turn on the principle that inventory you own represents cash tied up in a warehouse. Of course, there is truth in this concept; A slow turn means that you are sitting on unmoving (and expensive) stock. However, beware of undercalculating your stocking needs to achieve faster turn. An overly fast turn means you are probably missing sales because you are out of stock when a customer wants a particular item. This is especially true in businesses that offer an item in various sizes or colors.

You may have noticed in Table 3.9 that changing the assumptions of the operation from a traditional retail model (owned inventory) to a hybrid retail model (some owned inventory, some just-in-time inventory) increased the turn considerably. Web-based retail is still a very new environment, and it is difficult to predict how this phenomenon will play itself out over several seasons of selling. We would not call this "artificially inflated turn," but it is not a fully accurate representation of the state of the business either. Until more e-retail history clarifies the financial and stability impact of the hybrid forms of inventory management, it might be most prudent to track turn on your owned inventory separately, in addition to tracking the hybrid inventory.

Open to Buy

This receipt plan is now your open to buy (OTB), or the retail value of stock you need to purchase each month. Remember, you are actually purchasing at cost, but **tracking your purchases at retail value** for the purposes of your OTB and all other financial plans.

To folks new to the retail business (including the second author of this book), the fact that these plans track goods by retail dollars rather than the cost to acquire them seems counterintuitive at first. The key is to remember that these spreadsheets and planning tools are not tracking cash flow. Right now, you are laying the groundwork for inventory management.

The full retail value of your inventory remains the same over time, from when you acquire it, to when it sits in your warehouse, to when you sell it at full price or a discount. Only by making all your calculations in a single unit of measure (retail dollars) can you get an accurate understanding of your business.

Create your receipt plan however it makes the most sense for your business (e.g., by category or vendor). With your buy plan in place, you know exactly how much you can and should spend to support your assortment plans and goals. In Chapter 8, we develop additional planning tools to use when negotiating with vendors.

Once you have started selling, you can use the same plan and add a row for *actual* figures under each plan item. Table 3.10 is a buy plan for a completed season. The actual figures demonstrate that sales, receipts, and markdowns all exceeded plan for the season.

For subsequent years, you should add a third row so you can recap last year's numbers, as well as the current year's actuals. Table 3.11 is an example of a buy plan reflecting the previous year's numbers, the current season's plan and the current season's actual numbers through Month 3. In this example, the buyer plans for sales to increase a total of 17.5 percent over the same season last year. The BOS stock is higher than the previous year, so despite the minimal increase in receipts planned, turnover will be slower than in the previous year. Finally, the buyer is planning to lower the markdown rate (percentage), even though the dollar value of markdowns will increase by $2,000 this year compared with last year.

The assortment plan is a fluid plan. It is based on your sales and markdown expectations, which are bound to differ from reality. That is why it is important to continually check your actual results against your plan. Are sales higher than expected? You will need to increase your receipts (replenish stock in greater volume). Are sales lower than expected? You will need to decrease your receipts (slow down new stock purchases), or perhaps increase your markdown activity (move the stock faster).

Chapter 7 goes into more depth with profitability, but you now have the blueprints for the financial element of your assortment planning and a way of determining how much you should purchase to achieve your sales goals.

Table 3.10   Completed Season: Plan and Actuals

	Month 1	Month 2	Month 3	Month 4	Month 5	Month 6		
BOS stock	45							
BOM stock	45	55	60	65	63	66	58.6	Average stock
							1.20	Turn
Actual	40	56	62	64	63	65	50.0	
							1.60	
Sales (in thousands)	5	5	10	15	15	20	70	Total sales
Actual	4	4	12	18	20	22	80	
Markdowns	0	0	0	2	2	5	9	Total markdowns
							12.9%	Markdown percentage
Actual	0	0	1	3	3	6	13	
							16.3%	
Receipts	15	10	15	15	20	15	90	Total receipts
Actual	20	10	15	20	25	15	105	
EOM stock	55	60	65	63	66	56		
Actual	56	62	64	63	65	52		

Table 3.11   Plan, Last Year and Current Year Actuals

	Month 1	Month 2	Month 3	Month 4	Month 5	Month 6		
BOS stock	55							
BOM stock	55	70	75	75	74	74	68.9	Average stock
							1.37	Turn
LY	40	56	62	64	63	65	50.0	
							1.60	
Actual	55	71	77	76			39.9	
Sales	6	6	15	20	22	25	94	Total sales
LY	4	4	12	18	20	22	80	
Actual	6	5	13				24	
Markdowns	1	1	2	3	3	5	15	Total markdowns
							16.0%	Markdown percentage
LY	0	0	1	3	3	6	13	
							16.3%	
Actual	0	1	2				3	
							20.0%	
Receipts	22	12	17	22	25	15	113	Total receipts
LY	20	10	15	20	25	15	105	
Actual	22	12	14				48	
EOM stock	70	75	75	74	74	59		
LY	56	62	64	63	65	52		
Actual		71	77	76				

LY, last year.

Hypothetical Cases

Assortment Planning for ShoeWeb

ShoeWeb's retail strategy calls for an assortment that is as broad as it is deep. The e-retailer is building a reputation for having a wide selection of fashionable items, with hard-to-fit sizes guaranteed in stock. In addition, ShoeWeb is aiming for fast delivery, which means that the company will need to own much, if not all, of its inventory to manage fulfillment effectively.

What does this do to the assortment plan? The management team has its work cut out for it. Table 3.12 outlines the plan for a single manufacturer within the single subcategory of women's dress shoes.

Table 3.12   Assortment Planning Worksheet for ShoeWeb

Category: Women's

Subcategory: Dress

Product	Retail Price	Notes
Easy Spirit Dress Pump	$50 to $70	Black, navy, select fashion colors (obtain vendor's recommendations)
Nickels "Antonia"	Around (Ca.) $80	Black, navy; _-inch heel; square toe pump
Nickels "Sonia"	Ca. $80	Black, navy, brown; 1″ heel; square-toe pump
Nickels "Lucia"	Ca. $100	Black, navy, brown, burgundy; 1″ heel; low boot
Nickels "Raquela"	Ca. $80	Black, navy, brown; 1″ heel; square-toe oxford
Rockport "Laura"	Ca. $80	Black, navy, burgundy; flat; pump
DKNY "Venice"	Ca. $180	Black; 1″ heel; pump
DKNY "Verona"	Ca. $200	Black, brown; 1″ heel; moc-toe oxford

This is a preliminary list. Since the retail strategy for ShoeWeb calls for a broad assortment in each subcategory, the full assortment for this subcategory amounts to 15 or 20 different styles.

Until ShoeWeb's management team actually looks at the new style catalogs, it cannot know the precise retail value of the different styles they plan to stock and carry. Based on the team's experience, however, it can derive some ballpark figures that help create assortment tracking spreadsheets and buy plans, like the one in Table 3.13.

The goal at ShoeWeb is a 70 percent sell-through, so based on the expected sales units above, the team projects the quantity that should be ordered for the season. This quantity will be adjusted depending on the size runs, vendor suggestions, and so on, but the target sell-through rate provides the starting point for purchasing plans.

Bottom-up financial planning takes the sums on the order quantity and sales estimates and, after dividing them up by expected sales per month, builds the buy plan. Once these numbers are plugged into the sales and receipt rows, the buyer estimates the markdowns to be taken each month as well. At this point, the formulas give the merchant an idea of the turn and markdown percentage, which affects their profitability, for the season in question.

If these numbers are not acceptable (i.e., if they indicate the assortment will not be as profitable as planned), adjustments can be made until an acceptable result is reached. This process is the top-down portion of the planning—when buyers focus more on the overall results (sales, turn, profitability) than the individual items that create those results.

Thus, building workable assortment financial and forecasting plans involves a constant checking and re-checking from both a bottom-up and top-down perspective.

Assortment Planning for WebKidCare

WebKidCare is ready to begin planning its initial assortment of products. One of the key features in its competitive advantage analysis is its selection of classroom-grade equipment. Thus, the management team focuses its efforts on manufacturers that provide this kind of equipment. Additionally, the competitive advantage analysis relies on informative site content relevant to the site's target customer, the semiprofessional and professional caregiver. The team then seeks the guidance of expert product reviews and makes those reviews a key selling feature.

Table 3.13 Assortment Tracking for ShoeWeb

Category	Sub-category	Brand	Distributor	Description	Order quantity	Cost	Retail	Markup percentage	Expected sales units	Expected sales $
Women's	Dress	Easy Spirit	Easy Spirit	Dress Pump	285	32	65	50.8	200	13,000
Women's	Dress	Nickels	Nickels	Sonia 1" pump	110	42	85	50.6	75	6,375
Women's	Dress	Rockport	Rockport	Laura flat pump	115	39	79	50.6	80	6,320
Women's	Dress	Nickels	Nickels	Antonia 1/2" pump	70	42	85	50.6	50	4,250
Women's	Dress	Nickels	Nickels	Raquela 1" oxford	70	42	85	50.6	50	4,250
Women's	Dress	DKNY	DKNY	Verona oxford	30	75	180	58.3	20	3,600
Women's	Dress	DKNY	DKNY	Venice pump	30	70	150	53.3	20	3,000
Women's	Dress	Nickels	Nickels	Lucia 1" boot	45	47	95	50.5	30	2,850

NOTE: Sorted by expected sales.

Because the target market is accustomed to the occasional need to special-order equipment, the WebKidCare management team feels comfortable with a hybrid inventory model. Much of the inventory will be owned outright and shipped right from WebKidCare's warehouse, but some items will be ordered and shipped in response to customer demand, and certain vendors have agreed to this arrangement for some or all of their product lines. Table 3.14 reflects these choices.

WebKidCare's management team projects a 95 percent sell-through. Since the products do not come in small, medium, and large sizes and since the business is not fashion-driven, the team is more confident in the company's ability to sell its assortment down to the last unit without worrying about being left with odd sizes and items that don't sell.

Overall, WebKidCare seeks a 60 percent initial markup (IMU), which is consistent with industry standards and averages. Table 3.15 outlines a portion of the buy plan.

With the buy plan in place, WebKidCare is ready to move into merchandising the assortment.

Table 3.14   Assortment Planning Worksheet: WebKidCare

Category: Toddler

Subcategory: Large motor skills

Product	Retail price	Availability	Notes
Mini-trampoline with safety bar	$39	Warehouse	May require some customer support for safe assembly and safety guidance
Scooter-for-two	$53	Warehouse	Can we find a source domestically and lower the cost? Or shall we position this as a unique "high-end" item?
Climbing ramps: Solid color	$25	Warehouse	
Climbing ramps: Multicolor	$45	Vendor stock: 2 weeks	
Climbing ramps: Custom color	$65	Special Order: 4 to 6 weeks	

Table 3.15   Assortment Tracking: WebKidCare

Category	Sub-category	Brand	Distributor	Description	Preliminary order quantity	Cost	Retail	Markup %	Expected Sales Units	Expected Sales $
Smaller	Lg Motor Skills	Toddler World	PW Corp.	Solid color climbing ramp	210	10	25	60.6%	200	5,000
Smaller	Lg Motor Skills	Toddler World	PW Corp.	Multi-color climbing ramp	105	18	45	60.6%	100	4,500
Smaller	Lg Motor Skills	Bouncing Babies	PW Corp.	Mini tramp w/safety bar	105	16	39	59.0%	100	3,900
Smaller	Lg Motor Skills	Toddler World	PW Corp.	Custom color climbing ramp	52	25	65	61.5%	50	3,250
Smaller	Lg Motor Skills	Cycle-Tots	Universal Care	Scooter-for-two	52	20	53	62.3%	50	2,650

NOTE: Sorted by expected sales.

ASSORTMENT PLANNING CHECKLIST

- ❏ Define the products you want to offer. Use Worksheet 3.1, Assortment Planning, or Worksheet 3.2, Hybrid Assortment Planning.
  - ❏ Brainstorm potential products for each category and subcategory in your e-retail store.
  - ❏ Identify specific items you want to carry.
  - ❏ Research additional items to fill in areas of your assortment.
- ❏ Prioritize your assortment based on the items you think will be bestsellers.
  - ❏ Review your customer profile: What is the customer looking for?
  - ❏ Review your retail strategy: What items do you want associated with your operation?
- ❏ Identify product sources.
- ❏ Begin tracking assortment as you identify sources of product. Use Worksheet 3.2, Assortment Tracking.
  - ❏ TRACK EVERYTHING IN RETAIL DOLLARS.
  - ❏ Track availability of product, if you do not plan to own all of your inventory.
- ❏ Forecast total sales for each item you will carry over a period (i.e., a season of sales). Use Worksheet 3.4, Assortment Financial Planning.
  - ❏ Consider seasonal changes, market factors, and your promotional plans.
  - ❏ Check up on sell-through rates for your industry.
- ❏ Create buy plans for your products. Use Worksheet 3.5, Buy Plan.
  - ❏ Divide total seasonal sales across the months in your season, once again considering seasonal fluctuations, market factors, and your promotional plans.
  - ❏ Do an initial review of the turnover your buy plans create.
  - ❏ If you do not know what turn you need yet, aim for roughly 1.0.
  - ❏ Shuffle your plans and numbers to generate the turn you want.

CHAPTER FOUR

Merchandising

Chapter Preview

Not quite a catalog and not quite a storefront, e-retail sites have special merchandising considerations. Beginning with the knowledge base of traditional retail, coupled with the technical capabilities of a merchandising-savvy programmer, the expertise of talented Web designers, and effective copywriters, an e-retailer can make the most of the electronic selling environment. Our hypothetical e-retailers investigate their merchandising wants and needs.

Importance of Merchandising Decisions

Each store has its own atmosphere, by design or default. The same is true of a Web site, and you should design that atmosphere according to the image you want to project.

Think about your own regular shopping experiences to help you understand how merchandising decisions affect your customers' expectations regarding:

- Price
- Assortment
- Customer Service
- Efficiency
- Uniqueness

Compare, for example, a high-end, expensive food store with a discount supermarket. If you turn your attention to the details, you will spot differences in everything from store lighting, materials used in floors and shelving, shelf presentation, and a host of other elements. These differences affect your overall impression of the retailer, as well as your expectations when you shop there.

This is why it is important to keep your retail strategy in mind as you design the look and flow of your Web site. Your choices should always reflect and support your retail strategy and the competitive edge you have developed.

As with assortment planning, you should approach your merchandising by generating as many ideas as possible that are right for your concept. Later, time, technology, and financial constraints may limit what you can actually execute, but for now, you can dream up your ideal Web store (i.e., fabulous graphics, multiple search engines, fast image loading) with impunity.

Generate merchandising ideas by visiting other e-retail sites, studying merchandise catalogs that fill your snail-mailbox, and shopping ye olde brick and mortars. While you shop, take notes on what elements may create the image you want to project.

To start you off, Figures 4.1 through 4.3 are screen shots of e-retailers offering children's apparel and goods.

In an electronic environment, merchandising can also be personalized and thus is potentially more effective on a customer-by-customer basis than in a traditional store or through a printed catalog. Each mouse click can provide you with valuable data about the shopper at the other end of your Web connection. Use of this so-called "click-stream data" can dynamically drive the pages, products, and information your shopper finds right around the next virtual corner or the next time the shopper drops in to browse.

This capability does not come cheaply, as you may well imagine. The Appendix provides more information on resources to consider when building the back-end applications and functions that make your e-retail site effective.

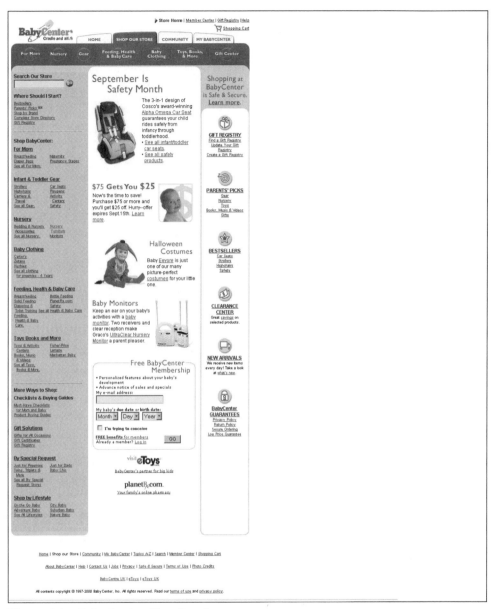

Figure 4.1   BabyCenter Storefront.

Description	Expectations created
Almost all text	Detailed product explanations, advice, and reviews
Newsletter layout	High-quality products

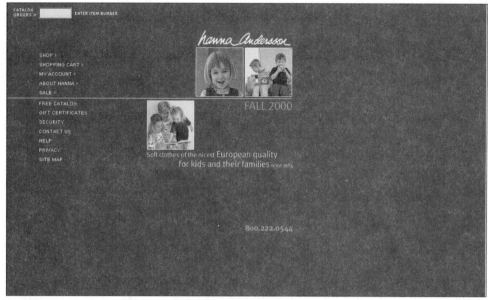

Figure 4.2   Hanna Andersson Storefront.

Description	Expectations created
Minimal text	High-quality products
Brand name emphasized	Fashion products
Lifestyle photos (relaxed group shots)	Selling a "look" as opposed to individual items

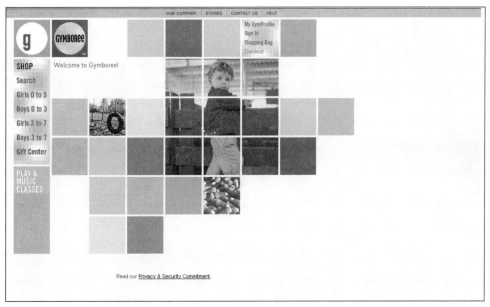

Figure 4.3   Gymboree Storefront.

Description	Expectations created
Color scheme and graphics match that of existing stores	Familiarity with existing operations
Light text	Fashion products
Flashing photo graphics	

SHOPPER'S ASSISTANCE: HIGH TECH, HIGH TOUCH

High-tech shopping is not necessarily cold and impersonal. e-Retail technical tools can include high-touch components that connect a shopper with a real live person. Your site may benefit from the inclusion of these tools:

- **Customer service e-mail.** The most common kind of interaction for e-retail sites is through the ubiquitous "contact us." Use it liberally on your site so that customers always know how they can get assistance, vent their complaints, or heap you with praise. Note: *Always* respond to customer's e-mail, preferably within 12 hours.
- **"Get telephone assistance now."** Many e-retail sites provide shoppers with the option of filling out a short online request form and getting an immediate call from a customer service representative who can assist them with their purchases.
- **"Get live assistance now."** A variation on the theme of telephone assistance, adapted to the Web environment. By clicking on a request for live chat assistance, a customer enters a queue for a chance at on-screen dialogue with a customer service representative. Chat assistance, like telephone assistance, can be provided on product selection or to answer a customer's questions.
- **"May I Help You?"** Monitoring software allows customer service personnel to keep track of real-time activity on your site. If a customer seems to be having difficulty locating a product or completing the steps to submit an order, an instant messaging box can pop up on the customer's screen, allowing the service representative to lend immediate assistance.

Your Partners in Merchandising

You will need a range of on-staff talents or a set of strong partnerships with access to the necessary tools for merchandising the assortment in your e-retail store. Each of these key functions must be taken on by individuals (or organizations) who understand consumer use of electronic media and the nuances of the retail industry, in addition to their area of special expertise. Minimum requirements are as follows:

- **Programmer, developer, strategist, and/or all-round Web guru:** This person must have an in-depth understanding of the capabilities and potential of Web technologies, such as click-stream data mining and other customization tools. Just having the knowledge, however, is not enough. Your guru must also be able to apply this knowledge to a retail merchandising application.
- **Designer:** This person must be able to create the visual and audio environment for effective merchandising.
- **Copywriter:** This person must understand the nuances of electronic communication, as well as how to use language to communicate product benefits to your customers.
- **Site production staff:** The person or people who can organize and implement ideas from a number of sources on your team are a critical factor in creating and maintaining a dynamic, effective site.
- **Image optimization staff:** For some organizations, these people are part of the site production staff. We list them separately here because of the vital importance of image optimization in Web-based retail. Images sell your products. You should ensure that your team can make the most of the digital environment.

If your retail strategy calls for editorial content, editors and/or writers can provide it. A panel of experts can provide expert product reviews, and an editor can help craft reviews for the Web environment. You may need chat room monitors or facilitators for community-building opportunities. Whatever additional features you have in your virtual store, they can contribute in the customer's mind to your overall store character. Therefore, they must be aligned with your merchandising plan and, ultimately, with your retail strategy.

There is a lot more to building an online store than merchandising, of course. Issues such as site security, shopping cart technology, and customer service are of vital importance to successful and effective e-retail sites. This, however, is not a chapter about how to build an e-retail site. Entire books have been written on that subject alone. *Our* task is to explore *merchandising;* the factors you need to consider and the decisions you must make simply to sell the products in your assortment.

The Elements of Merchandising

In a Web environment, the most important factor in considering the overriding impact of your e-retail site is its visual look and feel, with audio running a distant second. The following is a review of the critical design elements and the impressions they make.

Colors

Warm colors (red, yellow, brown) indicate a friendly, open atmosphere. Warm colors also encourage emotions over intellect. **Cool colors** (blue, green, silver) convey elegance and sophistication. Cool colors are also more appropriate when you want to emphasize the intellectual facets of your Web site.

Since users are visiting your store with a video monitor, give some thought to the effects of light from the monitor. Dark backgrounds tend to create less eyestrain for users who visit a site for an extended period (10 minutes or more). However, a dark background may be more difficult to read if a user prints out a page of product specifications, for example, for filing or future reference.

The reproduction of color through the Web has not yet reached state-of-the-art. e-Retailers, as well as all other sites, still have limited control over how colors look when they are displayed on the user's screen. Unlike catalogs, in which the ink color can be selected to best approximate the color of a product, e-retail sites face a greater degree of uncertainty in the leap from server to user. The result may not be what you intended, undermining your merchandising efforts and possibly resulting in customer dissatisfaction and product returns.

Several emerging technologies aim to address these concerns by integrating a "true color" application to a site. The application downloads to the user's computer and guarantees that the users see the colors that you want them to see. However, none of these new technologies has yet established itself as the industry leader.

Do you invest in one and hope it does not turn out to be a Betamax? Or do you live with the uncertainties of electronic color? It is up to you and the requirements of your retail strategy or course. If inaccurate color is going to be a deal-breaker for your audience, it may be worth the investment and the risk.

Layout

Open space creates a relaxed atmosphere and invites the visitor to slow down. **Filled space** (e.g., little white space) creates an exciting, high-energy environment.

Over the past few years, many of the early hiccups of Web site layouts have been overcome. For the most part, you can be confident that the customer sees the page as you have laid it out. The use of frames in page design can be a complication, as some Web browsers do not support their use or do so only clumsily.

Many sites offer users a "no frames" viewing option, which may require two layout design efforts instead of one.

Another layout consideration is if your users will be printing pages from your site. For example, if your e-retail site includes editorial content that users may want to print and file in hard copy, you should consider what those pages will look like on paper and in black and white, since not everyone owns a color printer.

Text

Heavy text indicates the site is information intensive. **Light text** means the site is relying on other elements to communicate. The implication is that the other elements (photos, brand logo) are sufficient to provide the information necessary for a wise purchase.

There are many uses for text on your e-retail site, and each use requires language consistent with its purpose, your user, and your retail strategy. You have an opportunity to share a great deal of product information with your users, in a way that catalogs (with space constraints) and traditional retailers (without a text-based selling feature) do not.

Understand the way online users deal with text before you generate paragraph after paragraph of text. Reading long blocks of text on a computer screen is the quick route to eyestrain, exhaustion, and all-round crankiness. Brevity is

---

DO NOT CLICK HERE

The two most overused words on the Web are "click here." You don't need 'em. You don't want 'em. Shel Holz, a national speaker and trainer on electronic communications, explains it best:

"Unfortunately, the nature of text-based hyperlinks makes [click here] stand out above just about anything else on a Web page. After all, in a sea of gray text, the hyperlink is blue and underlined! The scanning eye will inevitably track to the blue, underlined text. And does that text reinforce key messages? No! It tells you what to do with your mouse."[1]

Better to make a link out of a featured product, an attention-grabbing newsletter item or a benefit of buying from you!

the soul of the Web site; keep your text from getting so long that it requires scrolling.

In the electronic world, users tend to scan text rather than read every word. Make your text easy to scan. Use links and other interruptions to the text flow judiciously. Lists are a great scanning tool, helping users hone in on important topics, product categories, and the site functions they seek.

Animated Graphics

The advantages of animated graphics are that they grab the user's attention and convey energy and excitement. On the negative side, they can be distracting and/or confusing. Too many of them make an environment cluttered and difficult to navigate (to say nothing of the delay in load-times). Overkill also dilutes and destroys the impact you are trying to make, so use these sparingly and only when appropriate.

Audio

You may decide that your e-retail site would benefit from an audio component. This makes particular sense if there is an audio component to your product (e.g., music, recordings of poetry readings, bird calls) or if your editorial content includes things like speeches, live Web casts, and other audio-enhanced features.

Although we have not yet run into an e-retailer that has tried it, audio could also be used for overall ambiance. Shopping in a brick-and-mortar storefront is almost always an audio-enhanced experience, with trendy shops relying on rock music, and classic shops playing soothing classical or jazz. Would it work in an e-retail context? Someone will eventually try it and find out.

Just remember that not every Web user has an audio-enabled system, and even users who do have audio may have their speakers turned off or set too low to hear.

Site Navigation

You can think of site navigation in three components: sorting mechanisms, search mechanisms, and product presentation.

Sorting Mechanisms

The primary sorting of your product offerings has already been done via your assortment building—all those categories and subcategories. Use these categories as your starting point, but consider adding other means of grouping your products for customer convenience.

For example, BabyCenter.com (see Figure 4.1) offers the following options to its visitors looking for products:

- For Mom
- Nursery
- Infant and Toddler Gear
- Feeding, Health and Baby Care
- Baby Clothing
- Toys, Books and More
- Just for Preemies
- Twins, Triplets and More
- Just for Dads
- Baby Chic
- Shop by Lifestyle
- Gift Center
- Gift Registry
- Baby Center Parents Picks
- Bestsellers
- New Arrivals
- Checklists
- Buying Guides

Clearly, many products fall into more than one merchandising category. The idea is to create as many intuitive routes to the products as you can. Each sorting mechanism you create must make your site easier to shop for the customer using that criterion in their search for the right product. Use Worksheet 4.1, Product Groupings, to brainstorm the ways you can guide visitors to products.

Search Engines

Search engines, like sorting mechanisms, allow the customer to find the products they are most interested in buying. Search engines, however, can allow greater flexibility in allowing the shopper to narrow the search. They can, for example, allow the shopper to enter key words to locate a group of products, or combine several of your sorting categories.

If you must choose between a sorting mechanism like the one described above and a search engine, opt for the sorting mechanism. Search engines are

Worksheet 4.1   Product Groupings

_____	_____
(category)	(subcategory)
	_____
	_____
	_____
_____	_____
(category)	(subcategory)
	_____
	_____

_____
(other possible groupings)
_____
_____
_____

notorious for returning irrelevant results, and if your sorting mechanism is well-designed, shoppers will have no trouble finding products they want or browsing your selection. However, if your assortment is large, a search engine may be necessary to help customers find what they want quickly.

Product Presentation

Once customers have identified items they are interested in, they are going to want the right information to make a purchase decision. Make sure this information is clearly stated and all in one place. For example, do not list the specifications of a product on one screen, the sizes available on another screen, and the price on a third.

Be complete, but also concise. If certain terms are used repeatedly in product descriptions, you may want to add a key or glossary with more detailed explanations of what "combed cotton" or "burnished oak" means so you do not have to repeat a lengthy description with each relevant product.

HOW MANY CLICKS IN YOUR MIX?

It is no secret that online consumers tend to be impatient people without much tolerance for a lengthy, "clicky" search for products.

The trick is to minimize the clicks between your entry point and the item the customer wants to purchase without sacrificing the clarity of your site and sorting mechanisms. From your storefront, a customer expects to choose a product category (unless your e-retail site only carries one category of product). From that point, you have two more clicks to capture their attention, and that is all.

Here is where it is crucial for your whole team, the Web guru, designer, copywriter, and implementation staff, to be working together toward your merchandising goal. The successful integration of these three components keeps your customer engaged and moving on the path to purchase. Each member of the team must be plugged into a communication system that conveys not just *what* needs to be done but *why*. The merchandising logic behind the site should be crystal-clear to everyone working on the site. When programmers and designers understand why merchants make the choices they do, they can program and design a site in tune with those choices. The same goes for merchants who understand the potential and capabilities of the Web environment.

There is no such thing as too much communication, if it is effective communication and allows everyone on your team to do their best work.

Think of all the information that is helpful in making a purchase decision, and include it. Now imagine all of the hassles you have experienced while shopping (unclear pricing, incomplete information), and avoid the pitfalls in your e-retail store.

If you are carrying similar products, make it easy for the customer to compare his or her purchase options. If applicable, create a comparison chart of features and prices. If possible, let the shopper customize the chart to help them make their purchase decision.

When planning your product presentation, take a closer look at the work you did in Chapter 2 to define and understand your customers. Table 4.1 reiterates the primary and secondary motivators for purchasing certain products and adds a column for merchandising notes. Let the purchase motivators of your customers guide your product presentation choices.

Table 4.1   Product Purchase Motivation

Product	Primary purchase motivator	Secondary purchase motivator	e-Merchandising notes
Towels	Color	Price	Accurate color representation is very important; care instructions and impact on color of towel is required; customers need to be able to sort and compare choices by price
Lingerie	Gender	Age	Separate sections for women buying for themselves and men buying gifts for women; "lifestyle" (Urban Hip, Quiet Elegance, and so on) sorting mechanism can guide users by their age and preferences
Motorcycles	Interest	Brand	If customers are on the site, we know they are interested; emphasize brand of each model: use large logos at the head of the product description pages
Greeting cards	Brand	Season, occasion	Only carry preferred supplier; sort assortment by season and occasion to make cards easy to find

Never forget the cardinal rule of marketing copy: you are selling features, and customers are buying benefits. Customers buy your toothpaste because it gives them minty-fresh breath and a bright-white smile (benefits), not because it is made up of a long list of unpronounceable ingredients (features). In presenting your products, make it easy for your customers to want to buy. Emphasize the benefits, and make sure they are the benefits that matter to your customers.

For each item in your assortment, create a "features/benefits" card that lists the relevant selling information. This card can be found on the CD-ROM as Worksheet 4.2, Features/Benefits by SKU, or copy the blank worksheet here. A sample is provided in Table 4.2.

Worksheet 4.2   Features/Benefits by SKU

Product name
Model Number
Dimensions/sizing
Description
Delivery time
Price
Merchandising notes

Table 4.2   Features/Benefits by SKU

Product name	Silkessence full slip
Model number	SFF 3020
Dimensions/sizing	S, M, L
Description	Peach silk full slip with lace straps and hem
Delivery time	Immediate
Price	$45.95
Merchandising notes	Quiet Elegance, Anniversary, cross-sell with mules and robe

Finally, remember that your retail strategy defines how you present your assortment. Do not develop an atmosphere, sorting and search tools, or product information that run counter to your strategic goals. If you have determined that your Web store concept depends on offering the customer a wide range of choices, do not limit the shopper's ability to view many selections at once. If you expect your customers to buy merchandise at full-price, do not emphasize the "on-sale" category.

Customized Merchandising

e-Retail stores can have truly individual relationships with their customers, akin to the way a small boutique can have relationships with customers. When store owners and buyers understand an individual customer's interests and preferences, they can special-order items, offer the customer specific products they know the customer likes, and build that relationship one purchase at a time.

e-Retailers can do the same thing, for each and every customer, from the very first purchase (or even earlier, depending on the technology supporting your site). Remember that, even sitting at her computer, your customer takes a **more active** role in shopping your e-retail site than she does when browsing a catalog or a brick-and-mortar storefront. She must interact with the site, as well as by extension with you, to find products. That is a customer in a very different frame of mind from the one who takes your print catalog to bed at night as a counter-measure to insomnia or the one who hits the mall with a friend for a social excursion.

To capitalize on this relationship, you must get into the customer's frame of mind as she is visiting your e-retail site. What is she doing there? What does she hope to find? What are going to be the barriers that prevent her from placing an order? Then create the merchandising environment that meets those needs and overcomes those barriers, one customer at a time.

The interactive nature of Web sites allows you, the e-retailer, to recreate some of the better elements of in-store customer service and work with new cus-tomized models.

Quizzes and Product Selectors

These features allow a customer to enter her preferences, size, or other require-ments and get product recommendations. Some examples are as follows:

- Garden.com features a "plant finder," in which the shopper can enter such information as desired bloom color, her geographic location, and the charac-teristics of the planting site (sunny, shady, and so on) to create a list of suit-able plants.
- Title 9 Sports, a catalog retailer of women's athletic apparel, added an inter-active selector to its Web site (www.title9sports.com). With the "sports bra selector," women enter a size and the activities in which they participate to generate a list of suggested bra styles.
- House Beautiful (www.housebeautiful.com) features a "What's Your Deco-rating Style?" quiz. Visitors view different selections of furniture and fur-nishings and pick their favorites. Then the site aggregates their responses and names their style for them (traditionalist, eclectic, country living, and so on). Visitors can then ask to see products that suit their style.

Regardless of whether your quizzes and interactive features directly drive sales, they can be an invaluable addition to your site. Anything that engages visitors and involves them in the site is likely to capture their interests and stick in their memories. What they remember fondly, they are likely to revisit, or even tell a friend.

Quizzes and selectors do much more than guide customers through your assortment to the products they may want. These features indulge the customer in that wonderfully narcissistic pleasure of shopping: discovering herself in the image of merchandise.

Auto Customization

Because Web sites automatically collect information on all visitors, regardless of whether they make a purchase, you always have a chance to do some automatic customization. Your site may feature certain products based on the following:

- How a customer arrived at your site (through a search engine, by typing in the URL, or through a link from another site)
- What products the customer looked at most recently
- What content the customer looked at most recently

With the use of *cookies,* your site can recognize unique visitors when they return to the site, even if they did not buy anything the first time. You can then continue the customization of merchandising based on their last visit.

Elective Customization

Elective customization occurs when a shopper voluntarily provides information about his or her interests and needs, allowing you, the e-retailer, to present products and information in a way that appeals to that person.

Elective customization can be implemented many different ways. Some sites (e.g., BabyCenter) simply offer visitors the opportunity to "customize this site." Many sites offer elective customization at the point of purchase with an offer such as "notify via e-mail for similar products and updates" and so on. Sites can also entice visitors into elective customization through the use of contests, "members only" deals, or loss-leader sales. Any and all of these tactics may be appropriate for your site.

On the Web, information is the gold standard. Or rather, *accurate* information is the gold standard. Shoppers know this and for the most part keep a tight lid on their personal information. Do not be surprised if some of your "elective

THE RULES OF ENGAGEMENT

"... [T]he web truly makes possible new levels of attention to customer needs. Unlike print, broadcast, or even direct face-to-face communication with customers, the web is a fully interactive medium that produces its own written record. You can communicate in detail with a customer and retain each of the details. This means that the web enables individual, personalized attention to each customer. Web business customers understand this, and the fact changes their expectations. Engagement is no longer a delightful surprise; it is what it takes to do business."[2]

Bill Zoellick, in his book *Web Engagement: Connecting to Customers in e-Business,* explains clearly, for a "nontechie" audience, the technologies and tools that enable you to create responsive, personalized, engaged experiences for your customers.

Most of us are at least vaguely aware of cookies, which are packets of information a Web server sends to a user's browser as a record of interaction. When the browser next contacts the server (during the same visit or a subsequent visit), the cookie reminds the server of the details of the interaction. Cookies are the technology behind shopping carts, for example, since they are the means by which the browser saves information on items and quantities a customer wants to buy.

There is much more to engagement than cookies, however. Your server log file, which records each and every communication between your site and any computer in the world, can be analyzed to glean information on customers, either individually or in aggregate.

Delving into the potential and possibilities of Web engagement is far beyond the scope of this book, but in developing your site, your Web gurus must initiate you into the secrets of engagement. In fact, while your techies are reading *e-Merchant,* your merchants should be reading *Web Engagement.*

members" turn out to have provided fictitious information to get at the freebees and extras. A common technique for savvy shoppers is to set up a separate e-mail account used solely to register at sites. From the user's perspective, this keeps the junk mail down to a minimum.

How can you qualify the information you get through elective customization? Keep in mind that information gathered with an actual sale is most likely to be accurate, since the customer has to provide an accurate mailing address and/or e-mail address to confirm delivery. You can further qualify your customer data base by tracking your results over time and comparing the accuracy of information gathered through different methods. Finally, be sure that any promotional offers you send out based on elective customization really reflect accurately the preferences your customers have indicated. Keep the junk mail to a minimum; you want to earn a reputation as a valued resource, not a pest.

e-Merchandising Case Study: BabyCenter.com

Figure 4.4 shows two screens from a series used at the BabyCenter.com site to merchandise the popular glider rocker and ottoman.

BabyCenter offers three styles of rocker and ottoman, and the cushions for each piece are sold separately. The first level of information the shopper encounters is a basic listing of the items,wood finishes available, and the prices of each. To this point, the customer can navigate the merchandising easily.

Things become infinitely more complicated, however, when a shopper actually wants to select a glider, cushion, ottoman, and ottoman cushion for purchase. The e-retailer may want to make things as simple as possible, but the process now becomes convoluted. Say a shopper has selected a rocker to purchase. He or she puts it in the shopping cart. The list of items in the cart appears, and the shopper is offered the option of checking out or returning to shopping. If the shopper chooses to return to shopping, he or she is routed back to the page describing the chosen rocker. On that page, a link to "more rockers and ottomans" routes back to the general product list.

It is functional, because at that point, the shopper could select a cushion and move *it* to the shopping cart, but then the entire process has to be repeated in order to select an ottoman and ottoman cushion

Smart merchandising means making it easier for the customer to select all the items he or she wants at once. Hence, the product description page should consolidate these steps by including the following:

1. Photos of product, wood finishes, and fabric choices as done

2. Glider frame information (dimensions, assembly information)

3. Ottoman frame information (dimensions, assembly information)

4. Cushion information (materials, washing instructions)

5. Wood finishes (description of each)

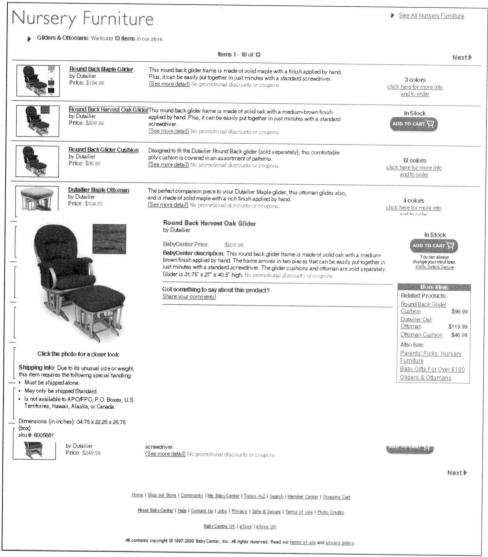

Figure 4.4   **Glider Rocker and Ottoman Merchandising Screens.**

6. Choose/order a glider (listed by wood finish with price)

7. Choose/order a glider cushion (listed by fabric with price)

8. Choose/order an ottomon (listed by wood finish with price)

9. Choose/order an ottomon cushion (listed by fabric with price)

Item 1 allows the customer to view the product on offer (with variations available).

Items 2 and 3 provide the information the customer needs to determine if the glider and/or ottoman will fit in the nursery. In addition, it provides the information that remains the same regardless of which wood finish or cushion is selected.

Item 4 provides information on the makeup and care of the cushions.

Item 5 gives descriptions (to complement the photos) of the wood finishes available. Items 6 through 9 is where the customer can both compare prices and place an order for the items selected.

From a design and programming perspective, it is a tougher challenge to create this kind of shopping experience. Yet consider how much easier it is for a customer to find what he or she wants and to purchase *all* of the items needed in a single step. Consider how much more likely that customer is to complete the purchase rather than abandon the cart, not to mention how much more likely that person is to buy a whole set of items rather than just a few.

e-Merchandising Case Study: Gap.com

Gap.com includes a number of helpful tools to help shoppers find the products they want. (The Gap chose not to grant permission to reprint an image from these tools. As of the publication of this book, these tools can be found at:

www.gap.com/html/tools/Pants/Pants.asp?wdid=2010)

Interactive features allow users to identify the colors, fit styles, and sizes and see what gap.com offers for each selection they make. The tools are not perfect, however, when it comes to sizing. The sizing chart lists women sizes 0 to 16, and lengths from x-short to x-long. No additional guidelines are available for defining these sizes, so the customer must guess what size provides the best fit, particularly with "x-short" and "x-long," which do not exist in the traditional Gap stores. The Gap needs to further define measurements that the consumer can check at home, such as waist size and inseam. If these measurements change from style to style (if Size 2 in Classic Fit has different measurements that Size 2 in Slim Fit), then The Gap has a problem in selling these items in an environment where the customer cannot try on the goods.

Using Offline Merchandising Online

When you are merchandising your online store, there are many offline merchandising techniques you can use:

- Placing your "key" items up front
- "Suggestive selling" complementary items
- Grouping similar products together
- Setting apart items on sale

When comparing your online concept to an offline competitor, note the disadvantages (Table 4.3) and advantages (Table 4.4) of selling your products online. Figure out how to *compensate* for the disadvantages and *capitalize* on the advantages.

Table 4.3   Disadvantages to Online Merchandising

Potential disadvantages to online merchandising	Suggestions to compensate
Customer has lost ability to touch, taste, and/or "play" with the product	Generous return policy Consumer reviews
Customer is used to trying on an item to determine exact fit OR customer is used to having alterations done (e.g., hems) at the place of purchase	Generous return policy Sizing assistance: charts which translate clothing sizes to body measurements Options to hem to requested inseam length prior to shipping
Item is usually purchased with the assistance of a sales associate who is well-versed in the available products (e.g., household appliances, fine art)	Comparison charts Detailed product descriptions Customer service available via phone or e-mail

Table 4.4 Advantages to Online Merchandising

Advantages to online merchandising	How to USE them
No physical space restrictions	If a product is right for your assortment, you can carry it—no need to first figure out onto "which shelf" it can be squeezed.
No physical placement of products necessary	Each item can appear in as many different groupings as you wish. The equivalent of "double" exposure in a bricks-and-mortar operation. There are more opportunities to cross-sell.
Ability to provide "personal" service to every visitor	The customer provides information with every click. Use this information to present complementary product options and services.
Minimal redesigning costs	Keep your site fresh and continually improve services and shopping aids.

WHEN YOU DO NOT OWN YOUR STOCK

By shopping via the Web, customers have already sacrificed one of the visceral plea-sures of shopping—instant gratification. When the item they want from your e-retail site is out of stock or on a delayed delivery schedule because of your arrangements with a vendor, you are grinding the salt and lemon juice into a raw wound.

If you rely on just-in-time inventory for some or all of your assortment, you have to be able to trust that the vendor will indeed deliver when promised, as promised. You also need to communicate realistic delivery timelines to your cus-tomers, and that is *not* just when they click "Submit Order."

Some e-retailers choose to put product availability with the first level of information a customer sees. Hence, from the beginning, the customer knows if an item is out of stock, available for immediate shipping, or how long before it is available for shipping. This is the most up-front method of presenting the infor-mation. However, you may want to consider placing product availability with the second level of information, that is, what the customer sees after clicking on a title or image. This gives the customer the opportunity to fall in love with an item before deciding if he or she wants to wait three to four weeks for delivery.

This tactic will backfire, however, if a sizable portion of your assortment is out of stock and cannot be special-ordered. Customers become frustrated if the majority of the items they are interested in purchasing are not actually available for purchase.

Long delivery times also mean you are likely to get more canceled orders. The longer the wait, the more "buyer's remorse" has a chance to kick in and foil the sale.

Organizing and Planning Your Efforts

Since merchandising requires the marriage of so many elements and the talents of so many individuals, it helps to create tracking mechanisms that monitor your progress. A blank copy is provided on the CD-ROM as Worksheet 4.3, Merchan-dising Plan. Table 4.5 shows a sample tracking form.

The information on this form has to be shared across several departments, including programming, design, and copy writing, at the bare minimum. At all points in the communication chain, the retail strategy is paramount, and all deci-sions must refer back to it.

Worksheet 4.3   Merchandising Plan

Product	SKU	Merchandising notes	Design status	Copy status	Program status

Table 4.5   Merchandising Plan

Product	SKU	Merchandising notes	Design status	Copy status	Program status
Silkessence full slip	SFF 3020	Quiet Elegance, Anniversary, cross-sell with mules and robe	Image optimization done; page layout draft	Complete and approved	Pending layout
Silkessence robe	SFF 4201	Quiet Elegance, Anniversary, cross-sell with mules and slip	Image optimization done; page layout done	Complete and approved	In process
Fire Engine Brassiere	JJF 1001	Urban Fire, Find Her a Gift, cross-sell with other Fire Engine items	Image optimization in process	Draft for approval	Pending

Hypothetical Cases

Merchandising Plan for ShoeWeb

Review Retail Strategy

The key elements of ShoeWeb's strategy are a wide assortment, guaranteed sizes, and fast delivery. (The "lowest prices" proposition has been rejected as incompatible with the other elements.) This means the assortment includes a wide range of brands and types of shoes (Table 4.6). The assortment will change seasonally.

Table 4.6   Product Groupings

Men's shoes	Dress
	Casual
	Athletic
	Seasonal (Call "sandals" and "summer shoes" or "boots")
Women's shoes	Dress
	Casual
	Athletic
	Seasonal (Call "sandals" and "summer shoes" or "boots")
Shoe care	Leather care products
	Polishes
	Laces
	Shoe trees
Leather Accessories	Handbags
	Belts

NOTE: Other sorting groups: By Brand, What's New, Sale, Comfort, Top Ten, Critic's Choice

The following are some of the initial merchandising ideas ShoeWeb's management team must consider:

- Shoes are mainly sold on appearance and (to a lesser extent) comfort. Photos must be high quality. Minimal text is appropriate.
- Create a "Comfort" flag and apply it to those shoes with special comfort features.
- Black is the most common color in footwear. Avoid darker backgrounds that minimize the impact of the product photography.
- Favor elements that create a relaxed, comfortable atmosphere.
- One area that does demand detailed explanation is sizing. This can include a brief description on how shoes are made and the reason this affects the "fit" of two different styles in the same numerical size. Tips for determining the right shoe size, using comparisons to shoes a customer may already own, should be included.

Search Engines

The sorting categories above are comprehensive and straightforward, so no additional search engine is needed at this time. For future development a search engine could respond to queries such as "Black pumps between $200 and $299" to assist consumers in narrowing their search. For now, however, it seems unnecessary.

Product Presentation

Quality product photography is a must. Additionally, products should be photographed in the same setting and position. This both adds to the professionalism of the merchandising look and assists consumers in comparing similar shoes. Image optimization is a vital part of implementing the site and merchandising the products effectively.

If a shoe style comes in multiple colors, each color should be photographed separately (or in a group shot) rather than relying on color swatches. This is particularly important for two-toned or multicolored shoes. It also reinforces the team's claim to carry the widest possible assortment.

Since each search category may collect a large number of selections (and that is the impression we want to make) the customer needs a way to hone in on the few styles to consider further. One possibility is a "weigh-station" between the product selection page and the shopping cart. By clicking on a style, the customer moves the item to a "consideration" area, and here can view the potential purchases side by side without the clutter of the rest of the assortment.

In this "consideration" area, the team has an opportunity to respond to the choices the customer has made by also presenting complementary items: shoe care accessories (as appropriate), belts, bags, and so on. Questions such as "Would you like to see other casual shoes in navy?" are helpful as well.

The following product information should be provided for each item:

- Product Name (brand and style name, if applicable)
- Description (e.g., leather captoe oxford)
- Material (e.g., brushed suede)
- Color(s)
- Price
- Sizes available

Disadvantages and Advantages

The ShoeWeb management team knows that it is up against some skepticism with regard to its ability to merchandise shoes on the Web. It contributes a great deal of time and energy to brainstorming the various advantages and disadvantages of its chosen business model (Tables 4.7 and 4.8).

Table 4.7   Disadvantages to Merchandising Online

Disadvantages	Compensate by . . .
Customer cannot touch product	Provide quality photography and material descriptions
Customer cannot try on product	Provide tips on determining the best size
	Direct customer to consider similar shoes already in their wardrobe
	Advise when a manufacturer tends to run long, wide, and so on
	Emphasize generous return policy
Customer requires sales assistance	Provide tips for shoe shopping
	Include information about shoe construction, technical elements of athletic or comfort technologies, and so on
	Create comparison charts for certain purchases, such as aerobic tennis shoes (compare features, cost, comfort, and so on)

Table 4.8   Advantages to Merchandising Online

Advantages	Capitalize on by . . .
No space/shelf limitations	Creating the widest assortment possible; emphasize this element in graphics, marketing materials, and so on
Multiple search avenues	Place each item in as many categories as appropriate
	Develop new category ideas whenever possible
Ability to respond to customer choices	Suggest complimentary products
	Ask if customer wants more information or needs to see additional selections similar to the ones already chosen

Merchandising Plan for WebKidCare

Review Retail Strategy

This strategy hinges on WebKidCare's niche market: the professional/semiprofessional caregiver. This audience wants information about its profession, the quality products WebKidCare provides, and low cost. The purchase decision is thought-driven, not emotionally based.

Initial merchandising ideas include the following:

- Space should be split between professional content and products
- Heavy text appropriate
- Suggest "sets" of equipment: "This slide, this seesaw, and this mini-trampoline for a value package price"
- Photos of product not essential; drawings can work well and could be easier to obtain and faster to download
- Suggest "floor plans": "If you have XX square feet in an indoor location, we can suggest a package of equipment for 5 children, 15 children or 25 children."

Table 4.9   Define Sorting Mechanisms

(Indoor) Playroom Equipment	Gross Motor Skills
	Fine Motor Skills
	Music Skills
	Reasoning
	Language
	Furniture
(Outdoor) Playground Equipment	Gross Motor Skills
	Water Play
	Sports Equipment
Caregiver Aids	Organizational Tools
	Activity Books
	Project Kits
	Health and Safety

NOTE: Additional sorting: By brand; Best Bets for 12 to 24 months; Best Bets for 24 to 48 months; Best Bets for 48 to 72 months; Favorite "Sets"; Special Offers

- Professional appearance, geared toward adults with a love for and professional interest in kids
- Extensive reviews of the products by expert panels and current users

Search Engine

With a professional target market, it makes sense to provide a search engine where the users can identify both information and products they would like to review.

Product Presentation

The presentation should be easy to read and facilitate comparison of similar products. Charts comparing similar products are a must. The site must not leave out any critical information such as dimensions, assembly requirements (if any), and delivery time. Photos of products may not be necessary, but at least drawings are needed.

The following product information should be provided for each item:

- Brand
- Model number (if applicable)
- Description
- Materials
- Dimensions and weight
- Assembly requirements
- Delivery time
- Price
- Reviews from expert panels, consumer reports, site editorial staff, and/or current customers

Advantages and Disadvantages

The most common sales channel for these types of products is via catalog, so there are fewer disadvantages to overcome in merchandising online, compared with current methods of distribution (Tables 4.10 and 4.11).

Table 4.10   Disadvantages to Merchandising Online

Disadvantages	Compensate by . . .
Not as portable as a catalog; customers have to be at their computers to use it	Make site content rich enough to compel users to spend the time with the site

Table 4.11   Advantages to Merchandising Online

Advantages	Capitalize on by . . .
Ability to create community for target market	Creating a credible information source, forum, and gathering place for professional and semi-professional caregivers
Site content and expert reviews	Emphasize the rich information and the objective product reviews in all marketing materials and make these aspects of the site easy to access
Easier to keep current than a printed catalog	Respond quickly to events in industry and send regular e-mail updates to customers to inform them of new product and events

MERCHANDISING CHECKLIST

- ❑ Review your retail strategy.
  - ❑ Shop other e-retailers and environments for ideas on merchandising that support your strategy.
  - ❑ Select your partners, if you do not have in-house staff to handle specialty tasks like programming, Web-specific strategy, design, copy writing, site implementation, and image optimization.
- ❑ Define your primary sorting mechanisms.
  - ❑ Review your assortment categories and subcategories. Will these make sense as merchandising categories? Use Worksheet 4.1, Product Groupings.
  - ❑ Consider other product groupings that will help your customer find items, such as Top Ten/Bestsellers; Gifts/Special packaging of multiple items; Products over or under a certain price; Sale items; and so on.
  - ❑ Do you need a search engine?
- ❑ Plan product presentation.
  - ❑ Will you have photos or drawings of every item?
  - ❑ How will you handle different color swatches of the same product?

(continued)

Merchandising Checklist (*continued*)

- ❑ What information does the customer need to be a satisfied customer?
- ❑ Create feature/benefit cards for each product; use Worksheet 4.2, Features/Benefits by SKU.
- ❑ Compensate for Online Disadvantages; list the possible barriers to online merchandising, and try to develop solutions or countermeasures.
- ❑ Capitalize on Online Advantages; list the opportunities that merchandising online can offer, and create features to make the most of these opportunities.
- ❑ Create an organization and planning document to tie together all the functions that go into merchandising; use Worksheet 4.3, Merchandising Plan.

Endnotes

1. Holtz, Shel. *Writing for the Wired World: The Communicator's Guide to Effective Online Content.* ©1999 International Association of Business Communicators. www.holtz.com
2. Zoellick, Bill. *Web Engagement: Connecting to Customers in e-Business.* ©2000, Addison-Wesley.

CHAPTER FIVE

Inventory

Chapter Preview

Inventory management must be approached from macro and micro levels. The nitty gritty of identifying the software and systems you need for inventory management is critical, as is a thorough understanding of how proper inventory management can help you run your business effectively and profitably. Our hypothetical e-retailers make decisions about relevant and effective inventory management categories and systems.

Why Worry about Inventory?

How you set up and manage your inventory will have a significant impact on many areas of your business. With effective inventory management systems in place, you are able to analyze and manage the following:

- Investment risk
- Product availability
- Delivery time
- Customer service
- Relationship to suppliers
- Future purchasing decisions
- Measurements of success and profitability

Inventory Models

For a consumer product retail operation, you must decide if you will employ the traditional retail method of purchasing and selling product, a retail "portal" method, or a hybrid of the two. Both models have advantages and disadvantages.

Traditional Retail Model

The *traditional retail model* calls for the retailer to purchase inventory, store it in a warehouse, then ship it to the customer when ordered and payment is made. Figure 5.1 lays out these ownership steps.

Advantages

- Retailer maintains control of product availability and delivery terms.
- With full control over product, retailer is able to provide better customer service.
- Some manufacturers prefer to do business this way, as this is what they are used to.

Disadvantages

- Retailer is investing in the product assortment and risks sitting on unsold merchandise.
- Retailer must come up with the payment up front to have the items in stock and ready for sales.

Retail Portal Model

The *retail portal model* calls for the retailer to merchandise and sell products. When orders come in from customers, the retailer purchases the goods from a manufacturer. Then the manufacturer ships the goods either to the retailer, to be sent on to the customer, or in some cases the manufacturer may ship directly to the customer. Figure 5.2 lays out these ownership steps.

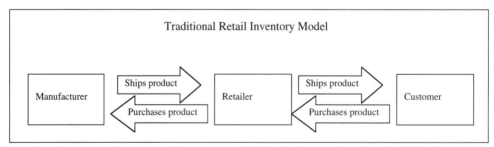

Figure 5.1   Traditional Retail Model.

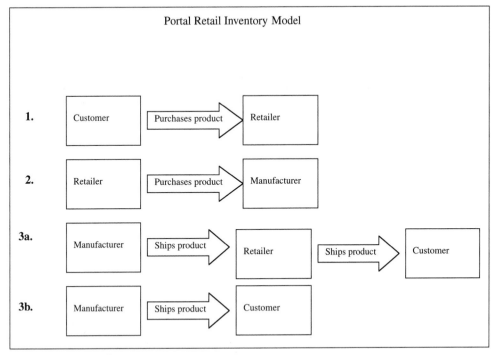

Figure 5.2   Retail Portal Model.

Advantages
- Manufacturer is carrying the risk of unsold product.
- This model eliminates the need for start-up investment in inventory.

Disadvantages
- Retailer loses control over supply. Manufacturer may not keep the right items in stock when needed or may have delays in shipping which the retailer cannot control.
- This model increases delivery time to customer.
- Some manufacturers may not be willing or able to set up and maintain this type of purchasing and shipping arrangement

Hybrid Retail Inventory Model

The *hybrid retail inventory model* blends the two models described above. The retailer stocks some items in a warehouse, as in the traditional model, and purchases some items from the manufacturer on a just-in-time basis when orders are placed. By understanding the advantages and disadvantages of each inventory model, you are in a better position to decide which items *need* to be in your warehouse, and which items can be ordered as needed.

In the early days of Web retailing, the prevailing assumption was that virtual stores would have virtual warehouses. Most e-retailers expected to function as retail portals, with manufacturers retaining ownership of the items until a customer order came in. However, as the selling seasons passed and customers demanded better service, delivery, and relationships with e-retailers, it became clear that e-retailers could not avoid dealing more directly with (i.e., owning) their inventory.

This evolution back to the traditional retail inventory model and to hybrids of the two has come about for several reasons. One very important element has been the manufacturers' willingness and ability to support just-in-time shipping arrangements. Not all manufacturers will take on the additional risk associated with portal inventory models. More to the point, manufacturers are generally not equipped to ship individual pieces or small orders on demand to customers or e-retailers.

At the same time, e-retailers have found that they need the control over their customer service and delivery that the traditional inventory model affords them. Product delivery delays and inadequate customer service have been the kiss of death for e-retailers unable to meet customer demands. It is worth noting that the most successful e-retailers—the ubiquitous Amazon.com immediately comes to mind—have invested in significant amounts of warehouse space.

Many e-retailers are currently betting on retaining—or gaining—control over their stocks and order fulfillment. Thus far, successes in e-retail have been based mainly on customer service and reliability—both features of the shopping experience which encourage repeat visitors. Thus, it makes sense for e-retailers to develop and control a key success element rather than rely on others (such as vendors or manufacturers) to perform this function for them.

Blend the two approaches if and when appropriate. For the hybrid model to work, just-in-time suppliers must have experience and competence in shipping quickly to customers. They must be willing and able to ship on demand. With this best-of-both-worlds model, e-retailers can decide which items (preferably fast-moving key items) they want to have in their stock and which items (slower-moving marginal items) they offer with longer delivery times and perhaps added shipping costs.

Tools to Use for Inventory Management

There is, of course, a vast pool of potential inventory management tools. You can purchase off-the-shelf e-commerce "shop in a box" software, which includes inventory reporting along with other back-end features (shopping cart, order verification, and so on) an e-retailer needs. You can create a simple tracking tool with any spreadsheet software. You can purchase or lease access to a customized Web-based management tool. Your choice of tool depends on many factors, including the size and type of your assortment, the kinds of ownership arrangements your company and vendors agree on, and your budget.

Inventory management may seem at first to be one element where you can save a bit of money by creating a simple "units in/units out" spreadsheet. However, inventory management is closely related to profitability management, which is explored in depth in Chapter 7. The tools you select at this stage will enable you to make informed, sophisticated decisions about promotional activity, future merchandise purchases, vendor negotiations, and more. Skimp at your own risk.

Software evolves constantly, and any tool you purchase today may be supplanted by a better tool some time down the road. For the purposes of e-retail, certain catalog management software packages may be effective; they have been perfected over the years, and are likely to be more "mature" (i.e., have "fewer bugs") than packages intended specifically for e-retail. Ernest H. Schell's *Guide to Catalog Management Software*[1] is an excellent place to begin your research.

Whether you purchase off-the-shelf software or build your own solution from scratch, you want to be sure your inventory management systems can perform a number of key merchant functions.

Data Management

Your system will be tracking data for you—but which data? Reported how? Verify that the system(s) you are considering can provide the following data:

Sales

Your program should report sales in at least two formats: (1) units sold and (2) retail dollars. In other words, you want access to both the number of units you sold and the total revenues of those sales. Keep in mind that the revenues may not necessarily equal the units sold multiplied by the retail value of the items if any of your sales were the result of promotional pricing.

HOW TO USE SELL-THROUGH DATA

Sell-through percentage makes the most sense when you track it on a week-to-week or month-to-month basis. Daily percentages can be useful but are also easily skewed by large deliveries. At the seasonal level, sell-through is not a particularly valuable measurement because it does not take into account goods received mid-season. For seasonal measurements, turnover is a better marker of the health of your business and a better guide for decision-making.

"Cost" of Your Markdown Activity

If you have an item that normally sells for $50 and you mark it down to $40 at the end of the season, how does your system record the value of that sale? You want to be sure you can get an accurate reading from your inventory management system as to the cost of your markdowns. Ideally, you want markdown reports in dollar amounts, as well as percentage of total sales.

Sell-Through Percentage

The sell-through percentage is calculated as the units sold during a given period (a day, a week, a month, a season, and so on), divided by the number of units on hand at the *beginning* of that period. Products delivered in the middle of a period (mid-week, for example, on a weekly sell-through calculation) are NOT included in the equation.

Receipts/Inflows to Stock

How will your inventory system identify when you take ownership of goods from a supplier? How are the goods "booked" to your stock? To maximize your profitability, you will need to watch and control this process as closely as you watch and control your sales and markdowns (see Chapter 7).

Reporting

Inventory management reports are your first indication of how your business is doing—as an entire store, department, or individual item. Without inventory reporting features that allow you to identify and manage performance challenges, it will be very difficult to make either strategic or tactical decisions.

Explore the ways in which any system under consideration can capture and deliver information to you. You need access to information at the SKU level and also at the level of wider classifications (departments or whole store as needed). Use the classifications that make the most sense for your business, but a good starting point would be a system that can track and deliver information at the following levels:

- Whole store
- Division and/or category
- Department
- Class

Let us consider, for example, an e-retailer that sells fashion jewelry and accessories. WebAccessories wants to be able to report at the levels named above. Therefore, the inventory management system must be able to generate reports for the following:

- **Whole store:** WebAccessories needs reporting on all products offered in the store.
- **Division:** WebAccessories would like to access reports by each of three divisions: jewelry, handbags and purses, and accessories. Each division can be further delineated as follows:
- **Departments**
  - *Jewelry:* Costume, gold, silver
  - *Handbags and purses:* Leather, sport, evening/special occasion, other
  - *Accessories:* Belts, scarves, hats, hosiery
- **Class:** Finally, WebAccessories wants to be able to identify inventory trends and needs by brand, so a class for brand names is created in the management program.

Your inventory management categories may or may not be identical to your merchandising categories. The categories you devise for merchandising are only one way to organize your product information. If it makes sense to organize your inventory management by different categories, then you should do so. For example, if WebAccessories directs customer selection of purses by brand rather than by style (leather, sport, and so on), then the company could choose to create a SKU-management structure that mirrors the online merchandising organization rather than the assortment planning categories.

Remember that whatever structure you choose for your inventory and sales management, you will likely have to live with it for quite a while. It is incredibly time-consuming and complicated to switch organizational systems mid-stream—to say nothing of the possible loss of historical information when you do this. So be sure you think through and choose your best option before committing yourself to a particular route.

Also remember that the whole purpose of this exercise is to give you *the best possible decision-making information for* your *business.* There is no "one-size-fits-all" solution, and you are likely to go through some trial and error before you are completely satisfied with your organizational structure. Maintaining some flexibility to change class, department, and division classifications is also useful as you start out.

You may be wondering why we present these options as "either/or." Theoretically, it should be possible to create an inventory management system that allows the users to categorize items in many ways, then run inventory reports on any one of a number of criteria. With such a system, WebAccessories could first run a report to see how purses are doing, then another report to see how all products, including selected purses, from a particular manufacturer are doing. In practice, however, retailers do not do this for a number of reasons. Since these are inventory systems, they must count each item exactly once in each report. Do not underestimate the expense of creating a system that can do one-to-one reporting for a large number of items, each classified in several ways.

More information is not necessarily better information. As it is, you will be constantly inundated with data, from which you will need to extract the salient information to make decisions. Do you really want to double your report load?

If you are able to report on your inventory by whole-store, category, department, and class, you have plenty of data to work with in making your decisions. You should play with your categories and inventory reporting structure until you are happy with the results, but be sure to settle on something workable for the long-term so you are not continually retooling your reporting structure. In doing so, you can save time (programming and entering inventory under multiple categories), cut down information clutter, and can more quickly achieve useful historical comparisons.

Report Frequency

Once you have ascertained that a system can provide the kind of information you need, ask yourself: Will it provide the information you need on a relevant timetable? Can it update sales daily, hourly, or as they occur?

Do not assume that you need the most frequent updates available. Over the course of a single day running your business, you will be subjected to an avalanche of information. Hourly sales reports may prove to be clutter rather than actionable data.

At times, you may want to track sales on an hourly basis (e.g., in conjunction with a media campaign or to provide information for organizational planning). In general, if you are getting your sales and markdown information on a daily basis, you will have the information you need for effective planning, analysis, and response to trends.

Too-frequent reporting can also cause headaches. For example, the ongoing receipt of new goods can result in widely fluctuating stock levels and sell-through percentages if reviewed on a short-term basis. Fretting over a low sell-through on a given day, which is actually just the result of a large receipt on the previous day, is a waste of effort. These numbers are most meaningful when averaged out over a longer period, such as a week or a month. Selecting an appropriate reporting period reduces the clutter and unnecessary or misleading information. It is better to review certain metrics over a longer period.

As you build up historical information, you will want your system to provide the following comparisons:

- Plan to Last Year
- Actual to Last Year
- Actual to Plan

As a general rule, you do not need to report these comparisons at a SKU level but rather at the level of classes, divisions, and whole store. For the most part you do not need to know if Item Number 3221, Pink Plastic Headband with Elephants, sold more this year or last year; but you should be able to track and compare sales and inventory for novelty hair accessories as a whole.

Compatibility

Your inventory management system is not functioning in a vacuum. In any system you choose, you should ensure that your inventory software can "talk" to your ordering system, your administrative tools, and possibly your vendors, among others.

Most manufacturers provide universal product codes (UPCs) or European article numbers (EANs) for each of their products. Your inventory management system should be able to track and verify UPCs. Each UPC is intended to designate or "point to" a single item, often down to the size and color of the item in question. Unfortunately, the reverse is not always true; a single item may have several UPCs assigned to it by the manufacturer. Unisex items, for instance, may have separate UPCs for the men's line and the women's line.

The first part of the UPC designates the manufacturer; each manufacturer has been "assigned" codes by the governing body. The last half of the code is comprised of the unique numbers chosen by the manufacturer to represent that item, and the final digit is a "check digit," which is calculated based on the first twelve numbers of the code. Therefore, a full UPC can only be assigned when you know the formula to apply to arrive at the correct "check digit."

Even if your manufacturers do not provide UPCs, consider assigning your own, using software that allows you to designate the first twelve digits, then assigns the correct check digit. The program can also alert you if you have already created an identical UPC and prevent you from assigning two different products the same code.

What is the value of using UPCs? It depends on your receiving procedures and how your warehouse is organized, but using (and scanning) UPCs is a quicker and more accurate method of recording the information on what comes in and what leaves your stock. To be useful, however, the information must be accurate, so be sure everyone working with UPCs (merchants, warehouse staff, manufacturers who offer to send the goods with the UPCs on attached tags) understands how they are used and the importance of accuracy. Set up protocols for receiving and picking/packing orders to customers that ensure that the right information enters the system. Then link the whole thing to your inventory management.

Your inventory management system should also be able to "talk to" your ordering/purchase order system. When you review and analyze current sales and stock positions, you are going to want to know how many items you have on order to replenish your stock. In this case, you will definitely need the information down to the SKU level so that you can verify whether additional orders need to be placed to respond to current trends. Of course, inventory management systems should communicate effectively with sales systems so that you know what is going out as well as what is coming in.

Depending on the intimacy of your relationships with your vendors, consider selecting and using inventory management systems that can tie in directly with your vendors' systems. This becomes particularly important the more you rely on just-in-time inventory instead of traditional inventory, or if you are selling highly fashionable or trendy products that could be the next Beanie Baby. Any time you need a vendor to work with you to change orders, add to orders, or cancel orders as quickly as possible, it will pay to have the vendor tied in directly with your inventory system.

Intelligent Decisions with Inventory Reporting

So you have every feature you could possibly want in an inventory management system. Now what do you do with all this information? Table 5.1 shows a sample inventory report for WebAccessories. To be most useful, this report would be produced on a regular (perhaps weekly) basis.

Let us review what is included here and how we can use this information.

First, the report covers sales over the first week of Spring 2001. The products listed are all in the Bags and Purses division and are part of the Leather department. WebAccessories carries bags and purses made by the designers Coach and DKNY and also produces its own "Private Label" merchandise, that is, items branded as "WebAccessories" products. The classes are determined by brand; the report subtotals each brand, as well as providing the department subtotal.

- **Item number:** This refers to the e-retailer's designated item number. Each SKU in the system has a unique identifying number.
- **Class/brand:** The name of the product class (brand) is listed in this column.
- **Description:** Shorthand description of the item.
- **Retail $:** This refers to the listed retail price for each SKU.
- **Units sold:** Records all the units sold during the designated period (in this case, the first week of the spring season).
- **ST%:** Sell-through percentage, or the number of units sold during the period divided by the number of units on hand (Units OH) at the beginning of the period.
- **$Sold:** Dollars sold, or revenues generated by sales of the particular item. Note that the $Sold for Coach and DKNY products equals the units sold multiplied by the retail price, but the $Sold for Private Label goods is equivalent to the units sold multiplied by something less than the owned retail. That's because Coach and DKNY goods are not sold at promotional prices, while Private Label goods are sometimes sold at promotional prices. (Chapters 6 and 7 will review promotional pricing in detail.)
- **Units OH:** Units On Hand, or the number of units of each item in the warehouse at the beginning of the period.
- **Units OO:** Units On Order, which reflects the number of units for which this retailer currently has purchase orders outstanding.

Table 5.1   Sample Inventory Report

Date: Today
Period: Week 1, Spring 01
Division: Bags and Purses
Department: Leather

Item #	Class/brand	Description	Retail $	Units sold	ST%	$Sold	Units OH	Units OO
55215	Coach	Black Evening Bag	89	2	4.4%	178	45	12
55216	Coach	Black Day Bag	89	5	14.3%	445	35	12
55217	Coach	Brown Day Bag	89	3	7.5%	267	40	0
55218	Coach	Red Day Bag	89	1	3.3%	89	30	0
55219	Coach	Black Tote Bag	129	2	6.7%	258	30	12
55220	Coach	Brn Tote Bag	129	4	18.2%	516	22	12
	CLASS SUBTOTAL			**17**	**8.4%**	**1753**	**202**	
22210	DKNY	Black Evening Bag	69	4	13.3%	276	30	0
22211	DKNY	Black Drawstring	79	5	12.5%	395	40	12
22212	DKNY	Brown Drawstring	79	5	12.5%	395	40	12
22213	DKNY	Tan Drawstring	79	6	30.0%	474	20	12
22214	DKNY	Tan Backpack	109	8	32.0%	872	25	0
	CLASS SUBTOTAL			**28**	**18.1%**	**2412**	**155**	
98990	Private Label	Black Backpack	89	4	10.0%	320	40	0
98991	Private Label	Tan Backpack	89	2	5.0%	160	40	0
98992	Private Label	Black Beltbag	49	3	8.6%	147	35	0
98993	Private Label	Black Tote Bag	99	8	25.0%	680	32	0
98994	Private Label	Brown Tote Bag	99	7	18.4%	630	38	0
	CLASS SUBTOTAL			**24**	**13.0%**	**1937**	**185**	
LEATHER DEPARTMENT SUBTOTAL				**69**	**12.7%**	**6102**	**542**	

By using this information the merchant can determine a number of things:

- Bestselling items
- Brand/class trends
- Department trends (compared with other departments in this division)
- Opportunities and/or missed products in the assortment
- Appropriate stock levels (to adjust Units OO accordingly)

Bestselling Items

Within DKNY, the bestsellers are both tan, and other big sellers are the Private Label tote bags. This tells the buyer to focus on tan goods for upcoming DKNY orders and that Private Label may be more appealing on the higher ticket items because it offers the greatest savings over the branded styles.

Brand/Class Trends

DKNY is producing the highest sales—both in units and retail dollars. Perhaps the assortment of DKNY leather products needs to be increased. Certainly DKNY's OH and OO need to be increased, since these numbers are currently lower than Coach and Private Label levels.

Department Trends

By comparing the information in this report to similar reports for other departments, the merchant could determine whether Leather as a whole is trending up or down in comparison with Sport, Evening/Special Occasion, and Other.

Opportunities and/or Missed Products in the Assortment

There seems to be an opportunity to increase the assortment available from DKNY. Tan products should be given special attention. Since tan is doing well, it would make sense to look into developing a tan drawstring or tote bag through the Private Label.

Appropriate Stock Levels

By reviewing this report, the merchant knows Coach stock levels should be closely watched. If current OO has not already shipped, the vendor can be approached about delaying or canceling the orders on the black evening bag and the black tote bag to avoid overstock.

DKNY tan backpacks are selling well, but there are no more units OO. The merchant will call the vendor to see if there are more tan backpacks available and, if so, will place a reorder.

> ## *HYBRID INVENTORY REPORTING*
>
> You may still be thinking that inventory reporting is not for you if you are planning on running your e-retail site as a portal for goods. We are betting, however, that as you source products in the marketplace, sell for a couple of seasons, and review your profitability (see Chapter 7), you will want to own as inventory some portion of your assortment. Additionally, even if you keep one product in your office and the rest are shipped directly from the manufacturer, you will need to track inventory effectively on that one product.
>
> For most e-retailers, it will be a lot more than one product. Whatever your mix of owned versus just-in-time, have the tools you need to manage your inventory effectively and profitably. Inventory is the blood of your business, the stuff customers buy from you, the stuff you invest in so that you have something to sell.

Private Label black tote bags are also doing well and no additional units are on order. Will it be possible to get more Private Label black tote bags this season?

Since it is early in the season, the buyer does not have to worry too much about end-of-season stocks yet but should be aware of which products will NOT be continuing into the fall season. The buyer should monitor orders and stocks accordingly.

Profitability Preview

In Chapter 7, we dissect the elements of a profitable e-retail organization. For any percentage of your assortment you plan to own in your warehouse (rather than relying on just-in-time arrangements), inventory management is intimately linked with profitability. This is because your inventory represents your cash investments, while profitability measures how quickly you are realizing a return on those investments.

Even if you rely in part or in whole on the retail portal inventory model, your ability to gather data on the goods that move through your portal will be an invaluable part of doing business. The more information you are able to share with your vendors, the better they can supply you with product on a just-in-time basis. Remember that you will generally earn a higher profit on goods you purchase outright, due to better terms on certainty and bulk shipping. Your inventory tracking will also help you spot the trends that tell you which best-sellers need to be in your warehouse and which items you can continue to order as needed.

However you adapt inventory data depends entirely on the specifics of your business. The point is to understand the potential power of the information available to you through careful planning and implementation of effective systems. It is not difficult to find and use a system that provides you with rich, critical information, if you know what to look for.

The inventory management you set up will control and influence all your future decisions based on ongoing stock and sales information, so spend time determining the most useful organization of this information. It is more efficient to manage a group of products than always going down to the individual product level to analyze performance. You will use your inventory management information to follow and respond to sales trends, assist in buying decisions, address stock liabilities, and in general make your stock investment more profitable and less risky.

Hypothetical Cases

Inventory Management for ShoeWeb

ShoeWeb has a couple of viable options when selecting how to track its inventory. The final choice will depend on how ShoeWeb's merchants intend to track purchases—by type of product or brand.

Both options have pros and cons. Shoes are a highly branded business, so it would make sense for ShoeWeb to make brands its primary reporting category. On the other hand, if ShoeWeb wants to emphasize department performances, the management may want to report primarily based on the type of shoe (e.g., casual, athletic, or dress shoe). The two possible inventory categorizations are illustrated in Figures 5.3 and 5.4. In Figure 5.3, a reporting system allows ShoeWeb to spot trends *within* dress, casual, and athletic categories. However, it will be much more difficult to compare the performance of dress versus casual styles of a single brand. The ShoeWeb management will be able to tell how well pumps are selling, compared with running shoes but will not be able to compare sales of Tommy's loafers to Tommy's dress shoes.

Figure 5.4 shows a reporting system that puts the emphasis on brands. With this reporting system, ShoeWeb's management will be able to identify which

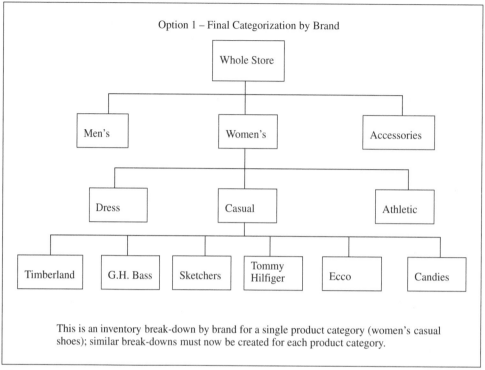

Option 1 – Final Categorization by Brand

This is an inventory break-down by brand for a single product category (women's casual shoes); similar break-downs must now be created for each product category.

Figure 5.3   Reporting System for Trends *Within*.

brands overall are selling well and which brands overall are doing poorly. The tradeoff, of course, is in the ability to track an entire type of shoe. How are sandals as a whole doing? It is hard to tell from this model.

Management may consider other options as well. Should there be tracking and analysis of stock and sales on all "comfort" shoes?

After reviewing the options, ShoeWeb's management decides it is more important to understand how casual, dress, and athletic shoes are doing as categories than it is to evaluate the performance of individual brands. The team selects Figure 5.3 as the model to track men's and women's shoes first by function then by brand.

In deciding how to track accessories, management uses a different set of criteria. For purchasing items like leather care, polish, shoelaces, and shoe trees, brand name takes a back seat to function. Therefore, it makes much more sense for ShoeWeb to track these product categories by function first and then by brand. Figure 5.5 shows the reporting structure for accessories.

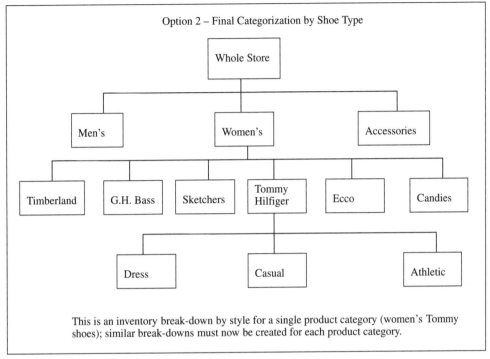

Figure 5.4   Reporting System Emphasizing Brands.

By experimenting with different groupings, ShoeWeb determines what yields the best decision-making information for the future. Each item in the assortment is assigned a single classification, and the standard reports and reporting frequency are designed.

Inventory Management for WebKidCare

The buyers for WebKidCare have no difficulty deciding how to classify their inventory for reporting purposes. In this environment, function takes precedence over brand. They create the reporting structure, as shown in Figure 5.6.

Each item in the assortment is assigned a single classification within the inventory management system. WebKidCare will be able to evaluate how Outdoor Playground is doing compared with Indoor Playground; how Fine Motor items are selling compared with Reading items; and how Climbing equipment is doing compared with Slides.

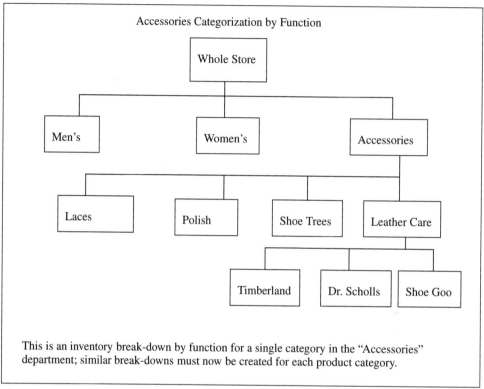

Accessories Categorization by Function

This is an inventory break-down by function for a single category in the "Accessories" department; similar break-downs must now be created for each product category.

Figure 5.5   Reporting Structure for Accessories.

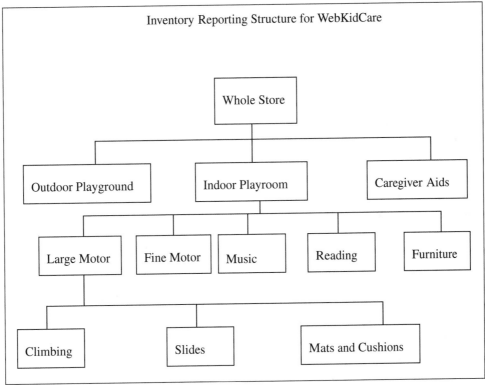

Figure 5.6   Classification of Inventory for Reporting Purposes.

INVENTORY CHECKLIST

- ❏ Review advantages and disadvantages of the traditional inventory model and the portal inventory model
- ❏ Research available inventory management tools and software, evaluating each option for its ability to:
    - ❏ Perform data management (sales, markdowns, sell-through, receipts)
    - ❏ Report on relevant data
    - ❏ Produce reports in an appropriate timeframe for decision-making
    - ❏ "Talk to" your other systems and possibly to your vendors
- ❏ Practice reading inventory reports for the intelligence they can provide about your business
    - ❏ What are your bestsellers?
    - ❏ What are the trends by brand or by class?
    - ❏ What are the trends by department?
    - ❏ What opportunities does your report suggest? Are products "missing" from your assortment?
    - ❏ Are you stocked at the appropriate levels for the season?

Endnotes

1. Schell, E. H. "Guide to Catalog Management Software," *Industry Publications International*, 10th edition, 2000.

CHAPTER SIX

Pricing and Promotional Strategy

Chapter Preview

The assortment planning phase laid the groundwork for pricing. In this chapter, we dissect the elements that go into determining prices, along with creating the promotional plans that relate to pricing. Our hypothetical e-retailers make pricing and promotional decisions based on industry standards and their knowledge of their customers and retail strategies.

The Elements of a Pricing Strategy

During the "Big Bang" days of Web commerce, the prevailing popular wisdom was that e-retailers would sell at dramatically lower prices than their brick-and-mortar counterparts. Even with these low prices, e-retailers would continue to enjoy fat profit margins because they would not be burdened with the pesky expenses of inventory and real estate. Furthermore, the online shopping population would be made up primarily of bargain-hungry shop-o-matics, seeking hot deals on obscure items.

Since then, the universe has expanded. e-Retailers have learned that they do need inventory, at least for some portion of their assortments. Real estate in Cyberspace is nearly as pricey as the kind on land—and can be just as expensive to maintain. Many individuals do indeed use the Web to find the lowest price, and price-comparison tools and sites even automate that process for them. However, many more use and shop the Web to look for unique or hard-to-find items, to access targeted editorial content, or to benefit from the convenience of 24/7 shopping and home delivery.

So if you feared your pricing strategy would consist mainly of undercutting the competition while struggling to remain solvent, take heart. It turns out that pricing strategies for e-retailers differ from those of traditional retailers only marginally, if at all.

Most other books on e-retail and Web-based commerce pay scant attention to the nuances of pricing and profitability, offering only general advice such as "shop the competition" or "plan for enough profit to cover your fixed expenses." In a nutshell, you should price at or below your competition, as well as buy low and sell high.

There is much more to profitable retail pricing than that. At the macro level, pricing results from a careful consideration of two values—the ceiling and floor. The price ceiling is the limit of what the market will bear, that is, what is the absolute most a customer will spend to purchase a particular item. The price floor is established by the cost of the goods plus all the expenses of doing business. The space between the ceiling and the floor is the room in which you make your profit.

So how do you find yourself within that space? That is the micro level, which takes into account all the nuances of your market, your customer base, your retail strategy and assortment, and more. The next two chapters examine all of the variables that go into determining a pricing strategy and how to pull the finances of your operation together to make your e-retail site profitable.

Pricing should be determined in conjunction with a careful analysis of each of the following elements:

- Cost of goods
- Initial mark-up
- Promotional strategy
- Competitor price
- Retail strategy

Cost of Goods

Buy Low, Sell High

Retailers make money by selling products at a higher price than that at which they purchased them. An exception to that rule, however, is when a retailer chooses to sell a particular item at or below cost. (By the way, they are not making it up on volume, as the old saying goes.) The product is a "loss-leader" and is intended to bring traffic into the shopping environment in the hope that shoppers will also purchase additional, profitable items.

Loss-leaders must be chosen carefully, however, and kept to a minimum if the retailer is going to remain profitable.

The vast majority of products are priced to provide a sufficient mark-up or margin with which the retailer can cover all costs of business and realize a net profit.

To be certain your prices allow for such a margin, you have to know the *full* cost of purchasing and owning a given item for sale.

LOSS-LEADER MERCHANDISING

When traditional retailers use loss-leader promotions, the loss-leaders are strategically positioned in the store so that customers will have to walk past more profitable items in order to get to the deals. If you are going to use loss-leaders in your e-retail store, you must find ways to drive customer traffic through your site so that they have an opportunity to see the other items in your assortment as well.

For example, a sporting goods e-retail store may decide to run a promotion offering athletic socks at cost. The store sends out an e-mail announcement to valued customers, announcing the special deal. When customers then visit the site, the screen offering the promotion on socks also merchandises the newest styles in running shoes (which are not promotionally priced).

Remember that the fine print of the promotion must be communicated with every promotional announcement. Be sure to indicate clearly if the special price is contingent on an additional purchase ("buy one, get one at half price"), if there is a time limit on the offer, or if customers are limited by quantity.

You may also consider loss-leaders as a way to gain information about your customers. For example, the sporting goods e-retailer may offer the socks at cost to any customer who fills out an online questionnaire indicating gender and sports preferences and provides an e-mail address.

Purchase Price

The first variable is the cost of purchase from the manufacturer or distributor. Does the price fluctuate over time? This is common with commodity-based products like gasoline. Do you have access to volume discounts, and are these quantities reasonable for your business? Perhaps the distributor offers a price break when you order 100 of an item at a time. That is great . . . unless your buy plan calls for you to sell 15 of the item for the entire season. Are there multiple sources of the product you can rely on at different times? For example, buying local is usually cheaper. However, if the product is strawberries, you live in Newfoundland, and it is January, you will need to find an alternative source for the ingredients for your homemade strawberry preserves.

If the answer to these questions indicates there will be variation in the price you pay to stock the product over time, select an average price to use in your calculations for the purposes of planning.

Of course, if your product costs change predictably and/or seasonally (as with fresh fruit and vegetables), your customers will also expect the retail price to fluctuate over the year. If your product costs are being affected by less predictable variations (e.g., exchange rate fluctuations), then you will not want to alter your retail price to reflect each adjustment, but you should revisit your retail price periodically to ensure that adverse changes have not eroded your margins.

Country of Origin

If the product is not manufactured in the United States or one of its territories, there will be duty costs. In most cases, your cost includes these fees, but if you are buying direct from an overseas source, your quoted price may not include this additional cost.

Freight

Someone is paying for the movement of products from manufacturer to retailer. The question is who and how. Does your supplier include freight in the price quote, or is it calculated (and billed) separately for each delivery?

Table 6.1 defines the critical terms that are variables included in price quotes.

Chapter 8 explores how to negotiate for the best terms possible to reduce these costs and more. For now it is merely important to note that you should include all of the above variables in determining what the average cost of goods is in making your pricing decisions.

Table 6.1   Freight Terms to Know

Term	What it is	What it means
FOB (Freight on Board)	Refers to the location where the buyer takes ownership of the goods	FOB Hong Kong means you become responsible for the merchandise, shipping, insurance, and duty/airport fees in Hong Kong; FOB LA means you become responsible for the goods in Los Angeles. FOB is always used in conjunction with a specific location.
Landed Cost	Cost at the U.S. port of entry	Freight from the country of origin to the United States, customs, and duty costs are included in the quoted price. Freight from the U.S. port of entry to the retailer is not included. You might have the option to use the vendor's freight service or to choose and arrange your own.
Ex Works	Cost at the manufacturer's (or supplier's) warehouse	Freight is not included in the quoted price. You might have the option to use the vendor's freight service, or choose and arrange your own.
Free Delivery	Cost as of delivery	Freight is included in quoted price. You may have a say in the method of transportation used.

If necessary customs charges and freight are *not* included in your purchase price, just keep in mind that these costs will need to be deducted from your gross margin—along with the other costs of doing business. If they are already included in your purchase price, however, you can forget about them for purposes of your profitability calculations in Chapter 7.

FREIGHT-FREE? NOT LIKELY

Some e-retailers may think they can avoid the extra costs of freight by requiring vendors to ship directly to customers. This is a highly unlikely scenario. First of all, if a vendor is willing to participate in such an agreement, you can bet that the vendor will charge you for the service—probably in addition to any shipping charges the customer pays. Second, most vendors are not equipped to pack and ship single items to individual customers; their operations are designed for bulk shipments to the retailer.

    If you are selling tangible goods, you are best off planning to pay for their movement from place to place, whether by air, sea, railroad, or camel.

Cost of Goods is merely the first variable to consider when establishing your pricing strategy. The other variables are just as important and more often overlooked by novice retailers.

Initial Markup (Margin)

Initial Mark-Up (IMU) is the difference between your retail price and your purchase price. It is calculated as a percentage of your retail price.

$$\frac{(\text{Retail price} - \text{Purchase price})}{\text{Retail price}} \times 100 = \text{IMU \%}$$

Thus, if you purchase an item for \$20 and retail it for \$50, your IMU is 60 percent.

$$\frac{(50-20)}{50} \times 100 = 60\%$$

"Usual" margins vary widely from retailer to retailer, and from product group to product group. Apparel mark-ups at traditional department stores usually range from 30 to 50 percent. Basic items such as socks and underwear tend to have higher margins in this environment. Extremely high-fashion items also tend toward higher margins in these sales channels. Warehouse chains such as Sam's Club or Costco aim for mark-ups between 20 and 40 percent on most non-food products. Grocery margins tend to be much more narrow, with mark-ups from

2 to 15 percent. Table 6.2 lays out the general mark-up standards traditional retailers have experienced.

Some retailers alter the stakes of mark-up by relying primarily on private label goods, which offer greater margins because a middleman is eliminated. The Gap and its subsidiaries (Banana Republic, Old Navy) use this strategy. These retailers treat almost their entire assortment as "fashion" (rather than "basic") and rely on frequent markdowns and constant change of styles and items. As a result, their stock turns over quickly, but IMUs start between 50 percent and 70 percent to make up for the heavy promotional activity.

As you are determining what your own initial mark-up should be, keep in mind that the *initial mark-up is not the same as your net margin*. Chapter 7 includes discussion on the factors that reduce IMU to Net Margin. Never forget that it is from your *net margin* that all fixed costs must be covered. Hence, you can see why it is important that your IMU is high enough to allow for all necessary costs of business *and* to generate a profit.

Promotional Strategy

Your promotional strategy—whether you plan to regularly put items on sale and what percentage of your assortment you then expect to sell at "full-price" versus sale price—will affect your net margin, so it must also be considered in establishing your retail price. Chapter 7 shows you how to make the exact calculations of

Table 6.2   Traditional Retail IMU Standards

Store Type	Standard IMU (%)
Specialty store	60 to 70
Department store	50 to 60
Mass store (i.e., Wal-Mart, K-Mart)	25 to 40
Warehouse store (i.e., Sam's Club, Costco)	10 to 20
Grocery store	15 to 20
Goods Type	
Soft goods (apparel)	60 to 80
Hard goods (gifts, stationery)	45 to 60
Food and Health/Beauty	10 to 25

the "cost" of promotional activity and permanent markdowns on items. For now, you must determine the overall strategy you want to follow with regard to realized sales prices.

There are a number of promotional strategies that you can use and/or adapt for your business and audience. Different promotional strategies communicate different messages to your customer. Be aware of the unspoken message in any method you choose. Table 6.3 summarizes some of the pricing and promotional options you have and how they are generally perceived by consumers.

Everyday low price is a strategy that communicates two primary messages to your customer:

- Items will not be put "on sale," so there is no reason to delay purchase to wait for a more attractive price
- On average, items are available at prices lower than the existing competition (otherwise, you would go out of business soon)

The main advantage to this system is that it prevents a customer from become a "sale-shopper" who rarely (if ever) purchases goods at full retail. The

Table 6.3   Pricing and Promotional Options and the Messages They Convey

No promotional (short-term sales) activity	Encourages the customer to believe the product is "worth" the asking price.
Frequent promotional activity	Generates excitement in customer—opens the possibility for "getting a great deal."
Little or no "clearance" product	Retailer limits the proportion of "fashion" in its assortment. Implies a stable assortment.
Low price compared with the competition	Retailer has found a way to cut costs. This may be by cutting quality or the cost of services. The retailer is advised to "explain" the reasons behind its lower costs if it wants to reassure its customers that quality of products has not been sacrificed.
High price compared with the competition	Retailer offers advantages that competitors do not. It is best if the retailer spells out what these advantages are . . . and *always* delivers on these promises.

disadvantage is that this retailer, in order to remain credible, cannot put items "on sale" to generate excitement or traffic, or to compete with special offerings from other retailers.

Although many retailers rely on the strategy of "everyday low price," Wal-Mart is the one who coined the phrase in the early 1990s.

With this type of strategy, there will be less of a difference between IMU and net margin. If *everyday low price* will be your calling card, you can afford to operate with a lower IMU than their competitors who choose other promotional strategies.

Hi-Low is the most common promotional strategy in today's retail environment, online and off. Full retail price is occasionally reduced for a specified "sales period," after which the price will return to the previous level. Some stores have weekly sales (you get the circulars with the Sunday paper), suggesting that customers should come in often to see what is on sale. Hi-Low can also be implemented through sales in conjunction with specific events—Mother's Day, Back-to-School, Holiday Rush, and so on. The same principles can be applied by e-retailers: communicate with your customers that a sale is happening (through advertising or a newsletter, or by other means), or make sales such a regular occurrence that shoppers naturally visit the site to find the latest deals.

The Hi-Low strategy is popular because "sales" are seen to increase shopper excitement and drive sales. If overused, however, shoppers are more likely to avoid ever purchasing at "full retail," and furthermore become suspicious of high retail prices in general. Hi-Low can also increase your customer service costs. When a sale ends, you will have to deal with customers who want to know if they can still get a sale price. Hi-Low can also complicate your returns activities, when customers return an item bought at full price during a sale period, or vice versa.

If you are going to pursue this strategy, be sure you are obeying the laws regarding promotional pricing. To protect consumers, there are rules about what can be considered *original retail price,* how long an item can be on sale in a given season, and how much time must elapse before an item is put on sale again.

Be sure you understand and *follow* these rules. Not only does it make you a more credible retailer, but the Federal Trade Commission can and does audit and penalize retailers who violate these rules.

If you would like to use a Hi-Low strategy, keep in mind that many brand owners have "rules" about if and when their products can be on sale. By ignoring these rules, you may jeopardize your relationship with a vendor and thus with the source of your product.

LAW AND ORDER IN CYBERSPACE

The Federal Trade Commission governs commercial activity in the United States, online and off. The FTC is the agency consumers complain to when they feel they've been ripped off. The agency is accessible via e-mail. If your customers have a complaint, it is very easy for them to let the FTC know.

Although the Web is still a relatively new selling medium, the FTC and the courts agree: All the laws that govern promotion, pricing, and consumer protection in print, TV, and radio also apply to the Web. Be sure you understand and follow the rules to avoid getting slapped with hefty fines—or even closed down.

Know and follow the basic principles of advertising law:

1. Advertising must be truthful and not misleading.

2. Advertisers must have evidence to back up their claims ("substantiation").

3. Advertisements cannot be unfair.

The FTC has published a concise guide to help e-retailers understand their obligations. "Dot Com Disclosures" can be found at www.ftc.gov/bcp/conline/pubs/buspubs/dotcom. In fact, the entire FTC site (www.ftc.gov) is full of helpful information and resources for e-retailers and consumers alike.

THE SUGGESTED RETAIL PRICE

Have you ever wondered what suggested retail price (SRP) really meant? Who is suggesting the price? Why are they "suggesting" it and not just "setting" it?

The federal laws governing fair trade state that retailers have the right to choose the price at which they sell their products. This means that the manufacturers and brand-holders that make the products you buy have, legally, no right to set the price the consumer ultimately pays.

They are, however, allowed to "suggest" a price to the retailers who purchase from them. Not all choose to do this, but many, particularly well-known brands, do.

So does that mean you, as a retailer, can ignore the suggested price and set whatever price you want? Yes and no. That is what the law intended. However, in practice, it seldom works that way.

If you want to set a price *higher* than the SRP, most brand owners and/or manufacturers will not have a problem with this. Since SRPs are often not communicated to the buying public, your customer base will not be aware of your choice to do this, unless the item is common and all your retail competitors have chosen to carry it at the SRP.

If you set a price *lower* than the SRP, technically the brand owner and/or manager has no legal recourse. However, brand owners are also legally permitted to choose with whom they do business and to whom they refuse to sell. Undercut their SRP, and you can forget about making future purchases from that brand.

In addition to providing SRPs, many brands want to control how often and at how deep a discount their products can be put on sale. These points should all be discussed during your negotiations with your vendors. The rules may be general guidelines (e.g., the number of days their product line can be sold at 20 percent off in the coming season), or specific rules (e.g., the exact dates their products can be put on sale).

Finally, in the case of "fashion" products that the manufacturer is planning to offer during a limited time, you may be "asked" to maintain the original SRP until a specified "break-date," which is the first time you are allowed to reduce the price. In fact, this "request" may apply even to "basic" items that are being phased out of manufacturer assortments. Vendors may allow you to "Hi-Low" after that date, but more likely they will also request that any price reductions are permanent. To them, these policies protect the integrity of their brands' prices.

Some brands protect their SRPs, promotional schedules, and permanent markdown break-dates more zealously than others. In general, the better known the brand, the more likely you are to jeopardize your future supply if you do not follow their rules.

Does all this mean that retailers are forever at the mercy of the brands they want to carry? Not entirely. While the suppliers are free to choose with whom they do business, retailers are free to choose as well. Just keep this in mind as you negotiate that you are building relationships with your product sources.

Finally, if you employ this strategy, the size of the impact on your IMU depends on how many items you sell at the promotional price versus how many items you sell at regular retail. If you anticipate a significant portion of your sales will come from promotional activity, you must increase your IMU accordingly.

Clearance pricing is used when an item is leaving a retailer's assortment. "Clearance" indicates that the new price is "permanent," and the retailer will not again raise the price. When you decide you will no longer be carrying a certain item, you will want to sell-through as much of your existing stock as possible. Most retailers attempt to do this by a series of permanent markdowns, in order to capture as many sales as possible at the highest price possible.

For example, you may have an item that originally retailed at $40. You have 100 left in stock when you decide not to reorder any more and sales at $40 have stalled.

Perhaps you have chosen 25 percent as the first level of markdowns. Your first permanent markdown takes the price to $30. You highlight this new price, reminding your shoppers that soon you will be out of stock on this item, and sell 40 units at this price over the next eight weeks. Your stock currently stands at 60 units, and sales in the last two weeks have slowed again.

You take your second permanent markdown to 50 percent off the original price and the item now costs $20. At this price you sell an additional 40 units over the next eight weeks. Your stock now stands at 20 units, which you can mark-down again or choose to "salvage" out of your stock.

Thus you have maximized the profit you can achieve as you try to reduce your on-hand stock to zero.

There are a couple of things to keep in mind in terms of clearance pricing. First, in the case of most branded items, the brand holder may "request" that you refrain from marking down their items until a set "break-date," which will be identical for all retailers carrying that item (see The Suggested Retail Price, above).

Second, it is not necessary to rely on markdowns to get rid of product you no longer want to have in stock. Your other options for eliminating unwanted stock include "returns to vendor" and "job-lotting."

Returns on unsold inventory can be negotiated at the time of purchase, or at the time you want to remove the item from your assortment. The latter is more likely to work if you have an ongoing relationship with that vendor, and are purchasing a new item to replace the one you are discontinuing.

Job-lotting is when you find a purchaser for your remaining stock. It will be unlikely that you will find a "jobber," who will pay you more than your original purchase price . . . but in some cases, getting $5 per unit for an item you purchased at $10 per unit is better than getting nothing at all.

Clearance, like Hi-Low promotional strategies, also affects your IMU. The more product you sell at less than the original retail price, the greater the difference between your IMU and your net margin.

Naturally, you purchase items you expect to sell, but you would be foolish to believe you will *always* sell *every* piece you have in stock. In fact, if you did, you probably did not purchase enough in the first place and are a victim of lost sales (and income) as a result.

If you are dealing in sized items (apparel, shoes), you are bound to be left with "odd sizes," which will never leave your stock unless you mark them down, sell them to a jobber, simply throw them away, or donate them to charitable causes.

EVERYWHERE AND NOWHERE: LIMITATIONS ON PROMOTIONAL STRATEGIES

The Web's global presence creates some potentially complicated legal issues for e-retailers. By operating in a global environment, e-retailers face potential exposure to laws governing promotional activities—even if they have no intention of selling to the markets in question. For example:

- Denmark bans advertising that targets children
- France bans advertising in English
- Germany bans advertising that explicitly compares prices with a competitor's prices

Will this affect most e-retailers? Probably not. However, it might not hurt to include in your policy statements something about the limitations on your marketing (e.g., "We market and sell solely to residents of North America."). If you do plan to market your products internationally, be sure you have in your corner a good international lawyer who can ensure that you are complying with all applicable laws.

Actually, you probably need a lawyer anyway! Make sure you bring up this issue in one of your discussions with said lawyer.

Talk to others in your industry to determine what percentage of your product you can expect to sell at clearance. The higher this number is, the higher your IMU will have to be to keep your business profitable.

Competitor Prices

You are, of course, not setting your prices in a vacuum. Other retailers will be offering the exact same items, similar items, or substitute items. Make a list of the most important of these retailers (important being the most important to your customers, of course) and visit them on a regular basis to check out their pricing and promotional activity. You do not have to slavishly compare item for item in your assortment. However, you should at least be aware of how key items in your assortment are priced by your competitors.

What you are aiming for is an understanding of how the customer regards her options. How does the marketplace look to the customer? How would she describe your prices in comparison to their other options for purchase? It all ties back to your initial retail strategy: why will the customer want to shop from your e-retail site rather than use any other method of acquiring a product? Elements like customer service and content are "softer" ways to position yourself in the marketplace. Price, on the other hand, can be objectively quantified and compared with the rest of the landscape.

Not that this translates into: undersell the competition at any cost. Remember that only a subset of Web shoppers use the Web to compare prices for each item they want to purchase—and perhaps none of your target market does this at all. Overall, shoppers are more likely to develop a general impression of prices in the marketplace, and your pricing image within that marketplace is far more important than the individual prices you set.

Returning to Retail Strategy

Knowing if you are establishing the right pricing and promotional image within your marketplace is only possible if you go back to your retail strategy. Your retail strategy has already helped you define the message you want to convey to your customers. Now is when you must verify that your pricing and promotional strategy supports and strengthens your retail strategy.

When we first considered retail strategy in Chapter 2 as the foundation for everything that followed, we laid out some of the benefits your e-retail site may offer consumers to compel them to shop at your site, including the following:

- Low/best price
- Broad selection (wide range of categories, features, price points, and so on)
- Deep selection (lots of colors and sizes of each item)
- Special/niche selection (e.g., special sizes, special-interest items)
- Delivery speed
- Customer service and support
- Product information/guarantees
- Rare or unique items
- Leverage from partners
- Brand recognition and loyalty
- Convenience/easy-to-find location
- Value of site content to users
- Loyalty programs

In the chapters that followed, we walked through the decisions necessary to flesh out that strategy. By this point, your e-retail concept has an easily recognized character, as every store, virtual or otherwise, has character. The character you build sets up the customer's expectations on pricing. No one expects Tiffany's to drop its prices just because Crazy Jim's Diamond Emporium is having a sale. In fact, Tiffany's would probably lose customers if the fine jeweler appeared to be competing with Crazy Jim.

When we begin to work on pricing and profitability, it is easy to lose sight of the overall character of the enterprise we are trying to build. When dealing with financials, it is common to think solely in terms of financials. However, you must keep tabs on the implied messages sent with the choices you make and how you present them to your customers. These are particularly important when you are starting out and creating the critical first impressions on your customer base.

Hypothetical Cases

Pricing and Promotional Strategies for ShoeWeb

Cost of Goods (COGs)

ShoeWeb is purchasing branded products from its authorized distributors. The products are mainly constructed overseas, but the vendors are responsible for all customs and duty liabilities, passing this cost on to the retailer in the purchase price. About half of the vendors include freight in their prices, and the rest bill the freight separately. For future profitability calculations, ShoeWeb management researches the usual freight costs and estimates that freight will equal four percent of the retail value of their purchases.

Initial Mark-Up

The industry standard for IMU is 50 percent, and most manufacturers' SRPs reflect this mark-up. The management does not want to jeopardize relationships with suppliers, so it has no plans to "break" any of the rules these manufacturers make about the pricing and promotional activity surrounding their product lines.

Promotional Strategy

ShoeWeb management will take advantage of promotional opportunities geared around seasonal events. For these events, a small selection of appropriate shoes will be featured and discounted to 20 percent off regular retail price. This will represent a small amount of the total assortment and offerings.

As its fashion products go out of season and the brands eliminate shoes from their lines, ShoeWeb management will practice a combination of returns to vendor and permanent markdowns to reduce stock levels. Clearance shoes will be merchandised separate from regular price offerings to preserve the integrity of the regular pricing structure.

Competitor Prices

ShoeWeb management keeps an ongoing check on their major competitors, both on and offline. The majority of their product is branded, and the competition observes the same SRP and promotional rules as ShoeWeb.

Retail Strategy

The key points of the retail strategy that relate the pricing and promotional strategy are as follows:

- An emphasis on service and selection rather than low price
- A need to maximize net margin to cover the expenses of selection, fashion products, quick delivery, and generous return policy
- A need to preserve the integrity of their products and their retail worth
- Fair prices, in line with the other retail options customers have

Pricing and Promotional Strategies for WebKidCare

WebKidCare is purchasing branded products and unbranded products that its buyers feel are of high enough quality for their customers. WebKidCare is also planning to develop and brand its own products to sell next to the other established brands.

Cost of Goods

The price from its vendors includes customs and duties charges. On its own line of products, however, which it will manufacture in the Far East and Eastern Europe, it will be responsible for the customs and duties charges, as well as the freight.

Due to the size and weight of the products, freight will be calculated separately for each delivery. No supplier includes this cost in its prices. Research indicates that, on average, freight charges will equal five percent of retail sales price.

Initial Mark-Up

Mark-ups in this industry tend to range from 50 percent to 80 percent. Products that require some form of professional installation are usually marked up more with an offer of "free installation" from the retailer.

WebKidCare, however, decides to separate this installation cost and bill it separately to the purchaser. Therefore, the buyer aims for an IMU of 60 percent across the board on all items. On products requiring installation, WebKidCare will arrange with a local subcontractor to perform the work and invoice the customer directly. Customers will also have the option of arranging installation on their own if they prefer.

Promotional Strategy

WebKidCare management does not carry fashion products, and its sales are not driven by impulse buying. Therefore, promotional sales activity is neither required nor desired. Instead, WebKidCare management will set a price on its product offerings and stick to it.

If a particular item is leaving the assortment, WebKidCare's preference will be to liquidate stock via returns to vendor or reselling to other outlets. As a last resource, leftover stock will be donated to non-profit facilities that cater to low-income families.

Competitor Prices

WebKidCare management keeps tabs on the offerings from its competitors, requesting price lists and catalogs from them as necessary. Its goal is to offer the best price in the market, so if a competitor publishes a lower price on an identical (or similar) item, it will change its price to beat the competitor's price. This applies only to everyday competitor prices and does not apply if the competitor is lowering its price for a short-term sale period.

Retail Strategy

The key points of the retail strategy that relate the pricing and promotional strategy are as follows:

- Emphasis on best price available on a quality product
- No promotional activity reinforces the fact that the original retail price is already the "best deal available."
- Donation of "leftover stock" to needy organizations (as opposed to clearance sales) reinforces commitment to community and its integrity

PRICING AND PROMOTIONAL CHECKLIST

❑ Evaluate all elements of price: COGs, IMU, promotional strategy, competitor prices, and retail strategy
  ❑ Consider all contributors to COGs, including purchase price, country of origin, and freight
  ❑ Research IMU for your industry and/or products
  ❑ Shop competition to gain an overview understanding of where your prices are in the marketplace
  ❑ Review your retail strategy to be sure that your prices are communicating a message that is aligned with your strategy
❑ Select a promotional strategy that is in tune with your retail strategy and your product line
  ❑ Are you an "Everyday Low Price" operation?
  ❑ Do you plan to "Hi-Low" your assortment?
  ❑ Will items be put on "Clearance"?

CHAPTER SEVEN

Profitability

Chapter Preview

Getting from revenues to profits requires attention to the many variables of pricing, vendor relations, market effects, and inventory management, to name a few. The e-retailer has control over these variables to a certain extent. To build a profitable organization, the e-retailer must learn how to exercise that control— how will changes made in one area of the operation affect profitability as a whole? Our hypothetical e-retailers dig into the nuances of their businesses as they build profitability plans.

So You Want to Make a Profit . . .

In running a retail operation, there are two key measurements for which you need to plan, calculate regularly, and analyze if you are to achieve and maintain profitability. These measurements are *turnover* and *maintained margin*. In this chapter we will review both concepts, including:

- How to calculate turnover and maintained margin
- How to interpret turnover and maintained margin
- How to adjust and improve turnover and maintained margin

It is impossible to overstate that *we can provide no magic formulas for profitability*. In preparing this book, this has been the most difficult chapter to write clearly and will probably be the most difficult chapter for those new to retail to grasp immediately.

Profitability also requires an intensive refresher of your math skills. Remember doing story problems in math class? Well, these are story problems from hell! You have to define all the variables and solve the problems. Like any skill, you will have to practice these principles before they become second nature to you.

Turnover

In previous chapters, we have already played with turnover, watched it move, and discussed its impact on retail operations. Now we are really going to work the concept hard and learn how to manipulate it for a healthy business. To review, turnover is calculated by dividing the total sales for a period by the average stock for the same period. Table 7.1 tracks stock, sales, markdowns, and receipts for six periods. The blank version of this table, Worksheet 7.1, includes all the appropriate formulas and is available on the CD-ROM.

Remember, all numbers (stock, sales, markdowns, and receipts) must be calculated in *retail dollars* for this spreadsheet to be accurate.

BOM stock is equal to the previous month's EOM stock.

EOM stock is calculated as follows:

BOM stock − sales − markdowns + receipts

Average stock is calculated by taking the BOM stock from each period *plus the EOM stock for the final period*. If you do not include this final number, you are only calculating average stock for the first five periods, instead of for all six. You divide this total by seven to arrive at the average stock for these six periods.

RETAIL DOLLARS REMINDER

As you calculate measurements of purchases, sales, and profitability, remember that all assumptions work with *retail dollars*. In planning for profitability, it is awkward and confusing to switch back and forth between the amount you paid to own an item and the amount for which you sold it. Therefore, you should standardize your calculations and refer to all elements in *retail dollars*. In other words, if you purchase an item for $40 and set a full-price retail on it at $80 (a 50 percent mark-up), this item should appear in your purchase and stock calculations at $80. Keep this in mind as you plan and build your financial analysis tools to avoid confusion later.

Table 7.1 Turnover Calculation

	Period 1	Period 2	Period 3	Period 4	Period 5	Period 6	Average Stock	Total	Turnover
BOM stock	100	105	119	119	87	65	91.14		1.87
Sales	20	30	30	40	30	20		170	
Markdowns	5	6	10	12	12	12		57	
Receipts	30	50	40	20	20	10		170	
EOM stock	105	119	119	87	65	43			

NOTE: Figures expressed in 1000s.

Turnover is then calculated by dividing the total sales for the period (in this example, $170,000) by the average stock value for the period ($91,140).

What Turnover Means

Turnover measures the profitability of your inventory. A turnover of 1.0 means that total sales equaled the average stock value. A turnover higher than 1.0 means sales exceeded average stock value. In Table 7.1, sales were almost twice as high as average stock value. This occurred even though receipts for the period actually equaled sales for the period.

Why is turnover higher than 1.0 in this case? The answer can be found in the row tracking markdowns. In achieving $170,000 in sales, some goods were sold at less than full retail. In this case, markdowns valued at $57,000 further reduced the value of stock.

Since stock numbers are calculated at the full-retail value of the inventory, every time you sell an item for less than full retail, you have to account for the difference. Let us say you have two gadgets in your stock with retail prices of $100. You sell SuperGadget at full retail. Table 7.2 shows the effect this has on your stock.

You sell MegaGadget, however, during a promotion for 20 percent off, so you actually received only $80 from the customer on this sale. However, you were carrying this item at $100 in your stock/inventory number. If you don't account for the "missing" $20, your EOM stock calculation will be $20 too high. So instead, you record the "cost" of the 20 percent discount in the markdown figure. Table 7.3 shows how to record the cost of the discount.

Table 7.1 shows retailer's stock reduced not just by sales, but by sales *and* markdowns. Hence, we see a turn higher than 1.0, despite the fact that receipts (inflows to stock inventory) equaled the sales figure. Inflows to stock (receipts) were less than outflows to stock (sales and markdowns).

Table 7.2   SuperGadget Sales

BOM stock	100
Sales	100
Markdowns	0
EOM stock	0

Table 7.3   MegaGadget Sales

BOM stock	100
Sales	80
Markdowns	20
EOM stock	0

Another important factor in determining turnover is the BOM stock figure. In the example above, if the BOM had been 200 instead of 100, overall turn would have dropped below 1.0. Table 7.4 calculates turnover based on this scenario.

In this example, although outflows (sales and markdowns) exceed inflows (receipts), the opening stock raises the average stock to a level where turnover drops below 1.0.

What does all this mean? Turnover shows you how quickly you are selling through your inventory. Since you have dollars invested in this inventory, it shows you how quickly you can expect a return on this investment.

Unfortunately, there is no one "right" turnover to aim for in each business. Turnover can be both too fast and too slow. If turnover is too slow it indicates you are holding on to too much stock that is not selling. On the other hand, if turnover is too fast, it means you are probably missing sales because you are out of stock when customers want to order product. Target turnover rates vary from business to business. Seasonal items need to turn faster than year-round items to ensure that they move during their shorter selling period.

Until you learn the nuances of customer demand over time on your product assortments, you should target a 1.0 turnover. You cannot go wrong if you are essentially selling through your stock during each period. However, do not let that number enslave you either. If you achieve a 1.0 turnover at the expense of being out of stock as you begin the next season, then you are not running a healthy business.

In Table 7.5, for example, the numbers generate a 1.0 turnover, but at the expense of running the business properly.

Here the BOM stock, sales, and markdowns are the same as in Table 7.4, where we hit a turn of 0.89. To increase the turn to 1.0, receipts must be reduced. To do so, the buyer decides to load up the receipts in the first three periods of the

Table 7.4 Turnover Calculation

	Period 1	Period 2	Period 3	Period 4	Period 5	Period 6	Average Stock	Total	Turnover
BOM stock	200	205	219	219	187	165	191.14		0.89
Sales	20	30	30	40	30	20		170	
Markdowns	5	6	10	12	12	12		57	
Receipts	30	50	40	20	20	10		170	
EOM stock	205	219	219	187	165	143			

NOTE: Figures expressed in 1000s.

Table 7.5   Turnover Calculation

	Period 1	Period 2	Period 3	Period 4	Period 5	Period 6	Average Stock	Total	Turnover
BOM stock	200	205	219	209	157	115	169.71		1.00
Sales	20	30	30	40	30	20		170	
Markdowns	5	6	10	12	12	12		57	
Receipts	30	50	30	0	0	0		110	
EOM stock	205	219	209	157	115	83			

NOTE: Figures expressed in 1000s.

season. While this achieves the 1.0 "desired" turn, this plan has the following serious drawbacks:

- **No new product receipts in periods 4, 5, and 6.** If this is a fashionable business, it is dangerous to go 12 weeks without fresh product. Additionally, what if a particular item is sold out by period 3? Under this plan, there are no receipt dollars available to purchase more of a hot-selling item (unless overall sales are higher than forecast).
- **EOM stock value in period 6 is $83,000.** Depending on the type of business and the expected sales for the coming season, this number may be too low to sustain sales goals for upcoming months.

Thus, although you should strive for a "healthy" turnover, becoming too focused on achieving a specific number may cause you to overlook and sacrifice other important elements of the business.

Over time, you will be able to determine which turnover rate best suits your business. It will probably end up between 0.7 and 1.5. The important thing to remember is that this is a valuable tool to prevent you from being over- or understocked in relation to your sales, markdown, and receipt goals.

Achieving a Turn Goal

To achieve a turnover goal, you can alter the following elements as you plan:

BOS stock (Beginning-of-Season stock). Do you pre-purchase for a season, or wait until the season begins? How much "old" stock will you have on hand, and how much of it can you get rid of via promotional activity, returning to vendors, or salvage? To increase your turnover, you may be tempted to force your BOS stock down as low as possible. Just keep in mind that without stock available, you cannot achieve sales. If the beginning of the season is a key sales period for you, you would be better off making sure you are fully stocked at this point, rather than being out-of-stock when the biggest orders come in.

Sales projections. Are you being aggressive or conservative? Which way would you rather err? Before you assume you want to be as conservative as possible with sales projections, remember this will limit your "open to buy" receipt budget. You either have to feel confident in sales figures that support your inventory purchases, or be prepared for an extremely low turn while you build your brand. This latter option is available to you, but you must have a timeframe within which your turnover will improve so that you can make a profit on your inventory and free up dollars for future receipts (e.g., next season).

Markdowns. Are you planning any promotional activity? Will you markdown older stock near the end of the season? When you permanently change the retail to a clearance level, you are effectively changing the retail dollar value and should take the reduction to your stock value at that time. Consider MegaGadget, which we decided originally retailed at $100. After five months, you decide to remove it from your stock and permanently reduce the price to $75. There is no chance you will now sell this item for $100, so you reduce your stock ownership total to reflect this. Table 7.6 illustrates this principle.

If in a later period you sell the item at $75, the sales will equal your stock amount, and your EOM stock will go to zero as it should.

Another way to think about it is to see your BOS stock number as your *maximum potential sales*. If you sold every item in inventory at full retail, this would equal your sales total. Markdowns reflect the difference between your maximum potential sales and your actual sales on the units that go out your door.

Does your markdown plan accurately reflect your promotional and clearance plans, as well as the amounts you expect to sell during promotional periods or on clearance? Again, are you being aggressive or conservative, and which way would you rather err?

Receipts. Receipts are usually the last item you add to your cash flow plans when calculating turnover. This is because you are often using this spreadsheet to calculate how much you can, and should, purchase, as well as when the purchases should occur within the season.

A general rule of thumb in many businesses is that each period you purchase the equivalent of the following period's sales and markdowns. Applying this assumption to our example, Table 7.7 shows us the results.

In period 2, sales are expected to be $30,000, and markdowns are projected at $6,000. Therefore, period 1 receipts are $36,000. For the final period (period 6), we assumed that period 7 sales and markdowns would be equivalent to Period 1 sales and markdowns—or $25,000.

Using this method gives us a turn of 0.79. The turn is lower than 1.0 (although the receipts are equal to the sales and markdowns over the period) because the

Table 7.6   MegaGadget Permanent Markdown

BOM stock	100
Sales	0
Markdowns	25
EOM stock	75

Table 7.7 Turnover Calculation

	Period 1	Period 2	Period 3	Period 4	Period 5	Period 6	Average Stock	Total	Turnover
BOM stock	200	211	215	227	227	217	215.29		0.79
Sales	20	30	30	40	30	20		170	
Markdowns	5	6	10	12	12	12		57	
Receipts	36	40	52	52	32	25		237	
EOM stock	211	215	227	227	217	210			

BOS stock is 200. In many businesses, this is too slow. Also of concern is the fact that the EOS stock is 210. If sales for the following season are not going to exceed sales for this season, the EOS figure is too high; we should be reducing overall stock levels instead of increasing them.

If BOS stock was firmly set and all sales and markdown forecasts are firm, the only way to improve the turnover will be to adjust the amount and flow of receipts, as shown in Table 7.8. Receipts received early in the season (periods 1 through 3) have a greater impact on average stock than receipts received in the last few periods. In the following example, the total number of receipts ($237,000) remains the same, but by shifting the time of receipt, turnover can be improved to 0.90.

This does not solve the EOS stock issue, as EOS remains at $210,000, but you can see that the turnover improves because during most of the season, the average stock is lower than in the first scenario.

There is no single right turnover goal, and no single correct way to achieve it. What is essential is that you know your options, and the levers you can toggle to adjust your plans to best reflect both your expectations and requirements for the business you are running.

All of these elements are interconnected, and you can improve your sales, decrease your markdown costs, maximize your receipt dollars, and achieve a healthy turnover by learning how these elements interact with one another and how they relate to your specific business.

Also, you can perform these analyses on the business as a whole, or for separate categories as necessary. It is an important tool for both planning and ongoing operating analyses.

Profit in a Post-Inventory Age

Turnover is a profitability consideration for e-retailers who are investing in owning some or all of their inventory. e-Retailers who manage to build relationships with vendors so that they do not need to own any inventory (they only purchase products they have already sold to customers, or they have arranged for direct-to-customer sales) can focus solely on maintained margin to determine their profitability requirements.

Your owned inventory and your just-in-time inventory represent two separate facets of your business that probably should be tracked separately as well as in aggregate. Only with separate accounting can you have a truly accurate understanding of the financial impact of owned stock versus just-in-time stock.

Table 7.8 Turnover Calculation

	Period 1	Period 2	Period 3	Period 4	Period 5	Period 6	Average Stock	Total	Turnover
BOM stock	200	195	179	179	177	185	189.29		0.90
Sales	20	30	30	40	30	20		170	
Markdowns	5	6	10	12	12	12		57	
Receipts	20	20	40	50	50	57		237	
EOM stock	195	179	179	177	185	210			

Maintained Margin

In Chapter 6, we introduced the concept of IMU, or initial mark-up. Your total sales, less your cost of goods sold, is your *gross margin*. There are additional costs associated with selling goods that must be calculated into a NET or MAINTAINED MARGIN (MM). It is from your MAINTAINED MARGIN that all overhead costs of doing business must be deducted before you can earn a profit on your operations. (FAIR WARNING: This part is math-intensive, and math-phobes may simply want to jump to the next section and have their CFOs deal with this material! At the minimum, please skim the discussion to get an idea of the scope and complexity of maintained margin. Then skip the calculations (assuming someone else in your organization will be handling this task for you). For those of you who love a good numbers challenge, you are in for a treat . . .

Maintained margin (MM) is a reflection of your operating profit: the money left over after covering the cost of goods, promotional and clearance activity, other reductions to stock, and any other costs directly associated with obtaining your stock (i.e., freight and/or duties if not included in purchase price from vendor). Because this figure already accounts for these deductions and costs, it is a better marker of profitability than your IMU will be.

Table 7.9 shows a calculation for maintained margin. To create this for your business, use Worksheet 7.2, Maintained Margin, which is provided on the CD-ROM.

Start with the retail dollar sales figure: the amount that came into your coffers due to sales. In this example, the retailer earned $2.8 million on sales. COGS (cost of goods sold) is what you paid to acquire the goods for sale. You get this number directly out of your purchase logs. Then we calculate IMU:

(Sales – COGS)/Sales

Now things become a bit trickier. To get an accurate assessment of your maintained margin and profitability, we determine the *cost complement*, a figure that neutralizes the effect of the IMU on your numbers before determining profits. The cost complement is defined as:

1 – IMU

In this case, the cost complement is 0.4286. If you use Worksheet 7.2 on the CD-ROM, the cost complement will calculate automatically for you.

Table 7.9   Maintained Margin

	Cost ($)	Retail ($)	Percentage (%)	Cost complement
SALES		2800		
COGS	1200			
IMU	1600		57.14	0.4286
Point-of-sale (POS) markdown		400		
Permanent markdown		500		
TOTAL MARKDOWN	385.74	900	32.14	
GROSS MARGIN (GM)	1214.26		43.36	
OTHER COSTS OF SALES				
Freight	84		3.00	
Salvage	28		1.00	
Other (e.g., duties)	0		0.00	
MAINTAINED MARGIN (MM)	1102.26		39.36	

NOTE: Figures expressed in 1000s.

Then we look at markdown activities. Point-of-sale (POS) markdowns and permanent markdowns are entered separately as shown. The cost of total markdowns is calculated as the retail value of the markdowns, multiplied by the cost complement. In the percentages column, markdowns are expressed as the retail value of the markdowns divided by the retail value of total sales.

To arrive at gross margin, we subtract the cost of the markdowns from the cost of the IMU. In this example, we get a result of $1,214,260, or 43.46 percent of retail sales. To check your calculations, you can also determine gross margin using the cost complement. Table 7.10 shows the alternatives for calculating gross margin. Multiply the cost complement by the total markdown percentage (in this case, 0.4286 x 32.14), then subtract that number from the IMU percentage (in this case, 57.14). The result should equal the gross margin percentage (in this case, 43.36). Slight rounding errors are of little concern.

The remaining items, freight, salvage, and other costs, are simply deducted from the gross margin to arrive at a final maintained margin. You can use an

Table 7.10   Alternatives for Calculating Gross Margin

	Method 1	Method 2
Formula	IMU$ − Total MKD (cost)$ = GM$	IMU% − (cost complement x Total MKD%) = GM%
Example	1600 − 385.74 = 1214.26	57.14 − (.4286 x 32.14) = 43.36

alternative method to check your calculations, as shown in Table 7.11. Relying on the percentages column, subtract freight, salvage, and other percentages from the gross margin percentage. The result should equal the value of maintained margin, expressed as a percentage of total retail sales. At the end of the day, this is the percentage of profits you have earned on your sales.

Whew! It's a workout. Do not be surprised if this exercise takes you a number of attempts to nail down.

Let us see how your financial plans can be evaluated for profitability. First, we should take another look at a financial plan that resulted in a 1.0 turn (Table 7.5). We will use this example to calculate maintained margin in Table 7.12.

To determine COGS, we need to know the vendor cost. Suppose we take a 50 percent IMU across the board on these items. This means our COGS is $85,000, and the IMU is $85,000 (50 percent). Conveniently, this makes the cost complement equal 0.5.

Total markdowns planned are $57,000. This will be made up of some breakdown between POS and Permanent. For this example, we will say that $40,000 in markdowns are permanent markdowns that we take in during the last two months of the season.

Table 7.11   Alternative Maintained Margin Calculations

	Method 1	Method 2
Formula	GM − Other Costs of Sales = MM$	GM% − Freight% − Salvage% − Other% = MM%
Example	1214.26 − 84 − 28 − 0 = 1102.26	46.36 − 3 − 1 − 0 = 39.36

Table 7.12   Sample Maintained Margin

	Cost ($)	Retail ($)	Percentage (%)	Cost complement
SALES		170		
COGS	85			
IMU	85		50.00	0.5
POS markdown		17		
Permanent markdown		40		
TOTAL MARKDOWN	28.5	57	33.53	
GM	56.5		33.24	
Freight	6.8		4.00	
Salvage	3.4		2.00	
Other (e.g., duties)	0		0.00	
MM	46.3		27.24	

NOTE: Figures expressed in 1000s. First, take the sales estimate directly from Table 7.5 ($170,000).

With this IMU and markdown rate, gross margin (GM) calculates to 33.24 percent, or $56,500. Freight is calculated (based on preliminary transportation research) at 4 percent of sales. Salvage is 2 percent of sales based on expected losses and damages to goods. In addition, there are no duty or other charges to consider.

With the sales and markdowns planned as above, MM will be 27.2 percent. Depending on the overhead costs of running this business, this may or may not be profitable enough to cover those expenses.

Let us say this is our plan, but then we check our IMU halfway through the season and realize that due to an increase in vendor prices, we are now only getting 48 percent in IMU. If we still must hit the 27.2 percent MM target, some of the permanent markdowns planned for the end of the season will have to be avoided to bring down our overall markdown rate. Alternatively, we need to negotiate with the vendor for assistance in paying for these markdowns to lower these drains on our margin.

Non-Mathletes May Rejoin Us Here . . .

The retailer in Table 7.9 earned $1,102,260, or 39.36 percent, on sales of $2.8 million. To turn a profit, $1,102,260 must be greater than all the retailer's overhead costs, including the following:

- Salaries
- Equipment
- Utilities and rent
- Distribution costs
- Marketing and advertising
- Insurance

If $1,102,260 is not sufficient to cover these expenses, the retailer must either generate additional sales without increasing markdown costs or increase the maintained margin percentage on the current sales. The first option to increase the maintained margin percentage is to increase the IMU. This can be done by raising prices and/or negotiating lower prices for the goods.

The second option is to lower the cost of markdowns by limiting promotional and/or clearance activity. The goal is to increase the proportion of sales at full-price.

Finally, although it is often difficult to achieve large gains in this area, the retailer may be able to lower freight costs by accepting slower delivery times or planning their orders to take advantage of the most economical freight options.

Using these formulas, you can determine if the IMU you have negotiated, combined with the promotional plans you have devised, will produce enough income to cover all necessary business expenses. If not, you have to go back to the drawing board. Alternatively, you can work backward. Once you know what maintained margin you must achieve, you can plan promotions or negotiate your IMU accordingly.

Another use of this tool is to calculate your financial position mid-season in order to make ongoing adjustments to promotional plans and other expenses. If midway through the season, your markdown percentage is running ahead of plan, you need to cut back on planned sales or permanent markdowns if you are to maintain your desired margin. At the same time, you may be able to improve your margin by taking advantage of an unexpected price deal from a vendor. This may allow you to devote more funds to marketing or distribution than you had originally planned.

Margins without Inventory

As noted above, e-retailers that do not invest in owning their inventory can focus on maintained margin rather than maintained margin *and* turnover in order to determine their profitability requirements. The easiest way to do this is to work the equation from both ends: what are your fixed costs, and how much product do you anticipate selling over a given period?

For example, take an e-retailer that specializes in handcrafted art from around the world. Through established relationships with artists, galleries, and clients, e-Xotiquè locates unique items. Once a match has been made between object and client, e-Xotiquè purchases the item, sells it to the client, and ships it—fully insured, of course.

Table 7.13 is a breakdown of e-Xotiquè's fixed costs for a six-month period. For the same six-month period, the principals forecast that they will achieve sales of $800,000 in retail dollars. Table 7.14 combines the sales forecast and the fixed costs to determine the minimum amount e-Xotiquè must earn to meet its expenses. An additional four percent of sales (a variable cost) is added as the expense of shipping and insuring product to clients.

Thus, e-Xotiquè must set a *minimum* IMU of 35 percent to cover the expenses of running the business.

No matter what business model your e-retail site uses, careful attention to your margins and profitability requirements is crucial. It should be clear that the work you do to determine your profitability works in tandem with your pricing

Table 7.13   e-Xotiquè's Fixed Costs for Six-Month Period

Line Item	Cost
Salaries	$150,000
Payroll and other taxes	15,000
Computer equipment and office supplies	25,000
Telephone and other utilities	5,000
Insurance	2,000
Rent	3,000
Marketing materials	50,000
TOTAL FIXED COSTS	$250,000

Table 7.14   e-Xotiquè's Maintained Margin

	Cost ($)	Retail ($)	Percentage
Sales		800	
COGS	516		
IMU	284		35.5
POS Mkd		0	
Perm Mkd		0	
Total Mkd	0		
Gross Margin	284		35.5
Other costs of sales			
Freight	17		2.13
Salvage	0		0.0
Other (Insurance)	17		2.13
Maintained Margin	250		31.25

and promotional strategies. If, after completing the worksheets for this chapter, you find that the numbers are not playing out right, revisit the work you did for Chapter 6, or go back to the assortment financial planning you did for Chapter 3. Or both! Lay all of the worksheets out side by side and do a careful evaluation. Which adjustments can you make to put your numbers on track? Now that you have figures in front of you, is there a fatal inconsistency somewhere in your plan that will hobble your operations down the road? Is there a profitable opportunity you have overlooked?

These planning tools are not Holy Writ of course, and you can make whatever changes you want to or need to, now or with a few selling seasons under your belt. However, it will be easier to alter your plans now, when you are in a planning mode, than to try to perform reconstructive surgery in the midst of running your e-retail operation.

Hypothetical Cases

Profitability Analysis for ShoeWeb

Turnover Considerations

Because ShoeWeb is a fashion-conscious business, it wants to maintain a turnover at or above 1.0. If the stock turns much above 1.2, ShoeWeb is potentially running out of stock on sizes and/or colors, so the management aims to keep turnover between 1.0 and 1.2. Overall sales season to season remain relatively similar, though different categories are strong in different seasons. For example, boot sales in the fall season are usually four times as high as boot sales in the spring. Likewise, sandal sales are practically nonexistent in the fall season.

Table 7.15 illustrates sales, markdown, receipt, and turnover plan for the men's shoe business (encompassing all categories).

A couple of critical aspects of this business are reflected in Table 7.15. First, the men's shoe business is a combination of fashion and basic items. In order to stay in stock on basic items, receipts must be planned for ALL months. ShoeWeb cannot afford to go a single month without filling into the basic styles, sizes, and colors of which it may have sold out.

Second, most fashion lines are introduced in the first few months of the season. The bulk of purchases are made in these months, and the fashion stock is then sold down through the rest of the season.

Promotional activity is fairly light (around 10 percent of sales) for the first half of the season, but as the season draws to a close, temporary sales and permanent markdowns are used to clear out fashion stock that will not be selling in the coming season. The markdown rate shoots up to 20 percent for these months.

Since next season's sales are also expected to be about $1 million, EOM stock of $800,000 leaves room for new purchases to start out the next season's fashions without endangering future turnover goals.

Table 7.16 illustrates the sandal shoe business, which is a piece of the above total business, and indicates how it differs from *total department* plans.

ShoeWeb begins the season with minimal leftover stock from the previous year or early purchases. No receipts are planned until the second period because sales do not really begin until period 3. Major sales periods are 4, 5, and 6, with an ever-increasing amount of sales coming from promotional activity and/or permanent clearance stock.

Turn nearly reaches 2.0, which is a good target for a seasonal product that sells almost nothing in the off-season. However, with this turn, ShoeWeb recognizes

Table 7.15   ShoeWeb Turnover Calculation

	Period 1	Period 2	Period 3	Period 4	Period 5	Period 6	Average Stock	Total	Turnover
BOM stock	800	1015	1305	1285	1005	820	100,429		1.00
Sales	75	100	200	300	225	100		1000	
Markdowns	10	10	20	60	40	20		160	
Receipts	300	400	200	80	80	100		1160	
EOM stock	1015	1305	1285	1005	820	800			

NOTE: Figures expressed in 1000s.

Table 7.16 Sandal Sales Only

	Period 1	Period 2	Period 3	Period 4	Period 5	Period 6	Average Stock	Total	Turnover
BOM stock	20	20	90	215	195	105	101.43		1.97
Sales	0	5	15	80	70	30		200	
Markdowns	0	0	0	10	20	10		40	
Receipts	0	75	140	70	0	0		285	
EOM stock	20	90	215	195	105	65			

NOTE: Figures expressed in 1000s.

that it *will* run out of bestselling styles, sizes, and colors before the season is over and is therefore forfeiting those sales. If ShoeWeb wants to avoid that scenario, its management will have to accept both a lower turnover and a higher EOS stock.

The EOM stock in period 6 is high, considering that essentially no sales are expected in the coming season. ShoeWeb can either negotiate to return this unsold stock to the suppliers or attempt to sell down as much as possible in the early months of the next season, by means of heavy promotional or clearance activity. ShoeWeb must have a plan in mind before the season begins, or next season's markdowns may be so expensive they wipe out whatever profits ShoeWeb makes on this line of business in the spring.

It is important to pay attention to the relationship between the two plans (total men's business versus sandal business). Note that with overall planned receipts of $400,000 for period 2, and planned receipts of $75,000 for sandals, that leaves $325,000 available for non-sandal purchases. In developing the turnover and receipt plans for each area of business, ShoeWeb's management must be careful not to exceed the totals already established. Alternatively, it could create all the subcategory plans first, then roll them into a total plan and see how the turnover, sales, and markdowns end up.

Markdown Effects on MM

ShoeWeb is running its business with monthly promotional sales planned (on limited items) and permanent markdowns on styles going out of stock. The purpose of this promotional strategy is to minimize the impact of off-price selling on the profitability of the business.

With the markdown plan above, the men's shoe business will have a markdown rate of 16 percent. If the IMU averages 50 percent, the business should achieve a maintained margin of 42 percent. The sandal business, in comparison, will experience a markdown rate of 20 percent. If ShoeWeb wants to target a maintained margin for this business as well, the IMU will have to be 52.5 percent. This is not unusual, as season and/or fashion product often commands a higher IMU to counteract this additional markdown activity required to clear stock.

Profitability Analysis for WebKidCare

WebKidCare is not in the fashion business and therefore can remain profitable with a lower turn rate (i.e., a higher stock investment in relation to sales) than ShoeWeb's. Additionally, WebKidCare will *not* be utilizing promotional sales or clearances, so its markdown liability will be minimal.

Table 7.17 shows what a seasonal plan for WebKidCare could look like.

Table 7.17   WebKidCare Turnover Calculation

	Period 1	Period 2	Period 3	Period 4	Period 5	Period 6	Average Stock	Total	Turnover
BOM stock	400	400	400	400	400	400	400.00		0.84
Sales	75	75	75	50	40	20		335	
Markdowns	0	0	0	0	0	0		0	
Receipts	75	75	75	50	40	20		335	
EOM stock	400	400	400	400	400	400			

NOTE: Figures expressed in 1000s.

Here is what this worksheet tells us about WebKidCare's business and profitability:

First, WebKidCare has chosen an assortment level maintained throughout the season by continually replacing its sales with new receipts. Furthermore, with no promotional or clearance activity, the company can sell profitably at a lower turnover rate than a promotional business can. If WebKidCare wants to increase its turnover, the management either needs to increase sales or decrease its starting stock level.

Markdown Effects on MM

Since WebKidCare has no promotional or clearance plans, it does not need to worry about this effect on its gross margin. When it chooses its IMU, it only needs to remember to deduct its freight, duty, and/or salvage costs to determine its operating profit, or net margin. Without the variability of promotional sales, there is less guesswork in its net margin forecasts. Since it can more accurately know its net margin, there is less need to "pad" IMU to provide breathing space to make a profit after all costs are deducted.

PROFITABILITY CHECKLIST

❑ Run a preliminary turnover calculation for your season, taking into account your pricing structure and promotional strategies. Use Worksheet 7.1, Turnover Calculation.
  ❑ MAKE ALL CALCULATIONS IN RETAIL DOLLARS.
  ❑ Review the turnover requirements of your business, taking into account industry standards, vendor agreements, and cash flow requirements
  ❑ Will you be aggressive or conservative in your forecasts for stocking, sales, and markdowns?
  ❑ What are the seasonal stocking requirements of your business?
❑ Calculate maintained margin for your business. Use Worksheet 7.2, Maintained Margin.
  ❑ Calculate the gross margin you are earning on your inventory.
  ❑ Factor in the costs of freight, salvage, and other fees to figure your maintained margin.
  ❑ Review fixed costs to determine if your maintained margin will suffice.
❑ Evaluate your options in Assortment Financial Planning, Pricing Strategy, and Profitability Calculations to determine how to improve the financial picture of your e-retail operation.

CHAPTER EIGHT

Vendor Relations

Chapter Preview

Building vendor relationships and negotiating for goods involves much more than getting a good price on the items you want in your e-store. We will examine all of the elements of a deal open for negotiation and how to evaluate your needs as you work with your vendors. Our hypothetical e-retailers address challenges in their vendor relationships as start-ups and in later negotiations.

Relationships That Help You Thrive

Successful retail is founded on your relationships with your customers, but it is sustained by your relationships with your suppliers. Vendors supply you with product, of course, but they are also your intimate partners on the road to profitability.

Your most important interactions with vendors will be in your negotiations for products and pricing. These negotiations lay the foundation for everything that follows—including the vendor's service and support of you as a customer. In addition to negotiating a good price for the goods you want to purchase, you may be able to create partnership opportunities, marketing leverages, exclusive products, and more.

Striking and maintaining a strong relationship thus does more than ensure that you have access to the products you want and need at terms that work for you. Strong vendor relationships can create the competitive advantages that separate you from your competition in the marketplace.

The cost of goods is usually your starting point. Although cost of goods is important, it is not the only element you will be negotiating on your purchases. Equally important are the following:

- Assortment choices
- Inventory status
- Quantity
- Delivery dates
- Freight
- Payment terms
- Damage allowance
- Marketing allowance
- Marketing materials and support
- Exclusives
- Markdown allowance
- Maintained margin
- Returns/damages
- Guarantee

Understand what is at stake with each element under negotiation. Assess your needs. Then assess the needs of your suppliers. Determine your negotiating position, as well as the position you anticipate your vendor will take.

The outcome of your negotiations affects your assortment, cash flow, and profitability, so it is very important to work carefully through all of the preparatory steps, including vendor-specific financial plans.

Elements Involved in Vendor Negotiations

Items to Purchase

You have received product sheets and made your choices. Occasionally, you may choose to carry everything in a supplier's product line, but usually you will want to purchase only selected items. Depending on the supplier and how they normally do business, you will have more or less freedom to choose only those items you desire for your assortment. Occasionally, however, suppliers may prefer to sell certain items as a set, or they may try to restrict your choices to a particular line they carry.

There are several things to keep in mind about item selection. First, you want to be aware of the supplier's goals. Is there an item that is overstocked, and the supplier needs to move it NOW? Are suppliers trying to differentiate their distribution channels by designating certain product lines or brands to specific types of retailers? Perhaps a supplier is positioning certain products for the Web channel and others for traditional stores or catalogs. By doing so, the vendor establishes separate product lines and avoids channel conflict.

The more you understand about your vendors' product assortments and distribution strategies, the better you can negotiate for the products that will perform best in your e-retail environment.

Also, remember that your suppliers are a great resource for product information and the relative merits of their product offerings. As you are building relationships with them, it is in their interest to sell you successful products. Share with them the details of your strategy as well as the logic that helped you define your assortment. Then listen to their advice on product selection.

This is not to say that suppliers are always right in their recommendations. You certainly should not buy something that you do not believe will sell on your e-retail site or that does not fit with your assortment. However, sometimes vendors adamantly insist that certain products will be the next automatic toaster. In that case, they should be willing to back up their confidence with a buy-back guarantee or other arrangement that lessens your risk.

In a similar vein, you can offer a supplier a chance to test market demand on new products. The vendor should be willing to assume all risks for unsold product if you purchase a new item on a "test" basis.

Sometimes a vendor will work to get you to buy into new products or categories, in addition to the ones you have carried in the past. They are trying to expand their relationship with you. If it makes sense in your assortment and financial plans, go for it. At the same time, you have an opportunity to leverage the supplier's interest in selling through you to create additional benefits for your e-retail operation. Perhaps you have old stock produced by that supplier that you want to return. Now is the time to do it.

Quantity

There may be quite a bit of give and take in determining the quantity of goods ordered. You will want to find out about volume discounts, if applicable, and how quickly you can reorder product if your initial purchase sells out quickly.

You will want to know if this is an item the vendor keeps in stock, or whether you have only one opportunity to order. Naturally, this information may influence the size of your order.

How frequently you wish to purchase will also affect your desired quantity.

If you are relying on just-in-time inventory for some quantity of product, you and any vendors that have agreed to this arrangement need clear communication as to market demand, flow of stock with order, quantity minimums and maximums, and more. Just-in-time inventory arrangements are far from standardized, and both parties will have to negotiate in good faith to come to agreement on these issues.

Delivery Date

You will want to know exactly when product will arrive so you can plan your stock levels and accounts payable accordingly. Ideally, you will want to establish a window of time in which the goods are delivered that is neither too soon, such as three months before their expected selling season, nor too late, such as after Christmas, if they are meant to be stocking stuffers. You should negotiate terms in which the order can be canceled if the vendor fails to deliver the goods before a specific deadline. This is particularly important with seasonal goods which, if they arrive too late, will never sell through in the appropriate season.

For just-in-time stock, you may want to negotiate delivery performance guarantees, such that vendors will compensate you if they fail to meet the shorter delivery schedules required by on-demand delivery. If vendors are shipping directly to your customers, you have a different set of negotiations ahead of you. Can you supply the vendor with branded packaging so that the merchandise arrives identified with you? By the same token, do you *need* to supply packaging, if the vendor is ill-equipped to ship single pieces?

Work out all the details of delivery, regardless of the inventory model you are using.

Cost

Find out what the list price is for an item. Then find out what discounts are available, and how to take advantage of them. If there are no "usual" discounts, try to create some on your own.

Hangups and hitches in service or delivery create discount opportunities. Say, for example, that WidgetWorld.com and the supplier, Widge, Inc., agree that the new summer-release widget will be delivered between May 1 and May 10.

WidgetWorld will pay $10 apiece for the widget shipment. If the shipment is delayed past May 10, the terms of the agreement call for the order to be canceled automatically.

On May 5, Widge, Inc. calls to say the goods are slightly delayed. They can, however, promise delivery by May 25, if the retailer will extend the delivery time.

WidgetWorld.com does not want to go all summer without the latest widget release, so the buyer agrees to take the shipment in despite the late delivery. To compensate for the fact that they will lose several weeks of selling time on the goods, however, WidgetWorld insists on a 10 percent discount. When the summer widgets arrive, WidgetWorld will pay only $9 apiece for the goods.

Depending on overall demand for the item with other purchasers, vendors may be quite willing to agree to this discount. Otherwise, they are stuck with the canceled order.

Freight

Find out what the usual freight terms are: who has responsibility for freight, who arranges it, and who pays for it. Negotiate changes that may be best for your operation. Remember, nothing is "free." If a supplier offers "free delivery," it just means the cost of freight is added to the purchase price.

Often suppliers do have access to the most economical transportation, but if you are investing a large amount of money in purchasing, it makes sense to check on your transportation options. If you arrange your own freight, then you should be getting a discount from those vendors whose price usually includes delivery.

Payment Terms

When suppliers are dealing with a new retailer, or any unknown quantity, they may demand payment before they are willing to ship the goods. Obviously, this arrangement does your cash flow no favors. Ideally, you order and receive goods, have several weeks of selling in which you earn money on your purchases, then pay for the purchases out of these earnings. Once you have established your credit-worthiness and relationship with suppliers, you should be able to command better payment terms—30 days, 45 days, or 60 days. This means that you are invoiced when the goods are shipped, but you have 30, 45, or 60 days to pay the bill.

When you get these payment terms, you may be able to benefit from additional discounts. Many suppliers offer discounts for paying early, such as 2 percent off the total due if you pay the invoice within 10 days. Your negotiations over payment may also cover returned and damaged goods. In this context, "damaged goods" means goods that a customer returns in a nonsaleable condition (e.g., shoes that have been worn, clothing that has been washed improperly, appliances that broke the first time they were switched on, and so on). Some agreements call for a damage "reserve," whereby you withhold full payment to leave a reserve for returned or damaged goods. For example, if you purchase $100,000 worth of goods and have agreed to a two percent damage reserve, you will only pay the vendor $98,000 when the bill is due. When vendors agree to a damage reserve, you do not return damaged or returned goods back to them, but will discard them or destroy them yourself. The vendor also will incur no additional liability on damages, even if the value of your total damaged products exceeds the $2,000 in reserve. The upside is that you will not have to worry about shipping stuff back to the vendor. The downside is that you could take a bath on it, if you are supplied with shoddy goods that fall apart right when the customer gets them.

Marketing Allowance

Does the vendor provide funds for marketing support based on the amount you purchase? What are the rules governing these funds and how can you get access to them? Many brands do make funds available based on the amount you purchase (e.g., with a purchase of $100,000, you get $10,000 in marketing support). However, the money almost always comes with strings attached; advertising must be full-price, the brand must be promoted individually, or other similar rules. You will need to provide proof that you have followed the rules to get the cash.

Marketing Materials and Support

Is the brand planning any promotional campaigns of which you should be aware? Can your site be "tagged" (mentioned in brand advertising) so that consumers know they can find these items with you?

What can the vendor supply you in terms of product information, product images, and selling support for your site presentation?

Exclusives

Are there any products for which you will be the only distribution outlet? Can you advertise this? Can you get any items for a period before they become available elsewhere?

Markdown Allowance

Vendors may put restrictions on promotional pricing, as we noted in Chapter 6. However, some vendors encourage promotional activity. If that is the case, are they willing to help pay for the cost of these markdowns? Can you agree on a deduction to the cost price to accomplish this, or would they prefer to receive a separate charge after the promotion has run its course?

Maintained Margin

Is the vendor willing to reach an agreement of a minimum margin performance on its products? With this agreement in place, at the end of each season you can determine the profitability of the product line using the tools developed in Chapter 7. If the goal margin is not reached, the vendor pays the difference.

Hello, retailer-Nirvana! You may have just decided to include a minimum margin performance clause in every deal you sign. Naturally, it is the kind of thing suppliers are not handing out like lollipops. This arrangement will not come your way every day, but it may be a possibility when you work with suppliers who are supremely confident in particular products or product lines and extremely eager to get them into the marketplace. They may be willing to agree to a maintained margin to get you to purchase and merchandise their offerings.

Returns and/or Damages

What is the vendor's policy on returns and/or damages? Will returned product have to be sent back to the supplier? Who pays for the freight in that case? Is a damage allowance a more cost-effective solution for you both? How about a damage claim, where you report and destroy the damaged items, but do not have to ship the items back to the supplier (saving on transportation costs)?

What about returns on goods that can be repaired? What makes the most sense on the given product category, and what approach will give the end-customer the best customer service?

Guarantees

What kinds of guarantees or warranties come with the purchase of these products? How is this information delivered to the purchaser? Remember that your customers will blame you as much as they blame the manufacturer if they are unhappy with the condition of their goods or if the customer service on defects, repairs, or replacements is shoddy. It is in your best interest to follow through on these issues with your manufacturers to ensure your reputation as a retailer is not damaged.

Obviously, not every subject above is critical on every purchase decision and/or vendor negotiation. The important thing to remember is that all of these are *possible* variables in your negotiating position. If you are reaching an impasse on a given point of negotiation, try to reach a compromise that makes use of another area of interest for you both.

For example, you may be willing to forgo marketing support in exchange for a better price, or you may want a 60-day payment period instead of a damages allowance. Your choices may vary from vendor to vendor and season to season as your business and your needs change.

Assessing Your Negotiating Position

Successfully negotiating a deal takes a lot of planning and preparations. Never underestimate the importance of evaluating the following:

- What you want
- What you can offer
- What your supplier wants
- What your supplier can offer

What You Want

You cannot possibly get what you want out of a negotiation unless you know what you want. You want the goods, of course, at a price at which you can successfully sell them and make a profit. That is the reason you are at the negotiating table in the first place. But there are sure to be other things that you need.

Do you want access to a certain item? Do you want the ability to reorder? What are your financial constraints and goals? You will find the financial planning portion particularly helpful in determining the answers to some of these questions, so do not skimp on that exercise.

What Can You Offer

You offer payment in negotiable tender for the supplier's products, as does every other business on the Web and in the real world. What else, besides your live check, makes you and your business important to suppliers? What is in it for them strategically?

Perhaps you can offer new and broader exposure for their products and brand. If you reach a new and different market for their products, you are helping them increase their overall sales without taking business away from other retailers. This is called *creating incremental sales*.

Can you help them improve their image or better align their image with their business goals? Can you find or create a market for their products where other distribution channels have failed? Can you help them take market share from their competitors?

Clearly, the larger and more successful your e-retail operation becomes, the more you can lay claim to being a valuable partner for your suppliers. As you grow, it will become easier for you to set the terms of purchase as you desire.

What Your Supplier Wants

Learn as much as you can about your supplier and how they do business. This will help you understand their needs and motivations. Are they looking for new markets for their products? Are they trying to improve or strengthen their brand image? Are they introducing new product lines? Who are their major competitors (and will you carry those competitors as well)?

By getting to know your suppliers you can anticipate their negotiation responses and devise compromises that serve both of your needs.

What Your Supplier Can Offer

What are your supplier's strengths? How can it help you do business better? Does it spend a lot of money supporting its brands? Is it developing new and interesting products for your consumers?

Go over the elements open for negotiation with this supplier. If it has not offered you an allowance for damages or marketing support, that does not mean it is unwilling to consider the idea. By knowing how it does business, you are more likely to think of ways this supplier can help you develop your business at little or no risk to it.

Preparing for Negotiations

You will need to prepare before you meet with vendors. First, research your potential vendors carefully. Ask around in your industry about vendors with whom you are interested in working—are they receptive to smaller businesses? Do they have an open or restrictive manner in dealing with negotiations and relationships? Remember from the assortment planning phase (see Chapter 3) that some larger vendors will be unwilling to work with small-scale retailers or will not want to use your e-retail site as a sales channel. Do not write off the reluctant ones completely; however, do not focus all your time and effort on them when starting out.

Additional "housekeeping" items you will want to attend to before meeting with vendors include having your credit checked, professionally preparing all presentation materials, and reviewing regulations governing retail in your geographic location(s) to be sure you have complied with all requirements (resale permits, licenses, and so on).

When you are ready to prepare for a specific meeting with a specific vendor, the single most important element is to develop a buy plan. This plan tells you how much you have to spend and when you can afford to receive the goods, given your turn requirements.

To create your buy plan, you must create your cash flow plan as you did in Chapter 7 (Worksheet 7.1, Turnover Calculation). Now, however, you must create a cash flow plan that mirrors your supplier relationships.

Evaluate the following example of a company that develops its financial plans by category:

- Books
- Toys
- CDs
- Clothing

For clothing, the department takes precedence over the manufacturer, so based on the relative importance of the various departments, the buyers develop sales plans for the following:

- Infant
- Toddler
- Little Kid
- Big Kid

When the buyers review the offerings from manufacturers, they will have to assign one of these categories to each item of clothing and then determine the quantity and/or timing of delivery so that each product fits into their overall plans. A given manufacturer may provide clothing for several departments.

During the purchasing meeting, the buyers will want to have each buy plan on hand to note purchase decisions.

Consider an example from the toy industry. Perhaps you are an e-retailer that wants to purchase toys from Mattel. Your assortment includes products from all of the major brands. Your business plans are developed based on the following categories of business:

- Dolls
- Board games
- Model kits
- Plush (stuffed) animals
- Electronic games
- Sports equipment

You have forecasted your sales, markdowns, turnover, and receipts in each of the above categories. However, when you meet with Mattel, you will want to have a buy plan tailored just for them.

Your preparation starts with consideration of the category of *Dolls*. Your overall doll buy plan should look like Table 8.1.

You know from your assortment planning that Mattel's dolls, particularly Barbie, will be your most important items within this category. You estimate that a full 80 percent of your total doll sales will come from Mattel dolls. You also know that Mattel does not allow promotional activity on any of its dolls, so you will not spend any of your markdown money on its products.

This means your Mattel doll cash flow would look like Table 8.2. This table shows that Mattel accounts for 80 percent of the stock, sales, and receipt figures from Table 8.1 and none of the markdown dollars.

Now you have to turn these numbers into something you can use as you make item and quantity decisions. Table 8.3 is a blank buy plan. Worksheet 8.1, Buy Plan by Vendor on the CD, includes all formulas you need to create this for any vendor you work with.

Use the top half of your buy plan to enter quantities for items in your current assortment that you will be continuing to sell. The lower part of the plan is for new products to be added to your assortment. By organizing your plan this way, you get a clear picture of how much of each month's budgeted receipts will be from existing products and how much you have to spend on new items.

Table 8.1 Dolls

	Period 1	Period 2	Period 3	Period 4	Period 5	Period 6	Average Stock	Total	Turnover
BOM stock	10	25	35	45	55	65	44		1.25
Sales	5	10	10	10	10	10		55	
Markdowns	0	0	0	0	0	2		2	
Receipts	20	20	20	20	20	20		120	
EOM stock	25	35	45	55	65	73			

NOTE: Figures expressed in 1000s.

Table 8.2   Mattel Cash Flow

	Period 1	Period 2	Period 3	Period 4	Period 5	Period 6	Average Stock	Total	Turnover
BOM stock	8	21	29	37	45	53	36		1.19
Sales	3	8	8	8	8	8		43	
Markdowns	0	0	0	0	0	0		0	
Receipts	16	16	16	16	16	16		96	
EOM stock	21	29	37	45	53	61			

Note: Figures expressed in 1000s.

Table 8.3   Buy Plan

BUY PLAN:

Season:

				Period 1		Period 2		Period 3		Period 4		Period 5		Period 6		TOTAL	
Item #	Description	Cost	Retail	Units	Retail	Units	Retail	Units	Retail	Units	Retail	Units	Retail	Units	Retail	Units	Retail
Current Assortment																	
New Products																	
TOTAL PURCHASES																	

The columns in your buy plan include the following:

- Item number
- Description
- Cost: The per-piece price you pay to the supplier
- Retail: The price you will list it and sell it for
- Period units: The number of pieces you will have delivered in that period
- Period retail: The total retail value of the items to be delivered in that period

If you use Worksheet 8.1, which is provided on the CD, the Total Purchases row will automatically calculate based on the data you enter. In the Buy Plan row, enter your buy plan budget for each period. The Difference row will also calculate automatically, telling you how much of your receipt budget you have left to spend.

Using this tool, your Mattel doll buy plan would look like Table 8.4.

If it is the first time you are purchasing from this vendor, you will have no current products and will be filling in the new products as you choose them.

Since your cash plans are developed in retail dollars, you will calculate how much you are buying in retail dollars as well. To do this, you must determine what retail you will set and multiply this by the units ordered in each period.

At the bottom of each retail dollar column, you will total the quantities and compare this to the cash plan receipt number. This is your budget, and you can spend up to this amount in each period.

If you already carry products from a particular vendor, you will want to start with a list of the products you will continue to sell in the coming season. Based on your selling statistics and your plans for the coming season, fill in the number of units you expect to purchase in each month. After you have spent this portion, you can use the rest of your budget to fill in new products that you select during the course of your meeting with the vendor.

Remember that you developed your receipt plans based on a turnover target, so you cannot shift receipts from one month to another without affecting the turnover. If you want to introduce a new product in a particular month and do not have enough money to cover that particular purchase, you will have to go back to receipt plans to try to find a way to increase the receipts in that month while maintaining your turn. It will involve increasing or decreasing your receipts in other months to affect your average stock.

By creating this plan and following it when you make purchasing decisions with your suppliers, you are building the right assortment to the right levels to support your sales and promotional plans. Without these tools you run the risk of over-stocking or under-stocking product you need to run your business.

Table 8.4 Sample Mattel Buy Plan

BUY PLAN Mattel, Dolls

Season Spr

Item #	Description	Cost	Retail	Period 1		Period 2		Period 3		Period 4		Period 5		Period 6		TOTAL	
				Units	Retail	Units	Retail	Units	Retail	Units	Retail	Units	Retail	Units	Retail	Units	Retail
Current Assortment																	
10101	Dress-Up Barbie	15	29.99	100	2999	100	2999	100	2999	100	2999	100	2999	100	2999	600	17994
10102	Make-Up Barbie	15	29.99	50	1499.5	0	0	0	0	50	1499.5	0	0	0	0	100	2999
10103	Suntan Barbie	15	29.99	20	599.8	20	599.8	20	599.8	0	0	0	0	0	0	60	1799.4
10104	Baby-Doll	12	24	100	2400	100	2400	100	2400	100	2400	100	2400	100	2400	600	14400
10105	Talking Baby	12	24	20	480	20	480	0	0	20	480	20	480	0	0	80	1920
10106	Napping Baby	9	19	20	380	10	190	10	190	10	190	10	190	10	190	70	1330
New Products																	
TOTAL PURCHASES					8358.3		6668.8		6188.8		7568.5		6069		5589		
BUY PLAN					16000		16000		16000		16000		16000		16000		

186

Although preparing your buy plan is the most important step, it is not the only preparation you will need to do before meeting with new or ongoing vendors.

Meeting with New and Prospective Vendors

You are going to have to be prepared to present your company and allay any doubts they may have about selling to you. The tools you have at your disposable to do this will depend on your site's stage of development. At the very least, you should have:

- A one-page outline of your concept,
- A list of the products (or brands) you have already secured, and
- Proof of your ability to pay (e.g., a letter of credit from a reputable bank for an amount that can reasonably cover the value of your projected inventory).

Your business plan and/or your retail strategy plan are good places to start in creating an effective presentation. Be honest and transparent with your information; you do not want to appear to be hiding anything. Your vendors will be your partners for the long haul; make your presentation to them as convincing as your presentation for financing or venture capital.

Be prepared for vendors who do not want to sell to you. Some may be unwilling to distribute via an e-retailer. Some may be spooked about e-retail stability, or the ability of a new business to pay. In any case, you may still be able to negotiate a "test" or an agreement to pay before shipment to get access to their product line.

Meeting with Current Vendors

In addition to purchasing new items, when you meet with current vendors it is important to recap and analyze business to date as well. It's helpful for both you and the vendor to see a regular "scorecard," like the one in Table 8.5, to see how their products measure up to sales, markdown, and margin goals.

By having these figures ready, you can discuss the growth and profitability of your business and determine the best way to improve both. Review Table 8.5 carefully to see what the previous season's figures tell us about this vendor's business. Table 8.6 is a blank vendor scorecard and is also available on the CD as Worksheet 8.2 to assist you in creating this document for each vendor you work with.

Table 8.5   Vendor Scorecard

	Season to Date		Previous Season	
	Actual	Plan	Actual	Plan
Sales	50	120	120	100
COG Sold	26	63	64.2	47.5
Mark-up	48%	47.50%	46.50%	52.50%
Mark-up dollars	24.00	57.00	55.80	52.50
Markdowns	25%	20%	21%	20%
Markdown dollars	12.50	24.00	20.00	20.00
Vendor Margin	35%	37%	35.30%	43%
Margin dollars	17.50	44.40	42.36	43.00

NOTE: Financial figures expressed in 1000s.

Worksheet 8.2   Vendor Scorecard

	Season to Date		Previous Season	
	Actual	Plan	Actual	Plan
Sales				
COG Sold				
Mark-up				
Mark-up dollars				
Markdowns				
Markdown dollars				
Vendor Margin				
Margin dollars				

NOTE: Financial figures expressed in 1000s.

The good news on the Vendor Scorecard in Table 8.5 is that sales exceeded plan. However, the cost of goods ran higher than expected, as did the amount spent on markdowns. As a result, the vendor margin ended at 35.3 percent instead of 43 percent as planned.

Since the overall sales were greater than expected, the retailer actually made almost as much money on the business as they had hoped: 43 percent of $100,000 is $43,000 and 35.3 percent of $120,000 is $42,360, so their net profit was only $640 less than management had planned.

It is also clear that when it came to the current season, management took the previous season's performance into account. The sales plan stayed at $120,000, but the buyer lowered mark-up expectations. Overall, the goal was to improve over last season's margin performance by reaching a 37 percent margin instead of a 35.3 percent.

To determine whether the sales goals can be achieved, we need to know how much time is left in the current season. With the information on hand, it looks like the mark-up is on plan, but the markdowns are running higher than expected. By having this information halfway through the season, the retailer and the vendor can work together to improve the markdown rate(or increase the markup) before the end of the season.

Sharing all of this information with your vendors is critical in making them an integral part of planning your business.

Handling Negotiations

You can think of each meeting with a vendor in terms of the following five steps:

1. Preparation

2. Opening meeting

3. Discussion of negotiation points

4. Agreement

5. Follow up

Each step is important for different reasons. We have already discussed the preparation that should go into each meeting. There are financial plans to develop. You should establish your goals and think about your vendor's goals. You should be prepared to present your retail concept or have past business quantified for discussion.

Try to start the meeting by listening to the other party. It is not uncommon for vendors to drop hints about their goals and concerns up front, which will make you better prepared when it is time to start negotiating. Ask about the vendor's business and answer any questions the vendor has about yours.

Now it's time to get down to business. Begin either by discussing previous business or by reviewing product assortments. Keep notes of the issues you discuss and make sure you have clear answers to your questions.

When you reach an agreement, make sure the details are understood by both of you and you each know what the next steps should be. Possible follow-up steps may be as follows:

- The vendor needs to send you samples and confirm delivery dates.
- You need to deliver a written order within 10 days.

After the meeting, follow up with a note or e-mail summarizing the main points and reiterating the next steps to be taken.

Negotiating Techniques

Many books on negotiation are available, as well as conferences and seminars to attend if you feel you lack negotiating skills. Professional sales coaches can also work with you to develop your negotiating skills.

In addition to doing your homework ahead of time, the most important thing to remember about negotiations in the retail environment (as opposed to negotiating to purchase a house) is that you can expect to have continuing contact with the same partners over many years. Your goal, therefore, should always be to create a working partnership and not to "beat" the other party in the negotiation.

This is not a zero-sum game. Your opponent does not have to "lose" for you to "win." In fact, if the supplier even feels like it lost, you have probably done yourself more damage in the long-run than any short-term gain you may have won.

Always be honest and fair. Reputations are made and kept in this business. You do not want the epitaph on your tombstone (or that of your e-retail site) to read: *Unreasonable Negotiator*. The community of your suppliers is usually quite small. If you are difficult or unpleasant to work with, the news will travel.

Hypothetical Cases

Vendor Relations for ShoeWeb

ShoeWeb, founded by shoe-retail veterans, begins its initial assortment planning with some advantages: its buyers already have relationships (from previous jobs) with the suppliers of the brands and styles they want to carry. The suppliers also know and have confidence in the management team.

On the other hand, many of ShoeWeb's suppliers are initially skeptical about consumer willingness to purchase shoes over the Web. In their initial negotiations, the buyers come prepared with an e-retail strategy presentation, outlined in the following box, and demonstrate that they have fully researched their market and will be able to overcome the challenges of Web-based retail.

Several selling seasons pass, shoe styles come and go, and now ShoeWeb is preparing for yet another spring and summer season. One of the buyers is preparing to meet with the sales representative for Rockport, a manufacturer of comfort shoes for men and women.

ShoeWeb business is planned at the brand level, and is already separated by gender. Therefore, the buyer already has financial plans for the men's Rockport business and the women's Rockport business.

ShoeWeb already carries 10 Rockport men's styles and 10 Rockport women's styles, which the buyer is continuing into the coming season. At a recent trade fair, a men's golf shoe was available, which can be added to the assortment in April (period 3), when the golf season begins.

According to the buy plan, the buyer's budget is used up on the 10 "basic" shoes during the last three periods of the season. This should not be a problem, however, since the spring seasonal shoes should be brought in at the beginning of

---

ShoeWeb PRESENTATION OUTLINE

I. Strategy Key Points

Broad and deep selection—The biggest shoe store on earth!

Web-enabled customization—Saving customers time by saving information about their shoe needs and buying habits, offering items that coordinate with items already in their wardrobes and providing a shopping service available anytime of the day or night.

II. Overcoming the Barriers

Will customers buy shoes over the Web? Customers already buy shoes and related products through catalogs. Our Web-enabled customization features will help overcome the inherent disadvantages of selling online.

    1. Provide catalog purchase statistics

    2. Share results of focus group research

    3. Share results of industry review research

III. Management Resumes

IV. Financials: Letter of Credit and/or Profitability Analyses, depending on audience

the season anyway. Since the buyer knows about the golf shoe and has an idea how many need to be purchased, it has already plugged that into the spreadsheet. However, until the cost is known (and a retail price can be chosen the impact on the company's financial plans cannot be calculated.

The buyer also knows the plan requires at least two sandals and one boat shoe in the assortment. Those are noted as well, so as to not be forgotten during the meeting.

Since this is an ongoing relationship with Rockport, the buyer will also use this opportunity to discuss Rockport's previous performance and will use this information to achieve the goals set in terms of marketing support.

Vendor Relations for WebKidCare

The management team of WebKidCare founded its company after years of running its own day care operation. It entered the e-retail arena with no existing supplier relationships, and with no particular credibility in the marketplace. In its initial vendor negotiations, it encounters a wide variety of responses from different suppliers.

For each sales meeting, the management team creates a full e-retail strategy presentation, outlined in the following box, including information on the management team and its expertise in the field of child care equipment.

WebKidCare's biggest challenge is to establish its credibility and creditworthiness in the marketplace. Once the company wins over suppliers, it can manage and maintain relationships skillfully.

WebKidCare PRESENTATION OUTLINE

I.   Company Mission

WebKidCare, founded in 2000 by John and Jane Smith, aims to be the leading Web-based resource for professional and semi-professional caregivers in the United States. Our visitors will be able to access complete, accurate, and timely information about the child care industry, child psychology and development, and best business practices while accessing a comprehensive selection of equipment and supplies for running a child care business. Our customers will look to us for reliable, one-stop shopping, supported by expert reviews, which will make day-to-day efforts easier and more professional.

II. Strategy Key Points
  1. Fragmented industry: We have an opportunity to define and lead.
  2. Busy customer with specialized needs: We have an opportunity to save them time and money, as well as increase their confidence in the value of their purchases.
  3. Expert reviews of products: Our customers will not have to spend their own time on product research because they know they can trust our experts.
  4. Low prices: Our virtual store and just-in-time inventory arrangements keep our overhead at a minimum, allowing us to pass some of the savings on to our customers.
  5. Targeted and effective site content: Our industry-specific content, professionally written and edited, will provide our customers with a unique, one-stop resource that can help them perform their jobs and run their businesses more effectively.

III. Management Resumes

IV. Advisory Board Members

V. Financials: Letter of Credit and/or Profitability Analyses, depending on audience

VI. Sample Articles:
  1. Financial recordkeeping for your home-based daycare
  2. What's a four-year-old's agenda?
  3. Top picks for outdoor equipment

VII. Editorial Policy

It is the policy of WebKidCare to publish and disseminate material that is of value to the professional and semi-professional caregiver. We do not publish "advertorial" materials intended to sell product. Our editorial goal is to create an online resource that caregivers can use with trust to improve their skills and their businesses. Anything that appears on WebKidCare, whether editorial content or products offered for sale, carries the KidCare Seal of Approval.

Our advisory board reviews all medical and similar claims, and approves all products and product recommendations. To request further information, nominate a professional for the advisory board, or appeal a board decision, *please contact our board chair*.

VENDOR RELATIONS CHECKLIST

❑ Evaluate your needs for each vendor's product line.

❑ Review negotiable variables for each vendor.

❑ Assess overall negotiating positions.

    ❑ What do you want?

    ❑ What can you offer?

    ❑ What does the vendor want?

    ❑ What can the vendor offer?

❑ Prepare financial plans by vendor and by product category, if appropriate (see Worksheet 7.1, Turnover Calculation).

❑ Prepare a buy plan based on your financial plans and assortment plans (use Worksheet 8.1, Buy Plan by Vendor).

    ❑ Reorder items you will be keeping in your assortment.

    ❑ List items you know you want to add to your assortment.

    ❑ Review receipt budgets to ensure you will meet your stocking and turn goals.

❑ Prepare a vendor scorecard for any vendors you have already worked with (use Worksheet 8.2, Vendor Scorecard).

❑ Sales Meeting

    ❑ Present e-retail strategy and backup materials to new and prospective vendors.

    ❑ Ask questions about their product lines and answer any questions they have about your business.

    ❑ Review vendor scorecards for vendors with whom you have been working.

    ❑ Review buy plans and place orders, evaluating all points of negotiation.

    ❑ Agree on post-meeting follow up.

❑ Follow Up

    ❑ Confirm order in writing, if necessary.

    ❑ Review product samples from vendor, if necessary.

    ❑ Other follow up as agreed.

❑ Ongoing

    ❑ Overall, is your relationship with your vendor healthy?

    ❑ Overall, are you accommodating your vendor within the parameters of running your business well?

CHAPTER NINE

Running a Retail Organization

Chapter Preview

From overall organization to the details of daily operation, careful planning and knowledge of the nature of the tasks at hand will create the environment you need to succeed. Know the projects you will need to tackle, the fires you may need to put out, and the responsibilities and communications structures you will need to establish. Our hypothetical e-retailers face the challenges of organizing and running their operations with creativity and professionalism.

Setting Up for Success

Whether your Web site is a pure e-retail operation or a combination of content and e-retail, you must give careful attention to the structure of your buying organization. Who will be responsible for which decisions? What is the most effective use of the people and talents you hire and develop?

In structuring your organization, you have a range of choices. The key is to lay out your expectations, job responsibilities, and communications structures as clearly as possible. Be willing to let the whole thing logically evolve, based on the particular mix of folks involved in your business at any given time.

The buyers or merchants are truly the vital organs of a retail operation, online or off. Figure 9.1 shows the many critical interactions and tasks for which the buyer is responsible. Your organization may not match this diagram exactly,

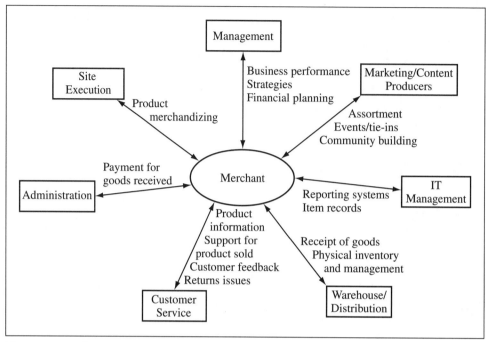

Figure 9.1 **Lines of Organizational Communication**

of course; in many smaller organizations, the management team is the same as the merchant team. However, this figure provides a starting point for discussion on the central role of the buyer.

Merchant Organization

As you develop your business, you should find (or train) buyers to assume responsibility for various categories of business. You can let your assortment structure dictate the division of responsibilities, but you should also keep in mind the possibility of using other divisions if these are more suited to your business. For example, if your business depends on several well-known brands and each brand offers a broad assortment of goods spanning a number of categories, you may prefer to set up a buying organization in which each vendor will work with a single buyer. Your buyers will have responsibilities that cut across product lines, but they will also have deeper brand knowledge and stronger relationships with the vendors.

You also need to consider the assortment organization you have set up for your record keeping and inventory management as discussed in Chapters 4 and 5. Your merchants must be able to gather the information they need for their areas of responsibility, so the choices you have made on naming the key categories for reporting statistics will have a huge impact on how your buyers' responsibilities should be delegated.

If your record-keeping and tracking systems do not gather the information "by brand" or "by vendor," it would be frustrating and inefficient to create a merchant organization divided along these lines. The merchants would have to spend a mammoth amount of time extracting the most basic of sales and stock information from your systems. It would be equally as challenging, if not impossible, to measure buyer performances.

Therefore, you can see that your assortment categories, your management systems, and your buying organization are all developed in tandem. They must work together, or nothing works at all.

Broad or Narrow Focus?

Will your buyers have a broad or narrow area of responsibility? There are pros and cons to either choice, as shown in Table 9.1.

Table 9.1   Broad or Narrow Focus

	Pro	Con
Broad: Responsibility for many categories of business	Improves rationalization of assortment—less likely to be unnecessary duplications	Difficult to remain aware of all the details of the business
Narrow: Responsibility for a narrow category of business	Buyer has the tools and the knowledge to make the best decisions possible.	Larger payroll costs; increased risks of assortment duplications in closely related buying categories

Whatever approach you end up choosing, you must be aware of the pitfalls and try to compensate for them.

For example, if you choose to set up broad areas of responsibility, the merchants will have their hands full selecting products and performing all of the upper-level management that goes along with negotiating and merchandising those products. In that case, you should establish adequate support systems and hire staff so that the merchants can focus on these critical tasks, leaving clerical and/or non-critical tasks to other specialists.

If your merchants have a narrow focus, on the other hand, your challenge is to establish communications systems that move information efficiently among the merchants. You want your overall assortment to have cohesion and logic, so your buyers had better be talking to each other and know what the overall strategy looks like. With a narrow merchant-focus, you may also have a larger payroll to support increased specialization among your buyers.

Merchant Responsibilities

Each retail organization will develop its own special needs, but the following are the tasks that one expects to fall under the buyer's supervision:

- Assortment choices
- Pricing
- Negotiating with vendors
- Purchasing goods/writing orders
- Promotional activity (planning and execution)
- Product merchandising/product information communication
- Supervising receipt of goods
- Financial planning
- Sales and stock analysis

Not only must the merchant's responsibilities be clearly laid out, but so too must the communications and interaction among the merchant organization and the other divisions of the business. See Figure 9.1 for an idea of the many lines of communication you must create in your e-retail business.

Remember, if areas of responsibility are large, you need the merchants to focus their efforts on the most critical activities—usually assortment and financial planning, as well as results analysis. You will need to designate others to

INCENTIVE PROGRAMS

In most traditional retail organizations, buyers are accustomed to receiving a portion of their compensation in the form of a bonus, which is directly tied to the business's performance. If you intend to recruit experienced buyers from the non-virtual world, you will have to consider incentive programs in putting together your compensation packages.

The usual tools of measurement for incentive programs are as follows:

- Sales
- Margin (usually some form of net margin)
- Turn

It is useful to measure performance by several factors such as these to prevent business decisions that run counter to the organization's goals.

For example, if buyers are rewarded strictly on sales performance, they may be tempted to maximize sales at the expense of margins or stock profitability. They may sell more units, but they may do so at a cost that is too high for the organization to maintain profitability.

If you intend to use a similar program in your organization, be sure the terms are spelled out clearly and everyone understands how the measurements will be calculated and evaluated. You need to decide how often bonuses will be calculated and who will be eligible to receive them.

For incentive programs to be effective, the people being rewarded must have control of reaching their goals. If you make someone responsible for the sales and margin performance of a particular area of business, you cannot allow someone else to make purchasing or markdown decisions within that area without obtaining consent.

Another option to the type of bonus system described above is to reward all employees based on the organization's performance, rather than singling out select employees for rewards. One advantage to this is that to function effectively, the entire organization must work together. A business line's success is not merely dependent on excellent buying decisions and management but on the combined efforts of everyone involved in creating the site, the community, and the customer's experience.

assume responsibility for activities such as writing orders, management of the receipt process, and/or management of IT information and records.

A Day in the Life of an e-Retail Organization

With the merchant the center of an e-retail organization, the day-to-day tasks fall into several primary categories:

- Performance/sales review
- Product-related tasks
- Order/shipping tasks
- Planning

In accomplishing these tasks, the merchant will interact with every department in an organization. Of course, there is no "typical" day, and in any given day, a merchant may perform only a few or all of these tasks, whirling through the office in crisis mode.

The point is not to tick each of these items off a to-do list but to have an understanding of the overall activity inside an e-retail operation. Merchants who consistently spend time with each of the tasks described can be assured they are on top of their business and are likely to achieve the results they desire.

Performance/Sales Review

In this category are all tasks relating directly to ongoing business, including review of current business and comparisons of current business with historical data.

Check Recent Business Performance (Sales, Markdowns, Stock) Versus Plan and/or Last Year

This is the critical information gathering you must do to make smart tactical decisions. On a daily basis, merchants will need to review inventory reports, sales reports, and profitability reports. Compare reports run on different subsets of information, by whole store, department, and division, to track the global picture on a day-to-day basis. On a weekly or biweekly basis, go down to the SKU-level and compare items, current year over last year, trends, and consumer response to marketing and promotional activity.

In these tasks, merchants review performances with management, marketing, and content producers and the site execution/technical teams for additional feedback. Did a marketing or editorial plan have a different effect on sales than expected? Did a change in page layout seem to make it easier or more difficult to complete a sale?

Note Variations (from Plan or Last Year) and Address Opportunities and/or Challenges

Analyze your business and make plans based on the information gathered above. Focus primarily on the aspects of the business you can still affect and control: orders planned but not placed yet, goals for market trips, changes to short-term promotional plans, and so on. Communicate changes you feel are necessary to improve your business and execute those plans. To improve sales, for example, you can add items to an ongoing sale, lengthen the period dates of an upcoming sale, increase the discount on a planned sale, and so on.

These plans must be shared with those responsible for successful execution. If the terms of a promotion or the items in a promotion will be changed, marketing and site execution will need to know, as well as your information technology (IT) department, depending on how your systems are structured. If you are increasing or decreasing quantities in a planned shipment, check with the warehouse to align your physical resources with your new plans. To the extent you can, share both the rationale and changes.

Product-Related Tasks

In this category are all tasks relating directly to choice, merchandising, and management of products.

Source/Review New Product Ideas and Merchandising Opportunities

Always watch for what is happening in your marketplace. Know what you are looking for to fill the gaps in your assortment. Capitalize on market trends. If everyone suddenly has a passion for purple, add some purple items to your assortment, perhaps by swapping out the orange ones that are not doing so well. Talk to existing and new suppliers. Visit trade shows. Shop the competition. Get feedback from your customers and from others within your organization.

As you identify opportunities, merchants must talk to their colleagues in site execution, marketing, content development, management, and warehouse. Are there cool merchandising concepts to adopt on the site? A new product that suggests a community-building opportunity? Is there space in the warehouse for those life-sized plush elephants that are certain to be the next kiddie craze?

Merchandise Assortment at the SKU Level, Including Decisions on Pricing, Bundling, and So On

The buyers make initial decisions on how best to sell the assortment they have chosen so carefully. In conjunction with marketing and site execution, the buyers flesh out and perfect these ideas. The better communication that goes on between these departments, the more efficiently they will be able to create effective merchandising.

Add New Products to the System, Making and Confirming Decisions on Pricing, Categorization, and Classifications

This is the nitty-gritty (but vitally important) information required to offer products for sale efficiently and accurately on your Web site. Your sales and stock reporting systems will depend on the information you input here. Make sure the merchants and the IT department are plugged into the same outlet when you create this system and work with it.

Ideally, you enter all products once into a single system and gather all the relevant information for selling and servicing them at this time. In addition to the information you need for stock and sales reporting, each product should be fully characterized with product dimensions (required for site execution, marketing, and warehouse), special product information (site execution, marketing, customer service) and possibly suppliers and costs (administration). Consider everyone's needs at the get-go to create the most efficient system possible.

Follow Up on Product Needs Such as Photos, Product Samples, Art, Product Descriptions, Merchandising Techniques, and So On

Throughout the process of selling, the merchants must continue to communicate with the Web designers, programmers, and copywriters, responding to their needs to merchandise the products in the most effective way to increase sales and customer satisfaction. Visit your site through an ordinary computer, with an ordinary modem connection so that you can evaluate the effect your merchandising has in its execution. It is also a good idea to check your site from both PC and Macintosh systems, through a variety of service providers, and to experiment with Internet Explorer, Netscape Navigator, and any other browser you believe your visitors might be using. The more the merchant understands about Web design and designers understand about the merchandise, the smoother and more successful the process will be.

Address Customer Questions or Programs with Products as They Arise;
Communicate Problems with Suppliers as Needed

Since the merchants are the "product experts" in the house, they must be available to support customer service whenever questions regarding performance, functions, and other issues arise. Merchants can create "fact sheets" to handle the basic questions but may occasionally be required to provide more extensive support. At the same time, any customer support that can be appropriately handled through an online frequently-asked-questions feature needs the input of merchants, customer service, and site execution.

Determine Appropriate Return Policies on Specific SKUs if Necessary

Depending on the category of business and the policies of the suppliers, different SKUs may require different return and/or service policies. It is the merchant's responsibility to communicate all of this with customer service and provide support as needed. General return policies need to be posted on the site; product-specific return, repair, and warranty policies need to be posted with the product. Obtain the assistance of site execution and customer service on this one.

Ordering/Shipping Tasks

These are tasks related to the logistics of sourcing and getting products to sell.

Discuss Specific Purchase Plans with Suppliers and Internal Checks as Needed;
Negotiate Terms and Place Orders

Once you have identified product to purchase (or repurchase) negotiate the deal and write the orders. Management needs to be involved to approve overall budgets, but it is most efficient for merchants to be free to order product within those budgets without needing management approval on each individual purchase.

If your site relies on a product advisory or product review board that vets potential new products, it would be the merchant's responsibility to shepherd the products through this process.

Track Shipment of Goods to Verify Product Availability and Location

So you ordered the product; will you actually receive it when it is due? Depending on your level of experience with a particular vendor, it is a good idea to stay on top of all shipments until they actually arrive at your door. That way, there are fewer unhappy surprises when the orders from customers start rolling in.

Address Changes to Orders Made by Suppliers Such as Short Shipments, Missing Colors and/or Styles, and So On

In addition to staying aware of when your orders arrive, you will need to know if the supplier made any changes to the order and/or did not deliver everything requested. Depending on the reasons for the changes and your current stock and sales situations, you may want to reorder what you did not receive the first time around or simply forget about it. Remember though that if you neither own it nor have immediate access to it, you cannot sell it, so be sure you know what you own.

Any changes to amounts, products, and other matters need to be acknowledged properly by warehouse and communicated appropriately to administration, marketing, and site execution. If your site offers green sweaters, your marketing department has been selling green sweaters, but the vendor came through with puce sweaters, then the information must flow from the warehouse, to the merchant, and to the marketing and site execution staff.

Answer Receiving Questions; Verify Goods Received Are Correct if Necessary

The merchants are the ones who ordered the goods, so if receiving has any questions, particularly if the goods received do not match the paperwork or purchase order information online, the merchant will have to help them resolve the discrepancies.

Verify Payables with Accounting Staff

If a shipment does not arrive according to the terms of the agreement, negotiate any changes in payment with your vendor and make sure your administrative staff understands changes and pays the correct amount. By the same token, be sure that your administrative staff pays vendors promptly and in full.

Planning

These are tasks related to ensuring future health and direction of the organization.

On a regular basis, merchants, management, marketing, content producers, and site execution teams must work together on strategic plans for the company. The input of all of these departments will define how the company moves from the present to the future, profitably and successfully. Financial plans must be hammered out between merchants and management, competitive analysis among merchants, management, and marketing, and overall strategy through collaboration of all.

For future planning, the long-term vision is what is at stake. What categories are trending up or down? How are whole classes, departments, or divisions doing? Now is not the time to fret over a single SKU. What does the big picture suggest?

It may be time to revisit the profitability analyses we created in Chapter 7. With a few seasons of data in your system, you will be in a much better position to forecast sales, determine optimal stock levels, and set turn goals that can make you profitable. It is also time to return to your promotional and pricing strategies (see Chapter 6) and see the real-world effect of decisions you may have made in the dark.

In fact, it would not be unthinkable to return to most of the decisions this book describes to evaluate their impact on your bottom line.

- Did you identify your market correctly? What have you learned about your customer that might suggest a different slant to your strategy?
- Is your assortment working for you as you expected? Do your customers often request products that you do not carry? Are there products customers never buy?
- Are your technical, marketing, IT, and merchandising teams speaking the same language? Is your site engaging visitors in the shopping experience, or is it static, too slow, or so terribly twentieth-century that they are bored?
- Do your inventory systems work the way you planned? Do you have items in stock that would be better ordered on a just-in-time basis? Are you missing sales or eating up your profits because you don't have good sellers on hand?
- Are your margins and promotional plans on target?
- Are you making revenue and profitability goals?
- Are you happy with your suppliers? Are they happy with you? If not, can it be fixed? Can you find alternative sources, if need be?

Just a day in the life? Hardly. More like a week in the life . . . or a month! e-Retail merchants and organizations must juggle all of these tasks, dealing with tactical, at-once, executional issues, as well as strategic long-term planning.

Because none of these decisions is made once and then set forevermore, especially in the changeable world of Web commerce, you need to create opportunities to evaluate each one, with the input of the proper people, on a regular basis. You cannot expect to fit in this kind of planning in between tactical tasks or when "everything else is done." It will not happen.

All businesses, all business owners, and certainly all e-retailers need to find the rhythm of planning and execution that works for their organizations. You may choose to review everything annually or semi-annually. You may need to pay more frequent attention to a fast-paced market or less attention to a market moving more slowly. Time, experience, and bald necessity will teach you the right rhythm for your business. Just know all the ingredients that need to be part of the recipe, if you want to feast at the end of the day.

Hypothetical Cases

Retail Organization for ShoeWeb

ShoeWeb is conceived as a "pure" e-retailer, with minimal non-retail content. The site includes some tips on selecting shoes and judging sizes, but all content is tied directly to their core business: selling shoes. In selecting merchandise, the buyers are driven purely by what sells or what *will* sell.

In Chapter 5, ShoeWeb decided that the inventory management system will report business based on shoe style rather than primarily by brand. This mirrors the buying structure created in Chapter 4. ShoeWeb has separate buyers for each of these departments: Men's, Women's, and Accessories.

Within the Men's and Women's departments, several buyers individually take on the responsibility for dress, casual, and athletic shoes. As business expands and the assortment warrants, the company will consider further specialization of their buyers. For example, ShoeWeb may hire several buyers within the dress category, then assign different buyers different brands to manage. This specialization will still be supported by the management systems, since each category (e.g., *Dress*) is further divided by a brand class.

Each buyer must manage a huge number of SKUs. To let the merchants focus on their most critical tasks, ShoeWeb must establish a support system to execute the lower-level buyer responsibilities. Support staff must include assistant buyers and clerical assistants. Additionally, the staff in the distribution center and in customer service will require additional, specialized training so that they can handle many of the receipt and/or customer questions that arise.

For example, while the buyer retains primary responsibility and control over assortment planning and merchandise selection, the assistant buyer and/or clerical assistant will execute the actual order writing, item maintenance, and receiving tasks. While the buyer determines the promotional calendar, the assistant buyer and clerical assistant are responsible for communication with the site execution team as well as the execution of the sales events.

All buyers report to the general merchandise manager (GMM) who in turn represents the buying organization within the company when planning and making decisions with operations, IT, finance, marketing, and so on.

Retail Organization for WebKidCare

WebKidCare is an e-retailer with a strong, possibly even dominant, focus on content. The site's mission is to provide early childhood caregivers with the resources they need to run their businesses, make good product choices, and create a networking community of ideas and solutions for the benefit of the industry as a whole.

In addition to the usual steps the merchants take to select products, they must also work closely with WebKidCare's advisory board, which reviews and vets all choices to ensure that the retail offerings are of the highest quality and best value for their site users. Merchants must build this step into their processes and be prepared for assortment additions and deletions that may result from it.

Currently, a single advisory board reviews all product categories; as the business grows, specialized subsets of the advisory board may focus on specific product categories. Additionally, WebKidCare must create communications systems that allow the members of the advisory board to contact the appropriate merchants if board members learn of products that should be carried on the site.

WebKidCare has separate buyers for three departments: Outdoor, Indoor, and Caregiver Aids. WebKidCare is more concerned with offering the "right" products than "all possible products," so their SKU count is relatively small for an e-retailer. Therefore, it is possible for the buyer to handle all of his or her responsibilities with only occasional clerical assistance.

The Indoor department soon establishes itself as the largest category, and as the assortment grows, WebKidCare employs new buyers to handle each of the subcategories: Large motor skills, Fine motor skills, Music, Reading, and Furniture.

Buyers at WebKidCare report to the Director of Merchandise, who in turn works closely with the content side to ensure that product offerings and content provide the best possible information and resources for site users. The relationship between the merchants and the content editors is an important one for this site. Merchants will want to know what products and categories are scheduled to be featured, and content editors will need to know what recommendations the advisory board has made to the merchants. Regular content/merchandise planning meetings are scheduled on a quarterly and as-needed basis.

ORGANIZATION CHECKLIST

❑   Review central role of merchant and/or buyer in your organization.

❑   Create communications systems and protocols to move information through the organization.

❑   Determine central issues of merchant structure:

  ❑   Is there a broad or narrow focus?

  ❑   What support staff and systems are required for business to work?

❑   Review ongoing tasks that make your business run, and create calendars that allow all tasks to be addressed.

  ❑   Performance/sales review tasks

  ❑   Product-related tasks

  ❑   Order/shipping tasks

  ❑   Planning tasks

CHAPTER TEN

The Virtual Real World: e-Retail Case Studies

Chapter Preview

Moving from the theoretical to the real world, we see how actual e-retailers plied their trade online. The following case studies demonstrate that there are many ways to apply retail concepts to Web-based retail—and many ways to innovate to make the most of the Web environment.

RedEnvelope

It began as an emergency service for those who were thoughtful and yet pressed for time—911gifts.com, where gifts ordered by midnight Eastern Standard Time would be delivered the following morning. Although RedEnvelope still has a 911gifts section in its Web-based retail store, the new incarnation of the company aims for total recognition as a unique gift source known for quality, style, and personality.

911gifts.com began in 1997 as the brainchild of Scott Galloway and R. Ian Chaplin. Galloway and Chaplin were co-founders of Prophet Brand Strategy, a consulting firm assisting companies with their electronic commerce and brand strategy efforts.

In the fall of 1999, the company evolved into RedEnvelope Gifts Online. The name refers to an Asian custom of presenting special gifts in a simple red envelope. The "urgency" feature of the assortment had been supplanted by an emphasis on meaningful gift-giving, simplified.

Figure 10.1   RedEnvelope Storefront.

Since the re-launch, several successful rounds of venture capital financing have enabled the company's dramatic growth.

RedEnvelope's management team has years of experience working for traditional and catalog retailers like Williams-Sonoma and its brands (Pottery Barn, Hold Everything, and others). With RedEnvelope, they have adapted traditional retail concepts to the Web environment. At the same time, they have embraced advanced technologies that enhance the consumer's shopping experience and added electronic touches such as e-mail gift reminders, which function elegantly in the Web environment.

Strategy

As 911gifts.com, the company targeted upscale customers with more money than time to do careful shopping. Chief Executive Officer Martin McClanan notes that the company's understanding of its market has not shifted in the evolution to

RedEnvelope. "We've found that the 'last-minute' aspects of our positioning were not necessarily the most important value proposition to the customer," he comments. "We found that our customers are more interested in a one-stop shopping experience where they can choose from a variety of high-quality gifts at approachable price-points."

What is an "approachable price-point"? Most gifts in RedEnvelope's assortment range in price from $30 to $300, indicating quality but not exorbitance.

McClanan describes the RedEnvelope brand as characterized by four key features:

- *Stylish products*—Products that are often unique and exclusive, since RedEnvelope works with suppliers and artisans to create gift items; customers know they are getting something special
- *Approachable price-points*—The range invites shoppers seeking gifts for all occasions, from "just because" or thank-you gifts to special occasion like weddings and anniversaries
- *Limited assortment*—Saves the customer time by making it easier and more convenient to shop because there are fewer items to sort through
- *Superlative customer service*—Live online customer service, personalized gift cards, on-time delivery, and the ability to send multiple items to multiple addresses with a single order form assure customers that they will be personally assisted throughout the transaction.

Assortment Planning

Merchant teams are responsible for developing and selecting the assortment for RedEnvelope. The assortment is organized around the primary shopping categories on the site: Home Décor; Office and Travel; Backyard; Flowers and Plants; Pet Gifts; Gift Baskets; Sweets; Personal Care; Jewelry and Accessories; Bar, Wine and Cigars; Gadgets and Tools; Sports and Games; Toys and Baby Gear.

Assortments are seasonal, and many items are exclusive to RedEnvelope. Assortment planning requires attention to gift-giving cycles (Christmas, Valentine's Day, June weddings, and so on), as well as changing fashion and customer tastes. Exclusives are designed specifically for RedEnvelope in most categories by artisans, working in concert with RedEnvelope's merchants.

Merchandising

On RedEnvelope's staff are Store Managers. Like their counterparts in the brick-and-mortar world, Store Managers are responsible for merchandising the assortment, developing cross-selling strategies, planning promotions, and other point-of-purchase tasks. In carrying out these responsibilities, they work closely with the merchant and buying staff.

In addition to the primary shopping categories, visitors to the site can sift through items using other criteria such as *for him, for her,* and by *occasion,* among others. The overall goal in merchandising, McClanan says, is to build the brand as an upscale, lifestyle brand.

That is accomplished through the details as much as through the overall merchandising strategy. "Photography is what sells the product," McClanan notes. "Years of experience have taught us that." Considering that RedEnvelope's management team includes some of the creative merchandising minds that pushed print catalogs toward lifestyle magazines, this emphasis on the visual presentation of the products is hardly surprising.

The years of experience have also yielded some other lessons that McClanan and his team consider carefully in developing the online store displays. "The more challenging items to merchandise effectively are those that are more complicated," he explains. "For example, [look at] some of our items in the Tools and Gadgets category: the more complicated the functions, the more the consumer wants to interact with the product prior to purchase.

"Also challenging are the 'commodity' products, such as toys and books, which are available from many well-known sites," he continues. When RedEnvelope does not develop exclusives for these commodity items, it can be difficult to sell the benefits of purchasing these items from their site rather than from alternative sources.

Overall, RedEnvelope has found that it does best with the categories in which a customer is truly browsing for ideas and does not yet have a definite plan to purchase a specific type of gift. Think of it as the classy, eclectic neighborhood boutique that always has something new and different—the place you always go when you are looking for ideas.

To help you get those ideas, RedEnvelope deployed a live customer representative system in November 1999. By clicking on a button conveniently located on all shopping pages, customers can get connected to a customer representative through a live chat feature. Customers can then get instant answers to any questions they may have on a product and obtain advice for locating the perfect gift.

McClanan recognizes a huge advantage to merchandising online, one that he and his colleagues could not duplicate in other environments. "You can truly test new product ideas in this medium," he explains. "We can purchase ten items, do the photography, add the item to the assortment and then judge its true popularity before investing in a huge number. This is a great advantage over traditional retailers."

Inventory Management

RedEnvelope owns its inventory, with the exception of a few items that are drop-shipped directly from the vendor. Its warehouse is located in Ohio, conveniently next door to the Airborne Express hub. Depending on the season, RedEnvelope may have anywhere from 600 to 1,500 SKUs in the assortment and available for sale.

To manage inventory effectively, RedEnvelope selected an off-the-shelf software product originally developed for catalog and direct mail retailers. "Although it's not as flexible as some of the other products recently created for online retailers," McClanan says, "it has the advantage of being a well-developed, well-tested, and robust system."

To address a common frustration with online shopping, RedEnvelope's inventory management system updates the site quickly, so that items merchandised and offered for sale are actually available when the customer places an order. However, when an order is placed, the first thing the system does is check inventory to confirm that the stock is available. When the credit card information has been validated, the system sends the customer an e-mail indicating that the order has been received and is being processed. The pick-and-pack instructions are generated at the warehouse. This can sometimes be a complex step, as individual orders may involve shipping to several addresses. The goods are shipped and the credit card is billed usually within 18 hours of order placement. With shipping, the customer receives another e-mail to confirm that the gifts are on their way.

Pricing and Promotion

The pricing structure for RedEnvelope reinforces the brand as a quality source of unique gifts. Initial mark ups (IMUs) and maintained margins (MMs) are in line with what consumers find at other upscale lifestyle retailers, online and off.

Vendor Relations

In the beginning, 911gifts.com found vendors reluctant to work with the company. Over time, as RedEnvelope has proven the solidity of its planning and execution, the reluctance has disappeared. "Now we have far more suppliers who want to work with us than we have room for in our assortment plans," McClanan says. Suppliers initially showed concern with financial stability and staying power—not channel conflict.

Structure

The organizational structure for RedEnvelope is solidly based on traditional retail structures. In addition to McClanan, the management team includes Hilary Billings, Chief Marketing Officer; Tom Bazzone, President and Chief Operating Officer; and Christopher Cunningham, Chief Information Officer. Each key individual has more than a dozen years' experience in his or her field.

The merchant teams are comprised of Creative Merchants and Control Buyers. Creative merchants own the financial responsibility for their assortment's margin performance, and they do the strategic planning, hunting for new gift ideas, and working with suppliers to develop unique products that establish RedEnvelope's brand. Control buyers handle the logistics of the supply chain, including everything from writing orders to working with suppliers to ensuring prompt delivery. Control buyers also have primary control over the inventory management aspects of managing the assortment.

Store managers take over at the level of site execution, planning how items will be merchandised and promoted to shoppers.

The Wisdom of Experience

"We've seen at least a dozen of our competitors go out of business in the last year, and it seems another five or six will be leaving the field shortly," McClanan observes. To weather the volatile e-retail environment for three years is its own accomplishment, one McClanan attributes to fundamental attention to the business of retail.

"We have always built our decision-making and plans around traditional retail metrics. We have refused to fall into the trap of sacrificing gross margins to achieve sales.

"Frankly, I've been surprised by the number of e-retailers who refute the sense of solid business decision-making," he continues. "The e-retail environment plays by the same rules as the so-called 'real world.' Yet quite a number of dot coms seemed to think they played by different rules, creating unsustainable growth plans or not thinking through how they would be able to earn a profit."

In the first ten months of its existence as RedEnvelope, the company achieved more than 400 percent sales growth and more than 40 percent increase in gross margins. "It's been a challenge to grow that quickly," McClanan admits. "Often we've wished we could slow down and test ideas more thoroughly before execution."

The only way such growth has been possible, let alone successful, is through balanced attention to each of the metrics at stake in a healthy business: sales, gross margin, maintained margin, turnover, marketing expenditures, and so on.

RedEnvelope is something of a test case in how much is possible in the e-retail environment in relatively little time. However, McClanan has cautionary words for would-be e-retailers: "Never grow beyond your business's ability to support the growth," he says. In other words, do not promise the universe if you can only deliver a galaxy or two!

garden.com

A big market without a dominating brand—sounds like a business opportunity. That is what Cliff and Lisa Sharples thought in 1995 when they were investigating industries for potential as e-retail opportunities. With friend and fellow recent business school graduate Jamie O'Neill, they chose the gardening industry ($47 billion a year in sales and no single entity with more than 1 percent of market share) and went to work.

A lot has changed since 1995. garden.com was a dot com before most of us had ever heard of such a thing. In the same five years, the gardening industry has in a word, blossomed, with retail sales now approaching $80 billion. Still, no single entity commands significant market share.

Gardeners are already accustomed to ordering product and having to wait, sometimes for months, for its arrival. With garden.com, they had an opportunity to consolidate ordering from a single source and at the same time, use site features like expert advice, garden and landscape planners, and an online gardening magazine. In addition to the site, garden.com mailed a periodic print catalog, primarily to promote seasonal specials and drive traffic to the site.

In 2000, the Sharples and O'Neill and company decided that garden.com had gone as far as they could take it and began seeking a buyer. With no suitors approaching by November 2000, the management team finally decided to gracefully bow out of the scene. By that time, it was hardly news for an e-retailer—even an established name—to decide that enough was enough. What was unique was garden.com's approach to closing up Cybershop. In gradual waves, the company laid off its work force, stopped accepting orders, and made payment

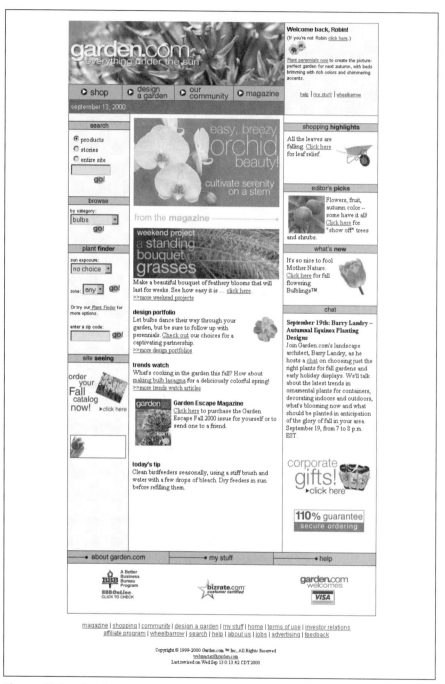

Figure 10.2   Garden.com Storefront.

arrangements with vendors and other creditors. The management team granted frank interviews with members of the press. The company would go down, but it would go down honorably.

Strategy

The strategy all along had been to overcome the existing limitations of the gardening industry (fragmented supply chains, perishable inventory, the need for geographically specific product information) while realizing the promise of the new selling medium. Garden.com sought to accomplish these goals and prove their staying power (five years!) in a highly variable environment. From the beginning, the founding trio took care to balance its management team with the right combination of skills and knowledge in technology, marketing, design, and startup management to make the venture successful.

The gardening market is largely made up of women who are relatively affluent and quite passionate about plants—not to mention ready to buy and hungry for information. Gardeners have had to contend with a fragmented supply chain by ordering items from multiple suppliers, then filling in their basic materials (tools, mulch, dirt, fertilizer) as necessary, often from area garden centers.

Garden.com's strategy of consolidation created a one-stop shop for consumers. At the same time, the company offered suppliers a Web-based sales channel. To complete the strategic picture, nearly all of garden.com's inventory was owned by the suppliers until the time an order was placed. With a virtual warehouse, garden.com did not carry the risk of unsold (or wilting) product.

"The arrangement lets everyone focus on their strengths," noted Bill Pond, director of Product Management for garden.com. "The supplier focuses on growing, packaging, and shipping the plants, and we focus on marketing and selling the product."

Initially, many of garden.com's suppliers were mail order retailers; by early 2000, the mix of suppliers had shifted to include more wholesalers, eliminating some conflicts of interest that retailers and the company were encountering. For the most part, however, the garden.com strategy seemed to be win-win: "We give them an e-commerce strategy without [them] having to invest in it themselves," noted Pond.

The revenue model for garden.com called for 85 percent of revenues to come from product sales, with the remainder made up by advertising. Financials published in June 2000 showed that revenues had grown 187 percent over the previous year, reaching $15.5 million. Cliff Sharples indicated in a postmortem interview that the company was on track to profitability by 2002. Garden.com simply ran out of time.

Assortment Planning

Pond headed up the assortment planning, conducted by the product management team. Approximately 18 people selected and procured products in seven product lines:

- Plants
- New growth (bulbs and seeds)
- Tools and essentials
- Garden décor (containers, furniture, trellises)
- Floral gifts
- Gifts
- Fresh stem (cut flowers)

Because the majority of the inventory was owned by suppliers until a sale was made, Pond's staff needed to work very closely with suppliers to plan the assortment and create sales projections. The intimacy of this supplier relationship offered additional benefits to garden.com as well. The company was able to build a uniquely broad and deep assortment by asking suppliers to source items they do not offer other retailers, providing garden.com with exclusives.

Merchandising

Garden.com was a garden planning tool, gardening magazine, master gardener lecture, garden club, and garden store all rolled into one. The comprehensive features of the site were an important aspect of merchandising, reinforcing the one-stop character of the site.

Customers could personalize their experience by opening up accounts, which provided them with customized product recommendations and targeted e-mail promotional offers.

Within the shopping section of the site, products were sorted by departments, categories, and subcategories and could also be searched by keyword. A plant finder feature allowed customers to enter their requirements (geographic zone, desired plant height, sunny or shady location, bloom color and period, and so on) to generate a list of suggested plants that fit their criteria. Garden.com also sold collections of plants to take the guesswork out of planning a garden; customers could select three seasons of color collections, butterfly-attracting collections, collections of single plant species such as hostas, and others.

In purchasing plants, consumers need a lot of vital statistics to ensure that their selections will not turn brown and crispy in their gardens. The product information page (Figure 10.3) delineated this information consistently so that it was easy to find and scan.

Garden.com also achieved successes in making the most of the interactive Web environment to merchandise product. For example, a holiday-season feature allowed customers to custom-construct a wreath. The customer was able to use the feature to select a base material, then cover it with plants, ornaments, and ribbons. Their individual wreath would then be constructed and sent directly to them.

The print catalog created one more offline reminder of garden.com and highlighted seasonal products, sales, and promotions.

Inventory Management

The close relationships between garden.com and its suppliers were critical to the inventory management systems and protocols. Inventory management began back at the assortment planning stage, Pond explained, because that was when suppliers allocated a portion of their supply to garden.com sales. All suppliers had, at minimum, one computer and printer at their site linked to garden.com's central ordering and inventory management system.

When an order came into garden.com via the Web site, if it was ready for delivery, it was immediately routed to the appropriate supplier. The supplier then assumed responsibility for picking and packing the goods. When packed, the supplier scanned the order back into the system, which printed out a mailing label. When the label was affixed to the shipment, it was scanned again, and an e-mail notification was automatically sent to the customer to announce product shipment.

At the time of order placement, the SKUs in the order were automatically deducted from the supplier's garden.com allocated inventory. The order briefly hit the financial inventory at garden.com before shifting to cost of goods sold.

The whole system was supported by a custom-built inventory management program that managed all the information links and generated inventory and sales reports for both garden.com and its suppliers.

Pricing and Promotion

Plants have highly variable costs and retail values. Other products in garden.com's assortment (tools, gifts, and so on) experienced fewer fluctuations in price. Thus mark-ups and maintained margins varied, depending on

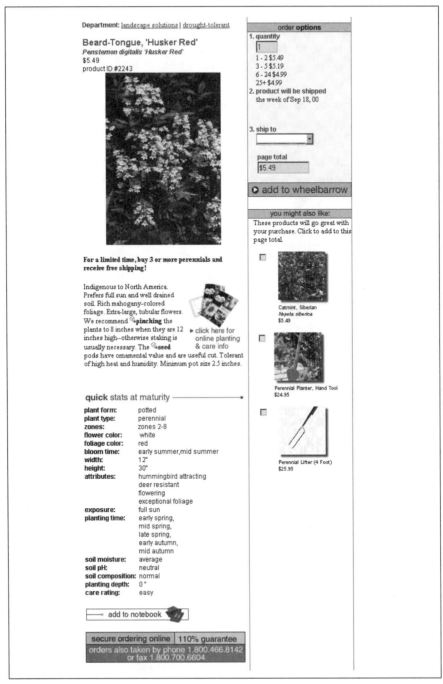

Figure 10.3   All product information presented in a consistent, easy to read format.

the characteristics of the product. IMU could be anywhere from 50 percent to 75 percent. Pond calculated MM as:

Product Revenue + Shipping Revenue – Product Cost – Shipping Cost – Returns – Handling and Package Fees.

Historically, MM ranged from 10 percent to 23 percent across the product lines.

With such a gap between IMU and MM, promotions clearly were a big aspect of garden.com's marketing program. "I came to garden.com without extensive retail experience," said Pond, "and if there's one thing I have learned, it's the power of promotions. The more creative, the more successful. We'll do better with a 'free gift with purchase' or 'we'll pay the shipping' than with a standard 'X-percent off' promotion."

Regular specials kept customers coming back to find out what was on sale, and promotions were highlighted in both the e-mail newsletter and print catalog.

Vendor Relations

Although some vendors were more reluctant to work with garden.com back in 1995, Pond reported that, by 2000, they were more than happy to work with the company. Since some suppliers also achieve direct-to-consumer sales, there were potential conflicts of interest, but for the most part, they were able to mitigate the effects of such conflicts effectively.

Structure

The Product Management team was part of the Marketing and Merchandising department. Also within Marketing and Merchandising was the Programming department, which worked closely with Product Management to determine how to present and promote the products in garden.com's assortment.

The three founders retained key roles in the management team to the end: Cliff Sharples as president and chief executive officer, Jamie O'Neill as chief operating officer, and Lisa Sharples as chief marketing officer. A fourth team member, Andy Martin, served as chief technology officer. Additional staffing divisions included landscape experts for content and customer service folks for customer interface.

The Wisdom of Experience

As one of the grandparents of Web-based retail, garden.com has been there, done that, and the wisdom of that experience is "back to basics."

"This is going to sound kind of 'Mickey Mouse,' but I think it is a trap that many e-retailers fell into," said Pond. "Number one, the point of selling product is to make money! Anytime you do anything different, you better have thought through the consequences. Negative gross margin to increase market share is sometimes short-sighted and certainly not sustainable. As a retailer, your entire product offering cannot be a loss-leader.

"Number two, fully load the costs of selling product. Understand the ramifications of doing anything possible to make revenue targets. The costs of product development, photography, copy, product shows, and the like are not free.

"Number three, it certainly feels like many dot coms were caught up in the 'anything goes' craze. Advertising campaigns that exceed revenue forecasts by a factor of two are inherently troubling. Even more so if the revenue forecast generates a negative gross margin."

It is not complicated advice, but it requires hard work and attention to the basics of retailing—the product, the costs, and the customer.

"If people come to your store for jeans or your site for plants, don't ever forget that," Pond concluded. "You need to exceed customer expectations in all categories, but you always need to be focused on your core products."

Does the end of garden.com signal a symbolic defeat for the concept of the online retail enterprise, for plants, or other consumer goods? Hardly. Many of garden.com's assets, including its list of 1.5 million loyal members, its proprietary back-end systems that linked the company to its suppliers, and other forms of intellectual property, were sold for an undisclosed sum to the venerable mail order garden operation, the W. Atlee Burpee Company. Like many a perennial, the concept of garden.com, tested five years in the real world, may yet produce live shoots and blooms, current appearances to the contrary.

FashionDish

If you want the latest celebrity gossip or a chance to buy Christina Aguilera's favorite ring, FashionDish.com is the place to go.

Launched in 1997 by Anne-Marie Otey, FashionDish dishes it out to a devoted readership and consumer base throughout the United States. The site is equal parts unique content, which the company also syndicates for additional revenues, and e-retail. Visitors turn to FashionDish to get specialized news and products they have a hard time finding elsewhere.

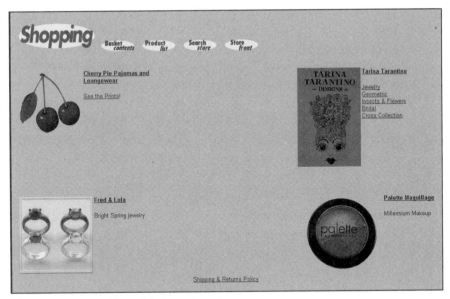

Figure 10.4   FashionDish Storefront

"Our visitors come from all over, though most of our sales come from places like Ohio, North Dakota, and Indiana and other non-urban areas," Otey notes. "Basically, they shop us because the products we offer just aren't available where they live."

Otey's background includes fashion journalism, reporting for *Elle* magazine and, most recently, for *People's* Stylewatch and Insider columns. "I wanted to combine fashion and gossip and create . . . fashion gossip," Otey recalls, "but I didn't want to do the *Women's Wear Daily* stuff about which designer fired whom. I wanted to focus on celebrities, their style quirks, sprees, and freebies."

Strategy

FashionDish's e-retail strategy is to marry up-to-the-minute, unique celebrity news with the opportunity to purchase the accessories celebrities wear. Included in the assortment mix are some lingerie and makeup items. Quickly changing content keeps visitors coming back regularly. FashionDish sells its products to a geographically diverse market with highly specialized desires.

"I started with the *People* demographic—women age 30 to mid 40s or mid 50s—and then skewed it five years younger to account for the Web environment," Otey says about her initial market identification. "It turned out, the Web skews the demographic more like 8 to 10 years younger. It's working for us; we're conscious of keeping it there."

Assortment Planning

Otey does all assortment planning herself, based increasingly on user feedback and historical sales data. "I've learned that *my* favorite color or style isn't always the customers' favorite color or style," she comments.

Merchandising

The site's content is a critical element in its merchandising. Content sets the product within the context of the celebrity lifestyle with which visitors want to identify. Otey writes most of the editorial content herself. FashionDish has access to as many celebrity photos as the company could ever wish to use.

Visitors are offered opportunities to click into the e-retail portion of the site from any content-oriented page. Once there, they can select a particular manufacturer's assortment to view or search products by keyword.

Since FashionDish sells primarily accessories, e-retail is not hampered by the need to provide extensive product information, dimensions, assembly, and so on.

"Our emphasis is on what's unique and on there being a story behind everything we sell," Otey comments. "We're also starting to work on private-label merchandise for the site. We'll commission a local designer to create pieces for us and then sell them alongside the rest of our assortment."

Otey has noticed that in her site's merchandising, sexy technology takes a back seat to well-thought-out merchandise and constant change. "People don't seem to care much if we're using the latest technology, but they do want rapid turnover and new merchandise on a regular basis," she says. "The real obstacles are not in technology but in the time and expense required to create a dynamic assortment."

Inventory Management

At first, Otey ran FashionDish as a portal site. She negotiated arrangements with her vendors, whereby the vendors maintained ownership of all goods until the customer orders came in. Then the vendors shipped the goods to FashionDish's offices, where staff would pack and ship orders to the customer.

The company is now developing a hybrid inventory model. "We have been burned frequently in the past when vendors have failed to inform us about stock-outs," says Otey. "That means that we've had to disappoint customers, and it's not the vendor they're disappointed with. It's us."

As FashionDish moves forward, Otey expects that some portion of the assortment will continue to be managed on a just-in-time basis, but an increasing percentage will be owned as inventory, especially in key selling seasons, such as the holidays. Bestselling items will be owned as year-around inventory.

Now that Otey is placing orders for inventory, she has the advantage of several seasons of historical sales data to help her make decisions. Additionally, sales data were collected during a period when FashionDish did *not* own inventory or carry the investment risk—not a bad way to test your assortment and your marketing . . .

To manage inventory and generate reports, FashionDish uses a spreadsheet that tracks units in and units out.

Pricing and Promotion

FashionDish aims to price its products in line with other potential sales channels (such as urban area department stores). However, FashionDish takes a smaller mark-up than the customer would encounter in the department store. (Department stores usually take 60 percent to 80 percent on jewelry and accessories.)

Occasionally, FashionDish will pass along savings to the customer when a really good volume discount comes their way. However, for the most part, the site does not employ any promotional pricing strategies.

Vendor Relations

In starting out, Otey was able to work primarily with vendors who had known her and her work in other settings. They had confidence in working with her and were willing to try the portal model of inventory management with her.

As noted above, the portal model did not work perfectly, either for FashionDish or its vendors. FashionDish is now purchasing more of its assortment as inventory—the system vendors are used to and able to accommodate most easily.

Since launching FashionDish, Otey has encountered one vendor that turned down flat her request for product. "It was a combination of factors," Otey recalls. "For one thing, we were ordering such small quantities that the vendor didn't think it was worth bothering with us. For another, the vendor wasn't willing to work with us on the portal model [of inventory management] and hold the goods until the orders came in."

Structure

FashionDish's sole buyer is Otey, who is also responsible for overall management of the company. A "shopping assistant" is responsible for all aspects of customer service including the following:

- Checking orders as they come in
- Pulling items in stock
- Ordering from suppliers any items that are not in stock
- Rechecking credit acceptance
- Packing goods
- Arranging for United Parcel Service shipping
- Handling customer product questions and returns

The Wisdom of Experience

"The biggest surprise for me has been the emotional involvement customers have in their purchases," Otey says. "Once they get their heart set on something, substitutions and delays are unacceptable.

"The other thing I've learned as an e-retailer after years of being a consumer is that the holiday selling seasons really *are* that important," she continues. "I used to think that retailers overdid the holiday sales hype, but the Christmas season can really make or break a retailer, e- or otherwise."

In short, plan your assortment, inventory, and cash flow carefully!

Craft.com

For the brief period between February 24, 2000 and June 30, 2000, craft enthusiasts had a unique alternative for finding craft projects and purchasing supplies. Craft.com, the brainchild of Brad Roberts, offered community, a craft idea library, and convenient purchase of all materials needed to complete craft and hobby projects. Unfortunately, Roberts and company did not have enough cash to sustain the company during the crucial period of entering the marketplace. A combination of timing (Craft.com started to seek investors just as Wall Street was turning sour on e-retail), and holes in the founding team finally put the kabosh on Craft.com.

Still, the concept was sound, and the work Roberts did to create and build the enterprise is worth a closer look.

Figure 10.5   Craft.com Storefront.

Strategy

Not just a craft store, Craft.com sought to create a community of craft enthusiasts. Some sites might try to accomplish this solely through chat rooms and featured crafters; Roberts' innovation was to involve the community itself in providing the most important feature of the site's content—the craft projects. Enthusiasts would submit their projects and receive some incentive such as revenue share or merchandise credit for sales made based on their ideas. Over time, Craft.com would command an unmatched library of craft projects (complete with one-stop shopping) and a loyal, engaged user base.

The strategy depended on the characteristics of the user base. Craft enthusiasts are eager for community, new ideas, and convenient purchases, and Craft.com promised to deliver on all counts. "We had a customer data base of over 70,000 individuals before we even launched the site," Roberts notes. "I recognized the Web as a vehicle to accomplish something unique, namely, to bring content together with commerce to drive a targeted sale. You can't do that in an offline store."

Financial plans called for 90 percent of revenues to come from merchandise sales, with another 10 percent from product placements and advertising. Over time, those numbers might change but never invert.

Assortment Planning

To launch Craft.com, materials and supplies for more than 150 craft projects were sourced, amounting to more than 7,000 SKUs. The business plan called for that to grow to more than 500 projects and 15,000 to 20,000 SKUs within 12 months.

Merchandising

The merchandising for Craft.com was structured around projects categorized by type. This structure made it easy for customers to find the kinds of projects and materials they needed.

At the same time, the emphasis of the site's home page was not on shopping or sales but on the crafts themselves, enhancing the site's positioning as a gathering place for enthusiasts. Customers could create accounts with personalized project suggestions and get helpful tips to learn more about the crafts and hobbies in which they were interested.

The project content was an ideal way to drive multiple sales, since any given craft would be likely to require several kinds of materials. Clicking on "Project of the Week," for example, a crafter would immediately get instructions on completing a project, uses for the project, skill level required, and a handy, complete shopping list just waiting to become an order.

What didn't work as well for the company, Roberts notes, was the unexpected time and cost associated with setting up and executing the site. "The merchandising took longer and the ongoing site development cost more than we had anticipated," he says. "Things like photos—there are no databases of good online photos of craft supplies, so we had to shoot them ourselves. At $75 per image, it adds up fast."

Inventory Management

"Our first model was 'guesstimation,'" Roberts sums up wryly, when asked what kinds of stock/inventory management systems the company used.

Figure 10.6 Craft.com's merchandising emphasis was on the crafts, not the individual products for sale.

The company owned approximately 10 percent of its inventory. The other 90 percent was owned by its distributor. Since the craft industry operates with a notoriously fragmented supply chain, Craft.com needed to find a way to create a broad assortment without the benefit of one integrated supply channel. The ownership relationship with the distributor was intended to circumvent that difficulty. "This partnership allowed Craft.com to leverage its inventory position and maximize its asset turns," Roberts notes, "but it left the business vulnerable to the assortment on-hand in an industry in which even a large distributor carries only 30 percent to 40 percent of what a full-line store stocks on any given day."

In the end, the arrangement did not pan out the way the company expected. The variable unit costs for the inventory stocked by the distributor turned out to be somewhat afield of projections. "On the cost side, our model had assumed a more efficient operation than what was ultimately achievable in this complex distribution channel. We were profitable at the level of gross margin from Day One, but funding this distribution arrangement cut into our margins more than we had anticipated."

This combination of unique factors—the project-based system and the distributor arrangements—made it impossible for Craft.com to rely on an off-the-shelf stock management package. With the clarity of hindsight, Roberts realizes how crippling the inventory management system (or, rather, the lack thereof) turned out to be. "For a start-up company, the costs of carrying inventory are very high. We focused on selling complete solutions and on emphasizing cross-sells, but we didn't have time to grow enough to make that deep across the board," he says. With a robust inventory management system, it would have been easier to identify assortment opportunities and the true cost of the inventory structure.

One success in inventory management that Craft.com achieved was the ability to keep the site updated in real time. The site reflected stock status based on information submitted directly from the distributor on an hourly basis.

Pricing and Promotion

Craft.com took a 50 percent IMU pretty much across the board on its assortment. Although the site did not use price promotions on products as such, it did offer free shipping promotions "almost the entire time we were operational," Roberts adds.

Vendor Relations

In approaching vendors, Roberts and his team prepared a full presentation outlining the competitive advantages of the site (category killer domain name, strong distributor partnership, community input, and involvement). Roberts was also consistently asked to provide credit references.

"Mostly, vendors were concerned about our ability to stay in the game," Roberts says, Wince.

The concept itself, of involving the consumers in a community and a dynamic library of resources,was an easy sell, however. Craft.com also had the early advantage of having no established competitors in the field and a vendor population anxious to use the Web sales channel to reach a substantial market.

Structure

Roberts, the founder, was the president of the organization. Departments focused on merchandising, content, production, logistics, operations, and marketing all reported directly to him. "In hindsight," he notes, "I should have brought on a couple of founding partners who could help share the load of the intense strategic and tactical efforts of building a young company. I did move quickly to build a management team of strong functional contributors, but as a team we had two limitations. First, a start-up is not a big business. You have to approach the game differently. It takes a real scrappy mentality. The leadership team had great backgrounds. Molding the processes, tactics, and team required of a new business out of their experience was a more laborious process than I had expected.

"It is very hard to get people who have the same deep commitment for the business as the founders," Roberts continues. "When times are busy or when they are tough, you want that passionate buy-in so that each manager can be that key evangelist or that key creative energy or that key trooper sweating in the trenches that a growing business constantly demands."

The Wisdom of Experience

There is no experience so wise as that which has seen a dream shut down. Roberts' vision of the e-retail environment is the result of his ten months of surfing its increasingly choppy waves.

Even with a sound concept and inspired execution, e-retail faces an uphill climb to profitability, Roberts warns, due to consumer behavior. "Right now, the online consumer population seems to be conditioned into a 'deals only' mentality," he believes. "Consumers will wait until you have an 'almost free' deal before they will shop with you. Maybe a strong offline brand can overcome this behavior pattern, but even strong brands will face this challenge."

He elaborates on the conundrum: "It seems increasingly likely that the only sites that will have the time and capital to survive to build a sustainable base business are those partnered or run by a strong traditional brand. On the other hand, most traditional brands have structured their business or systems in a way that is antithetical to the Web environment. For example, in the craft category, traditional store brands have underserved the customer for a long time. They are on the fast track to replicating that experience online. That approach sells short the ultimate customer value. To create an enterprise that can actually deliver on customer value, however, requires significant momentum simply to get into the game as a real player."

In short, be prepared for a very bumpy ride, and do not be surprised by the number of stalled vehicles in the ditch!

Gazoontite

Asthma or allergies acting up? Gazoontite! Founded on an e-retail site at gazoontite.com and expanded with Gazoontite retail stores and a Gazoontite catalog, the multichannel retailer sells products that help allergy sufferers breath more easily. Founder Soon-Chart Yu created Gazoontite in 1998 and from the very beginning, worked with the multichannel approach.

Considered a pioneer with the "clicks and bricks" strategy, Yu set about acquiring retail space when Wall Street was still in love with Web pure plays. He turned out to be way ahead of the learning curve. "Gazoontite would be a huge success story even without the Web site element," he notes.

Figure 10.7   Gazoontite Storefront.

Huge is right, and if you have ever had a bad bout of hay fever, you would know why. Yu's vision was to create a company that served as a central purchasing point for all kinds of products such as air filters, hypoallergenic linens, organic apparel, and more, which relieve the suffering of a sizable market of folks with money. The American College of Allergy, Asthma and Immunology reports that allergies affect 38 percent of all Americans, and at least 56 percent of U.S. households have at least one person with allergies. Niche, schmich. The "background and values" screen at gazoontite.com notes that the company reaches out ". . . to our customers and the breathing community at large." Non-breathers need not visit.

For a long time (i.e., long in Web terms), Gazoontite was the poster child for how multichannel retail was supposed to work. Yu relinquished management of the company in July 2000, and the management team that succeeded him was not able to raise cash to support the multichannel model. As of this writing, the catalog and the brick-and-mortar stores still operate; the e-retail site no longer supports online sales. Yu regained control of the company in October 2000, after Gazoontite filed for Chapter 11 protection. His goal is to revitalize the online sales component of the company, once reorganization has stabilized overall operations. In the meantime, Gazoontite focuses on strengthening its offline brand with successful retail stores and the catalog, now aimed primarily at the physician market.

Strategy

At the heart of Gazoontite's strategy has been the multichannel approach to sales. Gazoontite's intent was to be available however customers choose to shop: in person, through the catalog, or via the Web. Yu recognized that each channel offered benefits and faced challenges, and he was prepared to meet the consumer at each potential point of sale.

The success of the retail stores, Yu admits, has been a bit of a surprise. "We originally intended the flagship [San Francisco] store as part of the branding strategy for Gazoontite," Yu says. "But our offline marketing and sales efforts have proven to be hugely successful." Since the opening of the flagship store, the company has launched four additional retail locations on both coasts and in the Chicago area. Fifteen additional stores were planned before the Chapter 11 filing. Those expansion plans are now on hold.

Actually, the real surprise may be that someone had not thought of this earlier. Unlike other "niche" markets that can only achieve critical mass through Web or catalog marketing, the asthma-and-allergy market cuts across all geographic and demographic lines. Gazoontite's revenue mix demonstrates the way the retail stores have filled a void: until the Web site shut down sales, catalog and Web sales accounted for up to 50 percent of revenues. The other half came from the brick-and-mortar retail stores.

Assortment Planning

The Senior Vice President of Merchandising commands a team of merchants who are responsible for sourcing and selecting SKUs, determining the amount to purchase, and setting prices. The merchants each work in assigned categories to ensure that they develop comprehensive knowledge and understanding of their categories.

In any context other than under the rubric of "allergy products," the breadth of Gazoontite's assortment would make little sense. Bed pillows, shower squeegees, state-of-the-art air filters, books, plush toys, all-natural makeup and skin care products, all-natural household cleaners, essential oil diffusers. The logic of the assortment comes from the shared purpose of all the products. Indeed, a narrower assortment would not fill the needs of the niche as comprehensively.

Any new product must first be reviewed and approved by Gazoontite's product review board. If approved, it is purchased and made available through all Gazoontite sales channels. Some products are also reviewed by a medical advisory board, if the product makes any medical claims.

Currently, Gazoontite manages an assortment of nearly 3,000 SKUs.

Merchandising

The focus of gazoontite.com, as the home page makes clear, is the opportunity to purchase products. It is unfortunate that lack of cash in fall 2000 shut down the sales element of the site, since the site is so clearly a sales site rather than a pure information site. Worse yet, shoppers are not informed of the fact that they cannot actually *purchase* anything here until they click on an item they are interested in buying. (The sales screen directs them to "visit our retail stores" to purchase items.)

Luckily, the site's prominently featured community, library, and online nurse resources remain robust as ever, drawing customers to the site with additional features that they may want or need in coping with asthma and allergies or selecting products for purchase.

Products are organized in nine merchandising categories: bedding, cleaning, air and water purification, children's products, bath and beauty, books and education, aromatherapy, asthma management, and "Sale!" Products may actually appear in more than one category, but the sorting mechanism allows customers to find products wherever they happen to be looking.

Each of the different Gazoontite sales channels was intended to appeal to different customer needs. The stores appeal to the customer's need to touch a product

Air Purification

The average person inhales more than 2 tablespoons of airborne pollutants a day. Our air purifiers can help you breathe better by cleaning your air of dust mites, pollen, and other irritants. All of our air purifiers use HEPA (High Efficiency Particulate Air) filters, which capture 99.97% of all airborne particles down to 0.3 micron. (A human hair is about 50 microns wide.) For best performance, use air purifiers in rooms where all doors and windows are closed, and replace your filters regularly. For information on filter replacement cost, click on the name of each product.

how to use this chart:
Room size recommendations are based on Clean Air Delivery Rate (CADR), which tells how much clean air (in cubic feet per minute) the unit delivers to a room of a specified square footage. Ratings assume an 8-foot ceiling and at least 80% reduction in smoke particles. Given two air purifiers rated for rooms of equal size, the one with the higher CADR cleans more effectively. So, once you know your room size, you can make your selection based on CADR, plus other features you may want, such as portability. (CADR figures are based on testing by the Association of Home Appliance Manufacturers and verified by an independent lab.)

general description	room size	air changes/hour	CADR (dust)	CADR (tobacco smoke)	CADR (pollen)	filter lifespan	price
Blueair Air Purifier • Our top of the line model, independently rated the best of 150 air filters • Best choice for large rooms, open floor plans • Remarkably effective and absolutely silent • Patented Blueair system traps up to 99.9% of particles down to .1 micron • HEPA filter or special HEPA/SmokeStop Filter to remove smoke odors	20' x 30'	up to 21	330	350	310	HEPA/ SmokeStop: 6 months	$399.00
Honeywell QuietCare™ HEPA Cleaner • QuietCare™ technology is up to 30% quieter than similar cleaners • Ideal for bedrooms • Patented design for best airflow, least noise at all 3 speeds • Filter change indicator light • Three sizes to fit a variety of rooms • HEPA filter	12' x 14' 13' x 17' 15' x 19'	6 (for all sizes)	130 170 220	130 170 220	130 170 220	HEPA: 1-3 years Pre-filter: 3 months	$125.00 $190.00 $220.00
Honeywell QuietCare™ CPZ Air Cleaner • Special CPZ filter removes odors and gases while it cleans air • QuietCare™ technology is up to 30% quieter than similar cleaners • Patented design for best airflow, least noise • Ideal for kitchens • Filter change indicator light • HEPA filter	13' x 13'	6	135	135	135	HEPA: 1-3 years CPZ: 6-9 months	$250.00
DeLonghi DAP70 Air Purifier • The only air purifiers with 3 positions: vertical, horizontal, or wall-mounted • Compact and quiet -- perfect for offices or smaller rooms • Separately controlled ionizer freshens air • Filter change indicator light • HEPA filter	8' x 10' 9' x 10' 10' x 10'	7 6 5	70	70	70	HEPA: 2-3 years Carbon filter: 3 months Pre-filter: washable	$89.00

Figure 10.8   Gazoontite.com features product comparison screens that make it easy for customers to identify the right product for their needs.

and take it home immediately. The catalogs appeal to the customer who wants a portable shopping experience using to-the-point product information. But the Web? Hoo, boy—the Web is made for information junkies, and Gazoontite delivers. All of the information a customer could need to make a purchasing decision is clearly laid out on gazoontite.com. Even though it is not currently possible to purchase products, visitors can come to research items they are interested in and learn more about products that may help them. In addition to clearly written, concise product information, features like comparison tables are used throughout the site. For example, customers can compare the different features of the assortment of air filters to find the one that will best suit their needs.

Throughout the site, visitors are reminded that they can request a catalog or locate a retail store, reinforcing the commitment of Gazoontite to sell wherever the customer wants to buy.

Customer service was not slighted. While the online store was active, customers could call up a customer representative on a toll-free number to get assistance in selecting product and making a purchase, or they could hit the "online customer rep" button to be queued for online assistance. Connection times, like connection times for telephone representatives, varied based on the number of customers attempting to access help.

Customers visiting gazoontite.com seek information *and* product. Merchandising "extras," like the "Gazoontite forecast" providing pollen counts, fill that need.

Inventory Management

Gazoontite owns all of its assortment as inventory and services all three sales channels through a central warehouse. To manage inventory and generate a variety of reports, Gazoontite uses a custom-designed Web-based enterprise solution.

Pricing and Promotion

With a wide range of product types in its assortment, Gazoontite still manages to hit average IMUs of around 40 percent. "That number is trending upwards," Yu notes, "as we are able to negotiate more effectively and increase our volumes."

Hi-low promotional activity is a big part of the company's strategy. Regular home page features highlight the latest sale items, and all sale items are also grouped together in a "Sale" merchandising category. The company chooses not to discuss maintained margins, but the promotional activity must create a gap between IMU and MM.

Vendor Relations

When Yu's team began to approach vendors about selling through Gazoontite, vendors were as enthusiastic as their customers would later be. "Most of them were thrilled to have a retail outlet dedicated to this marketplace," Yu recalls. "It's great exposure for them and their products and a great improvement in building the consumer market."

Structure

All e-retailers will have structural challenges in getting technical teams and merchant teams to work effectively together. Gazoontite had all that and more, due to the multichannel sales strategy. "Each channel requires a different set of skills, and the teams didn't always know how to talk to each other," Yu says. "For the Web channel, the emphasis is on speed. For the stores, the emphasis is on detailed execution. For the catalog, the emphasis is on analytics. The result is that your organization has to be very detailed, very fast and very analytical all at once."

Constant, rapid, and clear communication is the only solution to making such a culturally mixed organization run successfully. An ongoing process of mutual training is also important: programmers must understand what merchants are trying to accomplish; store managers and telephone sales representatives must be presenting the same Gazoontite to the consumer. Merchants must understand the different nuances of presenting and promoting product through different sales channels.

"It's an ongoing process," Yu adds. "We're still learning."

Due to the current emphasis on the brick-and-mortar stores, Gazoontite will not have to contend with the distractions of trying to communicate cross-culturally for awhile. However, the new leadership team, headed by Craig P. Womack, former president of The Sharper Image and COO of Smith and Hawken, is not likely to forget the potential of the multichannel approach. As news of the reorganization trickled into the press, industry observers commented that Gazoontite had been distracted from its brick-and-mortar core by the promise of e-retail. e-Retail is as much at Gazoontite's core as any other sales channel. Gazoontite.com will not lie dormant forever.

The Wisdom of Experience

Yu did his homework before starting out, even spending several months as a sales associate in a Crate and Barrel store to understand firsthand the dynamic of point-of-sale customer relations. However, there were still surprises, particularly with regard to setting up and maintaining the Web sales channel.

"The full expense of setting up a fully functioning and robust e-commerce site was a surprise," he comments. "Everything is critical and everything is expensive—technology, content tools, and content itself—and the volume of information is overwhelming."

Make a budget. Double it. Set a time frame. Double it. Mostly, don't neglect the development of cultural relations among your departments.

BabyCenter

Questions and gear: that is what pregnancy and raising children seem to be all about these days. From the moment the home test changes color (or even earlier, if conception is elusive), parents are part of A Great Experiment that aims to create a healthy human being. Yet there is no official laboratory guide for this experiment, and the array of potential tools, decisions, and advice (solicited or otherwise) can be daunting.

BabyCenter aims to be the leading Web site for parents, whether they are looking to answer the questions or simply to purchase the gear. Founded in November 1997, BabyCenter was acquired in 2000 by e-retailer eToys. The acquisition has shifted some of the personnel in the San Francisco headquarters of BabyCenter, but the site continues to operate as it always has, with the enhancements of scale and financing that the acquisition affords.

Part newsletter, part library, part encounter group, and large part retail store, BabyCenter guides parents and parents-to-be through the maze of information and products for confident parenting and comfortable child-rearing.

Strategy

BabyCenter faces competition from a number of other resources on the Web, not to mention the myriad resources available offline. To differentiate itself in a busy marketplace, BabyCenter has focused on a subset of childcare information—preconception through the toddler years. By narrowing the focus to this subset, BabyCenter is better able to provide impressive depth in product assortment, as well as in information resources.

The key word for BabyCenter is guidance. Visitors are assured that they will be guided through the choices of parenthood, with expert advice on health, development, and products. Bulletin boards and chat sessions provide an important point of connection between parents and experts. Personalized e-mail

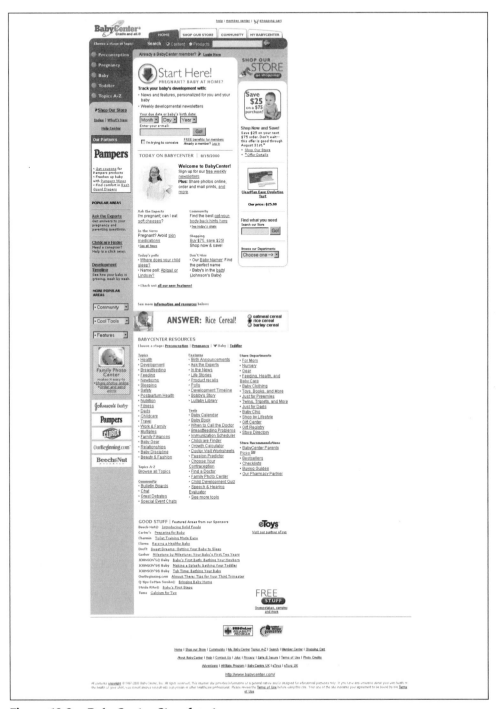

Figure 10.9   BabyCenter Storefront.

newsletters provide information tailored to the appropriate stage of pregnancy or child development.

Guidance, information, and community are the top-line, strategic positioning elements for BabyCenter. The bottom line, however, is retail. BabyCenter's revenue model calls for more than three-quarters of its revenues to come from product sales, with the remainder made up through advertising and sponsorships. (Product sales make up a smaller percentage of profits, however, as other income sources are more profitable.)

To manage the critical relationship between content and sales, BabyCenter runs its business through two departments: content/media and e-commerce. The branding of the organization accomplished through the content/media components of the business is what drives the sales on the e-commerce side of things. Through content, BabyCenter establishes its branding as a trusted, comprehensive resource; who *wouldn't* want to buy their child care products from such a source?

As one measure of success, BabyCenter gets more than 1.6 million unique visitors each month. The site's content and community-building features have indeed created the customer base to which BabyCenter can market its products.

Assortment Planning

To a certain degree, BabyCenter's strategic focus defines the range of products its merchants must seek to fill out the assortment—books, toys, clothing, nursery items, health care, and feeding items, along with the rest of the accoutrements that go along with modern parenthood. With a number of competitors, online and off, BabyCenter must have a comprehensive assortment to fulfill its promise of being a leading resource for parents.

Michael Schmier, vice president of Product Management, joined BabyCenter without previous experience in retail. He quickly came to respect the need for traditional merchant knowledge to make the business run effectively. "I've been surprised at the broad range of products and individual SKUs we have to carry and how merchants need to understand each SKU's demand curves and selling features," Schmier says.

The company's merchant knowledge has been acquired at times through difficult experience. "There are times I wish we'd had better product and category forecasts to avoid overbought situations," notes Josh Litwin, who served as vice president of Operations until the culmination of the eToys acquisition on September 1, 2000.

Merchants are divided into broad product categories, including hard goods, soft goods, and gear/nursery to select products for the assortment.

Merchandising

BabyCenter has created several creative merchandising techniques to draw customers into the store. In addition to the expected product categories (For Mom, Infant & Toddler Gear, Nursery, Baby Clothing, and so on), BabyCenter sorts products in the following ways:

Checklists and Buying Guides: Step-by-step guides point shoppers to the products they need for each stage of pregnancy and child rearing.

Gift Solutions: A selection of items appropriate for gift-giving for particular occasions is presented, along with a gift registry and a gift certificate program.

By Special Request: Special categories of products (preemies, multiple births, items for expectant fathers, and designer items) are merchandised separately to guide shoppers to exactly what they want.

Shop by Lifestyle: The most creative of the techniques, Shop by Lifestyle groups products according to lifestyle needs. "On the Go Baby" emphasizes travel gear. "Adventure Baby" emphasizes items that enable parents and infants to enjoy the great outdoors together. "Nature Baby" emphasizes all-natural and organic products.

In addition to its sorting mechanisms, BabyCenter uses many of the merchandising techniques that other e-retailers have found effective. Visitors can opt to view bestselling items in popular product categories, or shop the special list of products named by parents as the Best of Breed.

When visitors register for BabyCenter membership with an e-mail address and their baby's due date or date of birth, BabyCenter responds by providing targeted e-mail information on sales and special products appropriate for their stage of parenthood.

Inventory Management

Nearly all of the products offered at BabyCenter are owned by the company as inventory, with the exception of a few furniture items that are shipped to customers directly from the manufacturer. With the eToys acquisition, BabyCenter gained access to a wider warehouse and distribution network, with facilities on both coasts.

Without the limitations of space that traditional retailers face in selecting and merchandising their assortment, Web-based retailers face different kinds of inventory challenges, Schmier and Litwin note. "It's easy to get a huge number of SKUs, and then its very difficult to extract data and statistics about your SKUs in order to make intelligent business decisions," Schmier says.

From the operations standpoint, Litwin's observations are even more critical. "It was absolutely critical that we learned to manage our warehouse space and allocate it as a resource much like our financial resources," he recalls. "Some of our product SKUs take up a lot of room. Sometimes we were caught unprepared and unable to handle large receipts of strollers, for instance.

"The product/SKU database needed to have *all* the information in it," Litwin continues. "For pick-and-pack, we needed to have on hand all the information about a SKU's weight, country of origin, dimensions, and more."

Originally, BabyCenter developed all of its back-end inventory management programs and defined the reporting those programs would generate. Since the eToys acquisition, BabyCenter is folding its inventory management into eToys' system.

Pricing and Promotion

In the marketplace for parenting goods, there are many pricing strategies from which to choose. A number of retailers and e-retailers opt for the "guaranteed lowest price" proposition, while just as many go for the "best-of-the-best" strategy, with luxury prices to match. BabyCenter focuses on providing an important value-added information resource to its retail assortment at a reasonable price.

Across the product lines, BabyCenter shoots for an IMU of 35 percent to 40 percent, depending on the product category.

Schmier offers another reminder on the importance of pricing strategy: "You need to think through your pricing structure and margin considerations first," notes Schmier. "Be sure you have a model that can actually be profitable, even if things don't go exactly according to plan."

Promotions are an important part of BabyCenter's e-retail operations, but they are not used indiscriminately; they are targeted through the customized e-mail newsletter system and, occasionally, tied to time-limited offers. The site's clearance center moves items that are going out of stock at discounted prices.

Vendor Relations

BabyCenter had a difficult time breaking into the child care vendor community. It has been a struggle to convince suppliers that BabyCenter was not the sort of dot com to aggressively discount products and fight for the bargain-basement customer. "This is a highly competitive arena, and many retailers do take the 'sale, sale, sale' route with their assortments," Schmier says. "We were finally able to convince reluctant suppliers that we rely on a different model. Over the course of our relationships, we *have* avoided significant promotional activity, which has increased the confidence of our vendor partners. Overall, I'd say vendors find us a cooperative partner and much less aggressive with pricing and promotional activity than many of our retail competitors."

Structure

BabyCenter employs merchants who work in broad product categories. The merchants are also responsible for developing on-site merchandising and promotional techniques. Merchants report to directors of merchandising, and directors report to a senior vice president of e-commerce.

The medical advisory board is an additional layer in the decision-making structure. The board is more often called on to contribute to the content areas of BabyCenter, although board input may be sought to review the efficacy and/or safety of a product.

Communication across the organization has proven to be of central importance to running the business effectively. "You need merchants who understand the requirements of operations, and operations workers who understand what merchants do," notes Litwin.

The Wisdom of Experience

At the age of three, BabyCenter is a self-assured pre-schooler. However, it only got to that point through careful parenting. Schmier was not the only member of the management team who arrived at BabyCenter without extensive retail experience, but the company has learned on its feet and toddled into a leadership position.

At the heart of BabyCenter's success is knowledge of the customer on many levels. "You have to understand your customer," Schmier notes. "You have to understand how they shop for the categories you plan to carry in your assortment. What's more, you have to understand their attitudes regarding purchasing those products online."

With its community-building features and opportunities to rate and review products, BabyCenter also ensures that its customers understand each other, which is perhaps one of the most important of the intangible factors that make BabyCenter work.

Concepts and Resources

With our attention closely tuned to the details of retail, we have not been able to tend to so many other topics critical to the success of e-retail. The discussion and resources in this appendix are no substitute for the in-depth resources available on these subjects. Our overview here is intended to set you in the right direction to learn more and to help you ask some pointed questions along the way.

e-Business Overview

You will most likely want more of a bird's eye view of the e-business landscape than we provide in this book. In fact, understanding the e-business landscape is the kind of ongoing intelligence effort that will always make you more effective. In the process of conducting your research, you may uncover some Web sites that offer perspective on the direction and influences of e-business. Some news-oriented sites invite visitors to sign up for updates or get targeted news e-mailed to them. When you do so, pick just two or three sites to focus on, unless you can be reviewing information during the hours when ordinary humans require sleep.

There are, of course, plenty of books that can lay the framework for understanding e-business, some of which are listed in this book's bibliography, *A Few Good Books,* below. However, with such a dynamic environment as the Web, you will need to keep an eye on fresher news sources that can tell you about changing regulations and legislation, what your market is up to, what your competitors are up to, and the overall Zeitgeist in the global village. In addition to your traditional information sources (newspapers, conferences, networking, and so on), several online magazines can provide insight into the culture of the online world. Try *Salon Magazine* (www.salon.com), one of the longest publishing and best Web magazines out there.

At the very least, you want to be visiting the sites that your customers are visiting in order to keep track of how their universe expands and contracts.

Customer Relations

The Customer Rules

Without customers, there's no business. You already know that. You have also *been* a customer, so you probably already have some ideas of what you like and do not like from the customer's end of a retail relationship.

Why is it so easy to forget what it is like to be a frustrated customer as soon as we become retailers (e- or otherwise)? Probably because there is so much to do and so many details to handle that the softer elements of doing business seldom make it to the top of the priority list.

To make it in e-retail, however, customer service is critical. The winners of the first round of Web-based selling have all been organizations that have paid close attention to how they do customer service. They have invested in staffing and equipping customer representative departments even while operating on an overall deficit. They have bent over backward to make things right by customers. Furthermore they have created relationships with customers that are not solely based on merchandise. These are relationships that emphasize communication (both into and out of the business) for the enrichment of both parties.

The key word is trust. All customer-retailer relationships must be based on trust, which is inherently more difficult to establish and maintain in the electronic environment. As the saying goes, on the Internet, no one knows you're a dog. So your challenge in customer relations and customer service is to help your customer see that, if a dog, at least you are loyal, stalwart, and brave.

How can you create this trust with your market? Of course, most of the decisions you make will depend on the specifics of your business, assortment, and market. The following are some things to consider:

Remember Who Your Customer Is

Your customers are those who are ripe and ready to buy your product. Vendors are not your customers; they are your partners. The media are not your customers;

the media are a method of communicating with your customers. Consumers of your online content *may* be potential customers, but frankly, they are not as critical to your success and profitability unless you can convert them from readers/visitors into shoppers/buyers.

What does this mean for your e-retail business?

Every employee, no matter the department in which he or she works, must understand: who is the customer and what are his/her expectations. Site designers, writers, customer service representatives, warehouse personnel, media relations—whatever the job title, if it is on your payroll, that person is working to secure the business of your customer. If goods arrive mishandled, if your public relations efforts somehow stimulate bile in your target market, if the language on your site does not feel comfortable to your shoppers, they will leave your site without so much as a backward glance. And they will never come back.

Customer service begins the minute someone enters your site. Customer service is inherent in effective design of an e-retail site. Can new visitors easily find what they are looking for? Are new visitors made to feel welcome? Can they quickly access information and/or customer assistance if necessary?

Striking the right balance between informative and cluttered is the challenge for Web storefronts. If your customer is confronted every few centimeters with a "contact us!" prompt, she may get annoyed, much the way she might feel in a traditional store when salespeople get in her face. What is more, by pushing your "contact us!" in front of her repeatedly, you may actually be conditioning her to ignore the prompt when she really needs it. (Have you ever avoided asking a salesperson a question because she was too pushy when you first walked in the door?)

Of course, the tactics you deploy on your Web site will depend on your types of customers and products. Some products and target markets are better suited to the hands-on sell from the get-go. Yet the last thing you want to create is the electronic equivalent of the "I'm just looking" brush-off.

If your customers initiate their relationship with you to access your editorial content, do not overwhelm them on content pages with your Amazing Opportunities to Buy. They will not trust the validity of your content if it seems to drive them relentlessly to a request for their credit card numbers.

On the other hand, if customers are interested in buying, then make it easy for them. If they send you e-mail through a "contact us" feature, respond, preferably within 12 hours. Provide your company's telephone number and mailing address (a street address inspires more trust than a P.O. box number) on your Web site. Answer the phone when it rings. Return messages. Each point of contact that reinforces your identity as a credible and trustworthy entity will count in your favor when the customer is ready to buy.

Throughout the sales process up through and including product delivery, customers should be confident that they can ask questions and get answers they trust. The total experience of shopping with you, regardless of whether they buy something during each visit, should reinforce your branding as a reliable business with the customer's best interests at heart.

Editorial Policies

One way or another, any e-retail site will include a certain amount of copy, even if it is limited to product descriptions. As the Web evolves as a medium for selling, it is clear that e-retail stores can make the most of the environment by expanding their editorial reach far beyond product descriptions to encompass feature articles, product reviews, news, community centers, and other content of interest to the target market. That is the great advantage of e-retail over catalog and traditional brick-and-mortar retail: You have all the space you want to create the compelling content that will attract visitors and keep them at your site.

The use of editorial content creates a new kind of challenge for e-retail sites not faced by catalogs or traditional stores. Now you are a publisher, as well as a retailer.

Who Writes Your Content? Who Owns It?

Any site content that goes beyond basic product information will demand that you have a Web-savvy editor working for you, someone who understands not just language and your goals but how readers approach electronic material. Depending on the size and extent of your content requirements, you may also need a writer or two on staff, or at least a stable of reliable freelancers who understand your business and audience.

For any material you hire a freelancer to write, you will want to make sure that the terms of your agreement are for "work for hire." This means that you own the material once it is paid for. To be extra careful, have your freelancers confirm in writing that they have assigned copyright to you. Copyright assignment should include the writer's name, the name of the piece, and the date of payment.

You should know that work for hire is a different arrangement from what many freelance journalists are accustomed to for print articles. In the case of freelance print articles, publishers usually purchase first rights, but the journalist retains the copyright. You may need to negotiate over this, explain your need to maintain control over something that may be archived and accessed on your site for a long time, or hunt around for writers who are willing to work under these terms. This is very much an evolving question in the world of freelance communications. Professional writers are not of one mind as to rights associated with materials written expressly for the Web or other electronic media.

Do not let the uncertainties prevent you from hiring professional writers, however. Your readers can tell the difference between quality professional work and Amateur Hour. Similarly, if you have subject experts write articles for your site or if you solicit contributions from your community, have an editor work with the material before you publish it to make it as effective as possible.

How Connected Are Your Content and Merchandising?

This is a tricky area—the clear division of editorial policies and revenue-generators. In the creation of trust between you as e-retailer/content provider and your customers/readers, you want to identify clearly anything that is intended to sell product. Perhaps *all* of your content is designed to drive immediate sales. That is a valid strategic choice, but in that case do not create a façade of impartiality to convince readers that they are reading unbiased copy. Not only do you run the risk of attracting the unflattering attention of consumer watchdog groups (including the Federal Trade Commission), you are setting up an opportunity to disappoint your customer.

Not that your content should be held to standards of purity ordinarily reserved for juries. Go ahead and have an agenda. Just be honest about it.

In any event, have a written editorial policy that lays out your editorial mission and/or agenda, ownership of content, reprint and reuse guidelines, a method for contacting the site editor, and advertising policies if applicable. If your site features community input (consumer product reviews or a discussion board, for instance), you will also need policies governing acceptable use of these features, and laying out your rights as publisher and content manager to edit or expunge inappropriate material. Not to get all "Big Brother" about it, but if a user posts something obscene, libelous, or illegal, you want to be able to deal with it.

Legal Issues

By entering the world of e-commerce, you enter a complicated and at times, uncertain legal universe. In brief, get a good lawyer with experience in e-commerce, intellectual property, and/or consumer law. Then make sure that lawyer has good contacts in all the geographic areas in which you plan to do business.

Mom and Pop on Main Street do not need this kind of legal advice, but Mom-NPop.com sure do. The following are many of the key points you will want to go over with legal counsel to create and run your e-retail business effectively and safely.

Where Do You Do Business?

The everywhere-and-nowhere properties of the Web present challenges for e-retailer and consumer alike. In the United States alone, every state has its own consumer protection laws, under the "bare minimum" umbrella of the federal law. And of course, if you are doing business with customers in other countries, you need to be sure that you are complying with the laws of those countries as well.

Some e-retailers may cut their risk by voluntarily restricting their territory. You may have seen this kind of disclaimer or statement on an e-commerce site, stating that the company does business only in the United States or only in a particular region. If you opt for that kind of protection, it is only as strong as your commitment to it; if you have restricted your sales to the United States, when a customer wants a huge order sent to Mozambique, you must respectfully decline to fill it.

Keep in mind, too, that the legal system considers the *final destination* of the goods, not just the destination to which you, the e-retailer, ship them. For example, if your company restricts business to the United States and you get orders for goods to be shipped to P.O. boxes in Detroit, you might want to check up on the customers to find out if they are crossing the border from Ontario to buy your product. If so, the law may interpret the sale as *de facto* international.

The question of "where" is not simply one of collecting sales tax and/or duty fees. Your product liability is also at issue when you cross geographic boundaries. Each state has its own laws regarding product liability and the responsibilities of the retailer to the customer. Say that products are ordered by a customer in one state, processed by your home office in another state, assembled at a warehouse in a third, and then shipped by truck across multiple state lines. In the event of a defective product or injury, you have a tangled jurisdiction issue on your hands.

When Do You Own What You Own?

The question of jurisdiction comes into play when you ship goods to a customer, but also when you purchase goods from a vendor. As we discussed in Chapter 5, you may take possession of goods from your suppliers at any one of several points in the process of transporting them from the supplier's manufacturing facility to your warehouse. Your legal counsel must be able to help you sort out all of the questions that go along with the chain of ownership: foreign taxes and duties, liability, insurance, warehouse and transportation costs, and more.

Policies and Payments

To protect yourself and your customers, you must have site policies posted and available on your e-retail site. These policies should cover everything from consumer privacy to payment to shipping agreements to returns. Your goal is to create a transparent business, in which there are no foggy areas of who is responsible for what and when. As your lawyer will no doubt reiterate, creating transparency on the front end will save you no end of grief down the road.

You must know and understand the legal protections that allow consumers to stop payment or return items ordered remotely. If you are doing business internationally, you will also want to have the latest legal information on those countries in which you do business. It is also not a bad idea to have a separate letter of credit in each country in which you operate, to protect *your* interests in the event of a problem.

The policies may seem like an expensive pain in the neck (yes, have your lawyer write policies for *your* company; do not just copy them from another site). However, in addition to the protections they afford you and your customers, they enhance your credibility in the marketplace. They reaffirm your brand as an e-retailer with which people can safely do business.

The American Bar Association has committees in several of its practice sections that regularly review the impact of e-commerce on business. Web-based business will touch all areas of the law, and there is no single source that can provide you with every answer you need. Effective and targeted legal counsel should be your first move; then follow your counsel's directions as you progress.

Logistics

Logistics is where the virtual world gets real. How *do* you get physical products from here to there? How *do* you ensure you are paid in legal tender for those products? In the grand old days of bartering, there were no logistical challenges. As economic trade becomes increasingly abstract, successful follow-through on any given transaction requires attention to the details.

As we have made clear throughout this book, we believe that most, if not all, e-retailers will operate most profitably when they own at least some portion of their assortment as inventory, even if they rely on just-in-time arrangements for the majority of the assortment. The requirements for warehousing and shipping will vary depending on the geographic location of your market(s) and the size of your assortment, among other factors. If you are relying on a combination of just-in-time and on-hand inventory, you will also need to work to coordinate multiple logistics chains, integrating your distributors' shipments with your own to create a seamless customer experience.

The simplest approach may be to outsource the whole thing. The big shippers are chomping at the bit to take over the logistics requirements for the e-commerce sector. Let them court you. Get a sense of what those services have to offer or how you can combine them with in-house components (e.g., warehousing, personnel, payment processing) for a cost-effective solution.

Similarly, companies are vying for the privilege of handling your payment processing. Unless payment processing services are part of a total logistics package that works for you, it is unlikely that you will benefit from outsourcing this function. Once you have your merchant accounts and your site security established, you can automate many of the payment processing functions just as easily as an external company can do so.

In relation to moving goods and moving funds, logistics present certain legal challenges (e.g., insurance, consumer protection, and other issues) that you will want to address with legal counsel. Be sure that any company you trust to take care of logistics for you will protect your interests in the event of a problem with moving goods or banking payments.

Marketing

Marketing is its own entire library of information. We can hardly cover everything you need to know about marketing within the scope of this teeny-weeny resource section. For more information, refer to this book's bibliography, "A Few Good Books," and to the marketing expertise you have in (or hire into) your organization. When you plan and launch your e-retail store, there are two primary considerations we can reiterate here.

Consistent, Targeted Messages

Confused customers are not likely to buy anything. They need to know what you are all about. If there is a primary law to marketing communications, it is to keep the message consistent and targeted to the interests of your audience.

Naturally, your brochures, ads for your site, and catalogs are marketing materials, but your emphasis on consistent and targeted messages should not end with them. Marketing is a living, breathing aspect of total brand management, which manifests itself in everything that "stands" for your company, online and off. If marketing messages are not reinforced at every point of potential contact with your audience (e.g., site policies, product packaging, sponsorships, and so on), then all the targeted marketing in the world will not overcome the inconsistency customers associate with your brand.

Benefits, Benefits, Benefits

The corollary to the above principle is the concept of communicating benefits. The interests of your audience lie in what your product can do for them, and in how buying from you improves their very existence. Always review your marketing communications materials to ensure that they make the leap from features to benefits. Communications should take your customers by the hand and lead them through the decision to buy from you. Do not make it any harder than absolutely necessary for them to reach that decision.

Technical Partners

You would not try to open up a brick-and-mortar store without an architect, a contractor, and a host of other expert assistants. Once up and running, a brick-and-mortar store would also need janitorial and landscaping services, utilities (with upgrades as necessary), and repairs.

In setting up and running your e-retail site, you need just as much expert assistance as if you were building a "real world" store. However, it is difficult to know what you really need and what, in the greater scheme of things, is less important, especially at the cash-crunched outset. The world of Web design, execution, and hosting is changing so rapidly that it is difficult even to characterize the changes!

There are many good books that can help you work through the specifics of what your site needs and how to get it. Several are listed in this book's bibliography, "A Few Good Books." Start with these questions, and always work with technical resources you trust.

Do It Yourself or Not?

It is true that anyone with a computer, an Internet connection, and a certain degree of common sense can set up a functioning Web site. On a small scale, you can even get away with it. It gets out of hand quickly, however. Web management, like property or building management, is definitely a full-time job.

So do not even consider the "do it yourself" approach, unless you are willing to hire, train, and retain the kind of talent you need to keep the enterprise up and running over the long haul. The next question then is: in-house or outsource?

Both options have their advantages. Bringing the execution of the site in-house affords you ongoing control at the day-to-day level; outsourcing allows you to spend your hiring dollars elsewhere. Some of the questions to ask in addressing this conundrum include the following:

- How complex do you expect your site to be? If you are planning on a site that is primarily product and includes few interactive features, you may be in a better position to bring this work in-house.
- Does your business plan call for significant changes in the scale and/or scope of the site in the next 12 to 18 months? If so, do you feel more confident in your staff's abilities to keep up with the changes or in an external company's abilities to stay with you through transition?

Finding and Hiring the Right Technical Partners

Whether you choose to execute your site in-house or hire an outside firm to handle it, chances are you will need external assistance at some point in the process of planning, setting up, and running your e-retail site. It might be for a one-time project, such as setting up an underlying database for your site; it might be an ongoing consultant relationship. The Web is a complex environment, and your Web-based retail is bound to hit some area that you simply do not have in-house expertise to address.

Many practitioners and firms in the creative arts have added "Web work" to their list of accomplishments, but finding the right skills for your task at hand means going beyond the resume. Advertising firms do a lot of site designs and treatments, but they are unlikely to have the programming staff on hand to build applications. Some Web developers do just programming; some do programming and copywriting and layout. To make the process just a wee bit more challenging, the industry is still young enough that there are few agreed-on industry standards for training or certification.

Your best bet may be to establish a relationship with one or two Web commerce consultants who can guide your choices as you go. Additionally, if your operation is big enough to warrant the expense, you can bring someone with

Web commerce expertise into your organization as Chief Technology Officer or the equivalent. However, one way or another, you need to give the development and ongoing care of your Web site primary importance; it is your storefront, your customer interface, your window to the world.

Care and Feeding of a Web Site

Building a Web site is an ongoing proposition, not a project that is put on the calendar, measured through a timeline, and completed. Current industry reviews suggest that, on average, companies should allocate an annual maintenance budget equal to 70 percent of the cost of initial site development.

As a consumer-oriented site, your online store needs to feature fresh merchandise and content on a regular basis. Daily additions are ideal; weekly additions would be the minimum in most markets. You need to give your customers a reason to come back.

From that perspective, it only makes sense to bring your Web maintenance staff (e.g., designers, programmers, writers, and editors) primarily in-house. You depend on these functions to keep your business interacting effectively with the customer. At the very least, you need to have your point-people in-house (e.g., an editor, a lead programmer, and a lead designer). Do not trust the lifeblood of your business to someone else's blood bank.

Glossary of Common Retail Terms

Average Unit Cost: For SKUs with variable unit costs, the average cost over time (used for planning purposes).

Basic Items: SKUs that are always in stock, can be reordered from manufacturer, are often purchased more than once and remain the same from season to season. Contrast with "Fashion Items."

BOM Stock: The value of stock, in retail dollars, at the beginning of the month.

BOS Stock: The value of stock, in retail dollars, at the beginning of the season.

Broad Assortment: Describes a retailer with products in many different categories. The "everything under one roof" concept describes a broad assortment.

Buy Plan: Financial road map for product purchases. Determines both amount (in retail dollars) and timing of receipts. May be created at the level of whole store, department, category, vendor, and so on, as needed.

Clearance: Indicates an item's retail price has been permanently lowered to help move remaining quantities out of retailer's stock.

COG/COGS: Cost of goods/cost of goods sold. Actual unit purchase cost. May or may not be equivalent to list price, depending on whether the vendor offers purchasing discounts.

Damages: Product deemed nonsellable after customer return. Depending on vendor agreement, may be returned to supplier or "salvaged" out of stock.

Deep Assortment: Describes a retailer with many variations (e.g., color, sizes) of each article. "Your size guaranteed in stock" describes a deep assortment.

EAN: European Article Number. European version of the UPC.

EDI: Electronic Data Interchange. This term is used broadly to describe systems that allow vendors and retailers to share information.

EOM Stock: Value of stock, in retail dollars, at the end of the month.

EOS Stock: Value of stock, in retail dollars, at the end of the season.

Fashion Items: SKUs that are usually available for a single season, or two at the most. Contrast with "Basic Items."

FOB: Freight On Board. Designates the point at which the retailer assumes possession, financial responsibility, and legal responsibility for the goods. Expressed as "FOB Hong Kong" or "FOB Los Angeles."

FTC: Federal Trade Commission. The United States agency that regulates consumer law and has jurisdiction over Internet commerce.

GM: Gross Margin. Figured as: Sales – COGS – markdown costs = GM.

GMM: General Merchandise Manager. Often the person in a retail organization responsible for merchant and/or buying functions.

Hi-Low (or Hi-Lo): Promotional pricing strategy whereby goods are periodically put on sale/discounted for a defined and limited promotional period, then returned to the original retail price.

IMU: Initial Mark Up. Also referred to as Mark-up or Marking. Expressed as a percentage and figured: (Retail – Cost) / Retail = IMU.

Landed Cost: Cost of goods as of arrival in U.S. port of entry. Freight from point of entry to retailer will be added to this cost.

Line List: Manufacturers' and/or distributors' list of available products.

List Price: Cost of item offered by a manufacturer or distributor. List price is before any discounts.

Markdowns: Difference between the full retail value of an item and the revenue actually generated by selling the item. Markdowns may be the result of promotional pricing (Hi-Low) or clearance.

Merchandising: Presentation of merchandise for sale.

Merchant/Buyer: Used interchangeably in this text. The person responsible for procurement of product.

MM: Maintained Margin. GM less product costs such as freight, duties, and salvage.

OTB: Open to Buy. The amount in your buy plan designated for purchase of fresh merchandise; expressed in retail dollars.

POS: Point of Sale. Can refer to merchandising, promotional activity, or other product-specific activities.

Receipts: Incoming stock retail value.

Retail $: Valuations based on retail price of goods.

Sales Channel: The path of goods from manufacturer to consumer.

Salvage: Product destroyed or otherwise removed from saleable stock without generating income.

Sell-Through Percentage (Sell-Thru, Sell-Thru %): A measure of how quickly inventory moves in a short time frame, such as a week or a month. Does not include mid-period receipts. Figured as: Sales (Period X) / BOS Stock (Period X) = Sell-Thru %

SKU: Stock Keeping Unit. A flexible term that can be defined to suit a retailer's business. May or may not align with a vendor's definition of a product.

SRP (Suggested Retail Price): The price a manufacturer or distributor "suggests" retailers use to sell an item. Retailers are legally entitled to ignore the SRP but may jeopardize vendor relations if they do not honor SRPs.

Turnover (Turn): A measure of how quickly investment in inventory is realizing a profit. Most traditional retailers aim for a turnover between 0.7 and 1.6, although seasonal items require higher turns to be profitable. Figured as: Sales (Period X) / Average Stock (Period X) = Turn.

Units BOH: Number of units owned at the beginning of the period.

Units OH: Number of units owned.

Units OO: Units On Order. Units ordered but not yet received.

UPC: Universal Product Code. A 13-digit code that designates a single product, often defined down to the color and size level. In other words, the black dress (size 4), black dress (size 8), and red dress (size 8) will all have unique UPC numbers.

Variable Unit Cost: A SKU cost that fluctuates over time. Commodity-based products or products subject to exchange rate fluctuations are common examples, but the cost of any product can change over time.

Bibliography

A Few Good Books

Amor, Daniel. *The E-Business (R)evolution*. Prentice Hall, 1999.

Bazerman, Max H. and Neale, Margaret A. *Negotiating Rationally*. Free Press, 1993.

Beckwith, Harry. *Selling the Invisible: A Field Guide to Modern Marketing*. Warner Books, 1997. Even if you are selling the visible (i.e., consumer goods), Beckwith provides an invaluable perspective on the factors that motivate sales.

Brown, Stanley A. *Customer Relationship Management: A Strategic Imperative in the World of E-Business*. John Wiley & Sons, 2000.

De Kare-Silver, Michael. *E-Shock: The Electronic Shopping Revolution: Strategies for Retailers and Manufacturers*. AMACOM, 1999.

Godin, Seth. *Permission Marketing: Turning Strangers into Friends, and Friends into Customers*. Simon & Schuster, 1999. Godin is the vice president of direct marketing for Yahoo!

Kalakota, Ravi and Robinson, Marcia. *e-Business: Roadmap for Success*. Addison-Wesley, 1999.

Means, Grady and Schneider, David. *Meta-Capitalism: The E-Business Revolution and the Design of 21st Century Companies and Markets*. John Wiley & Sons, 2000.

Minoli, Dan and Emma. *Web Commerce Technology Handbook*. McGraw-Hill, 1998.

Newell, Frederick. *Loyalty.com: Customer Relationship Management in the New Era of Internet Marketing*. McGraw-Hill, 2000.

Schell, Ernest H. *Guide to Catalog Management Software (10th edition)*. Industry Publications International, 2000.

Shaw, Jack and Sperry, Judy. *Surviving the Digital Jungle: What Every Executive Needs to Know About eCommerce and eBusiness*. Electronic Commerce Strategies, Inc., 2000.

Tiernan, Bernadette. *E-Tailing*. Dearborn Financial Publishing, 2000.

Treese, Winfield and Stewart, Lawrence. *Designing Systems for Internet Commerce*. Addison-Wesley, 1998.

Yesil, Magdalena. *Creating the Virtual Store: Taking Your Web Site from Browsing to Buying*. John Wiley & Sons, 1997.

Zoellick, Bill. *Web Engagement: Connecting to Customers in e-Business*. Addison-Wesley, 2000.

Additional Resources

American Bar Association (www.abanet.org)

The Business Law section of the ABA has a Committee on Cyberspace Law and a Subcommittee on E-Commerce; one of their projects is the consumer-oriented Safe Shopping site (www.safeshopping.org). Of more particular interest to e-retailers may be the Committee on Cyberspace Law's informational site (www.abanet.org/buslaw/cyber), where legislative reporters recap legislative proposals and action on such topics as taxation of e-commerce, digital signatures, encryption, and more. The Subcommittee on E-Commerce (www.abanet.org/buslaw/cyber/ecommerce/ecommerce.html) provides information on ABA activities to review and understand the changing business world. The ABA also has a searchable online directory of lawyers across the country.

Federal Trade Commission (www.ftc.gov)

The Federal Trade Commission's section on Business Guidance (www.ftc.gov/ftc/business.htm) is worth a visit. In addition to general reference and guidance materials to help you run your business in accordance with trade laws, a series of publications aimed directly at e-commerce issues (www.ftc.gov/bcp/menu-internet.htm) is available for free download.

Logistics Resources

Cahner's Business Information publishes Logistics Management and Distribution Report and provides such services as a logistics buyers' guide on its Web site (www.logistics-buyers-guide.com).

The major players in logistics have set up special divisions to cater to e-commerce needs:

UPS has an e-commerce division (www.ec.ups.com).

Federal Express offers a menu of e-commerce tools (www.federalexpress.com/us/ebusiness).

Airborne Express runs a subsidiary company, Airborne Logistics Services (www.als.airborne.com).

Index

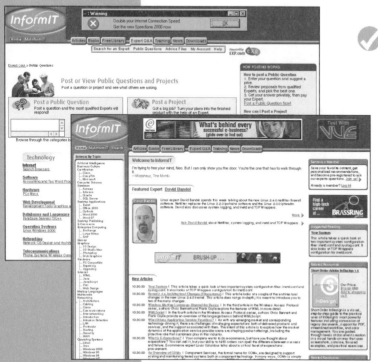

Register Your Book

at www.aw.com/cseng/register

You may be eligible to receive:

- Advance notice of forthcoming editions of the book
- Related book recommendations
- Chapter excerpts and supplements of forthcoming titles
- Information about special contests and promotions throughout the year
- Notices and reminders about author appearances, tradeshows, and online chats with special guests

Contact us

If you are interested in writing a book or reviewing manuscripts prior to publication, please write to us at:

Editorial Department
Addison-Wesley Professional
75 Arlington Street, Suite 300
Boston, MA 02116 USA
Email: AWPro@aw.com

Addison-Wesley

Visit us on the Web: http://www.aw.com/cseng

CD-ROM Warranty

Addison-Wesley warrants the enclosed disc to be free of defects in materials and faulty workmanship under normal use for a period of ninety days after purchase. If a defect is discovered in the disc during this warranty period, a replacement disc can be obtained at no charge by sending the defective disc, postage prepaid, with proof of purchase to:

Editorial Department
Addison-Wesley Professional
Pearson Technology Group
75 Arlington Street, Suite 300
Boston, MA 02116
Email: AWPro

Addison-Wesley makes no warranty or representation, either expressed or implied, with respect to this software, its quality, performance, merchantability, or fitness for a particular purpose. In no event will Addison Wesley, its distributors, or dealers be liable for direct, indirect, special, incidental, or consequential damages arising out of the use or inability to use the software. The exclusion of implied warranties is not permitted in some states. Therefore, the above exclusion may not apply to you. This warranty provides you with specific legal rights. There may be other rights that you may have that vary from state to state. The contents of this CD-ROM are intended for personal use only.

More information and updates are available at:
http://www.awl.com/cseng/titles/0-201-72169-4